MW01118872

"Whether you are a new designer or an established one, Shilov's masterpiece is a step by step blueprint for success to literally landing your dream design job. Starting right from understanding the role, through navigating the design interview process till you ship your first project as a product designer; the book guides you through the 'what', 'why,' and 'how' of the journey."

— Aniruddha Kadam, Product Design Manager, LinkedIn

"Land Your Dream Design Job is a timely bible for any designer who wants to break into the field. The book is filled with a variety of easy-to-understand principles, examples, tips, and tricks that uncover the ambiguous land of portfolio-building and design interviewing. Even better, you will learn how to define your career goals and pursue the job that's right for you."

— Hang Le, Head of Design, HelloSign

"Dan has summed up the ins and outs of the design interview process, for any designer looking to crack the code on nailing a portfolio review. It's also a must-read for any hiring manager or product designer involved in the interview process. If your team wants to win, you have to set your candidates up for success, and this book will help you do just that."

— Zain Ali, YCombinator

"Whether you're a product designer at the beginning of your career or an experienced designer looking to refresh your portfolio and redefine your career goals, Land Your Dream Design Job is a comprehensive book that helps you approach your design career with intention. This book gives you full perspective on the whole interview process and challenges you with questions for self-reflection."

— Julie Stanescu, Founder, Rethink

"Finding genuinely thoughtful and thorough insights on design interviewing is rare. Shilov's book is a gem that does that and more with a comprehensive yet pragmatic approach from career aspiration to job offer and beyond. Sage advice for both the early career designer and design veteran (and a refresher course for design managers hiring talent too!)."

— Melissa Hui, Founder, Context Leap

Other Books Available at Holloway.com

The Holloway Guide to Remote Work

Katie Womersley, Juan Pablo Buriticá et al.

A comprehensive guide to building, managing, and adapting to working with distributed teams.

The Holloway Guide to Equity Compensation

Joshua Levy, Joe Wallin et al.

Stock options, RSUs, job offers, and taxes—a detailed reference, explained from the ground up.

The Holloway Guide to Technical Recruiting and Hiring

Osman (Ozzie) Osman et al.

A practical, expert-reviewed guide to growing software engineering teams effectively, written by and for hiring managers, recruiters, interviewers, and candidates.

The Holloway Guide to Raising Venture Capital

Andy Sparks et al.

A current and comprehensive resource for entrepreneurs, with technical detail, practical knowledge, real-world scenarios, and pitfalls to avoid.

Founding Sales: The Early-Stage Go-To-Market Handbook

Pete Kazanjy

This tactical handbook distills early sales first principles, and teaches the skills required for going from being a founder to early salesperson, and eventually becoming an early sales leader.

Angel Investing: Start to Finish

Joe Wallin, Pete Baltaxe

A journey through the perils and rewards of angel investing, from fundamentals to finding deals, financings, and term sheets.

Land Your Dream Design Job

Land Your Dream Design Job

A GUIDE FOR PRODUCT DESIGNERS, FROM PORTFOLIO TO INTERVIEW TO JOB OFFER

Dan Shilov

Whether you're looking for your first job or your fifteenth, you can find an opportunity that plays to your strengths, matches with your values, and provides support for professional growth.

COURTNEY NASH, EDITOR

HOLLOWAY

Published in the United States by Holloway, San Francisco
Holloway.com

Cover design by Order (New York) and Andy Sparks
Interior design by Joshua Levy and Jennifer Durrant
Print engineering by Titus Wormer

Typefaces: Tiempos Text and National 2
by Kris Sowersby of Klim Type Foundry

Print version 1.0 · Digital version e1.0.3
doc c6305f · pipeline cdbb9a · genbook 4fa043 · 2023-10-10

Want More Out of This Book?

Holloway publishes books online. As a reader of this special full-access print edition, you are granted personal access to the paid digital edition, which you can read and share on the web, and offers commentary, updates, and corrections. A Holloway account also gives access to search, definitions of key terms, bookmarks, highlights, and other features. Claim your account by visiting: **holloway.com/print20299**

If you wish to recommend the book to others, suggest they visit **holloway.com/ddj** to learn more and purchase their own digital or print copy.

The author welcomes your feedback! Please consider adding comments or suggestions to the book online so others can benefit. Or say hello@holloway.com. Thank you for reading.

The Holloway team

LEGEND

Some elements in the text are marked for special significance:

IMPORTANT	Important or often overlooked tip
CAUTION	Caution, limitation, or problem
CONFUSION	Common confusion or misunderstanding, such as confusing terminology
NEW	New or recent developments
STORY	A personal anecdote or story

Web links appear as numbered footnotes in print.

References to other related sections are indicated by superscript section numbers, prefixed with §.

OVERVIEW

TABLE OF CONTENTS

INTRODUCTION

I have a confession to make. Early on in my career I was terrible at interviewing. I would take months obsessing over every pixel in my online portfolio only to fail in the last round of interviews. That is, if I got lucky to get to that final round in the first place. Most of the time, after submitting my application, I never heard anything back. As a designer I was comfortable generating ideas on a whiteboard with colleagues, but doing a whiteboard design challenge in front of an interview panel gave me performance anxiety. And don't get me started on the take-home design exercise assignment. Trying to read the lines of what the company was looking for while balancing a looming work deadline always put me in a tight spot.

Much has changed since then. Over the past decade I've personally interviewed with many companies, from small startups to large corporations. Beyond my own experience of interviewing, I had the privilege of being on the other side of the table. I conducted app critiques, whiteboard challenges, sat in on portfolio presentations, and talked with countless designers and design managers. If there was one thing that I learned, it's that everyone struggles with interviews. Even senior candidates—strong in their craft with years of experience behind them—tend to hit some speed bumps in their interview process.

Designing is hard. We spend considerable time, effort, and money learning the craft, whether it's through traditional education, new boot camps, or on the job. We invest time in our education because we believe the payoff will be worth it. But when it comes to looking for work, we frequently find ourselves on our own. Unfortunately, the job search and design interviewing process can sometimes feel just as mysterious, understood only by a select few. It can feel downright elitist. And, of course, the lack of feedback on how we've done or what we could have done better doesn't help.

But it doesn't have to be this way.

With the right approach we can take control of the job search process to land a role that's both exciting and helps us grow. You can improve your interviewing skills and communicate in such a way that puts your best foot forward to let your skills and talents shine.

1 Who This Book Is For

This book is geared toward individual contributor designers who are looking to transition to their next or first role. If you're a current manager or a manager-to-be, you may still find this information useful, but note that this material doesn't cover manager-specific design interviews.

CONFUSION Throughout the book, for the purpose of brevity, I use the term "product designer" as a catchall for various industry terms such as "interaction designer," "UX/UI designer," "experience designer," among others.

1.1 *New Designers*

If you're starting out as a designer, congrats! You're on an exciting journey. To set you up for success we'll look into strategies for approaching the job search in a way that gives you more autonomy. I recommend paying close attention to the first part of the book, which will help you think through your ideal role based on your strengths, growth areas, and interests. Starting with the end in my mind will sharpen your senses and get the most out of your search. And of course, the book is chock full of interview examples to help you on your journey.

1.2 *Experienced Designers*

You may think you already know how to prepare and what to expect from interviews, having been through the process a few times. This may be true, but design expertise does not always equate to excellent interview performance. So don't leave this to chance. Whether it's how to represent yourself during your final presentation or how to solve design exercises without missing a beat, you can skip around to sections that you may need more practice on or are looking for ways to distinguish yourself.

1.3 *Teachers, Mentors, and Design Educators*

Having been once a design student, I know the value of a solid education. Nothing beats dedicating the time and effort to learn design through and through. But beyond classes, few design programs help students in navigating the world post-graduation. Unfortunately, too often, students are left to their own devices. This book aims to bridge the gap between the two worlds—academia and professional practice—and will give you useful information for helping today's students succeed in the competitive marketplace.

2 What Is Covered

This book takes the approach of covering the product design job search process from beginning to end. It's meant to be your guide throughout the process, from when you first start thinking about where you want to go all the way to how you can create your new job and get up to speed quickly—and it's chock-full of tips in-between.

You don't have to read the book from cover to cover. In fact I encourage you to skip around. Go to the sections that are the most relevant to you now or where you need the most help.

- **Part I: The Modern Product Designer.** Before firing up that portfolio, it helps to first understand who you are as a designer. We'll look into the skills and traits of today's product designers. We'll also do a detailed breakdown of key job characteristics you should consider for your next role. By defining your ideal role upfront, you'll be able to tailor your application thus increasing your chances of landing the dream job.
- **Part II: Taking Action and Finding Opportunities.** We'll build on the previous section by uncovering your superpowers, which will lay the groundwork for your pitch. You'll use your pitch across various channels to communicate your unique competitive advantage as a designer. I'll show you how you can tailor your portfolio to practically speak to your strengths. Lastly, we'll cover several strategies for how to apply to roles.

- **Part III: Preparing for Design Interviews.** You'll get to know how to speak the language of people you'll be interviewing with, whether it's engineers, researchers, or product managers. By knowing what to expect, you'll be able to interview confidently. Lastly, you'll learn how to use storytelling and public speaking techniques to make your portfolio presentation stand out.
- **Part IV: Acing Design Exercises.** Design interviews are sometimes known for their notorious exercises: the app critique, the whiteboard challenge, and the take-home assignment. Many have stumped an experienced designer. But fear not! In this section, we'll cover everything you need to know about them. Aside from sharing frameworks that will help you solve any challenge in your path I've also included detailed solutions and walkthroughs.
- **Part V: After the Interviews.** No design process is complete without feedback, and interviewing is no exception. In this part, we'll cover the actions you should take after an interview to improve your performance. We'll also consider strategies for how to deal with setbacks. If you received an offer, you'll find advice on navigating negotiation, getting insider info, and helping you navigate the transition to your next role.

Good luck and enjoy the journey—you got this!

PART I: THE MODERN PRODUCT DESIGNER

3 Product Design Skills, Traits, and Responsibilities

Product designer. UX designer. UI/UX designer. Interaction designer. Experience designer. There are just some of the many titles designers call themselves these days. But look deeper and you'll quickly realize that one company's product designer is very different from another's. Before diving into titles, it helps to step back and start by asking yourself:

- What type of designer are you?
- What are your strengths and what are your growth areas?
- What traits are second nature and what doesn't come as easy?
- If you were to make up your own title, how would you describe yourself?

By understanding yourself, your skills, you'll be able to come up with a compelling value proposition that gets companies excited to work with you. Yes, this will take some time upfront to think about. But by taking a focused approach you'll not only target opportunities that are a good fit but also increase your chances of landing an offer that's closer to your ideal role.

Product design is a field that requires a combination of many skills and traits. It might seem overwhelming at first to realize how much there is to learn, but the good news is that no one is expected to master everything. Even if someone hypothetically did, they wouldn't have the time to get everything done.

This natural constraint is a good thing, as it allows you to focus on mastering a couple of skills that are **in demand** and **meaningful** to you. As a designer, you have to think about ways to creatively combine your skills to synthesize, identify the right problems, and solve them efficiently.

3.1 *What Does a Product Designer Do?*

The design industry has evolved significantly over the last few decades. Significant innovations in mobile computing have increased design scope to native and wearable devices. Larger tech companies translated psychology principles with the help of design into engaging, and at times addictive, products. All of this is to say that the roles and responsibilities of designers have significantly changed over the last few years.

The titles of design have also evolved. Previously, specialist skills present in roles such as web designer, service designer, interaction designer, UX designer, UI designer, and information architect are now commonly seen collapsed under the title of "product designer." This sometimes adds more to the confusion since product design expectations vary by company.

CONFUSION To keep things focused and less wordy, throughout the book I'll be using the term product design to refer to UX/UI design as well.

While the definition of a product designer is in flux, here are some general things to keep in mind if you're applying for this role:

- **Craft skills.** Baseline visual design and interaction design skills, sometimes with fundamental user research skills mixed in.
- **Collaboration skills.** The ability to work with other designers and cross-functional stakeholders to ensure everyone is on the same page and is able to deliver a great product together.
- **Professional traits.** The ability to lead, take initiative, and handle complex situations.
- **Strategy.** Also known as "product thinking," it's thinking about business implications of your design decisions and ensuring your work influences positive business outcomes, such as scaling the company's team to help the company grow or reduce costs.

There's more to being a great designer than having a collection of skills, of course. Having the ability to execute and deliver work that leads to impact is the ultimate marker of success. Everything ladders up to why a designer is hired by a company in the first place, to either improve or grow the business.

3.2 *What's Your Design Shape?*

Different models exist out there to map out design skills. It's a rough science and more of an art. IDEO popularized the T-shaped designer[1]—someone who has deep knowledge and expertise in one or two areas (for example, interaction design and research) but has broad knowledge of other areas (for example, service design and brand design). Larger companies, usually with bigger teams, are composed of a mix of designers. Some of those designers tend to be I-shaped—deep specialists in their domain (motion graphics experts, for instance).

FIGURE: ASSESSING YOUR DESIGN SKILLS

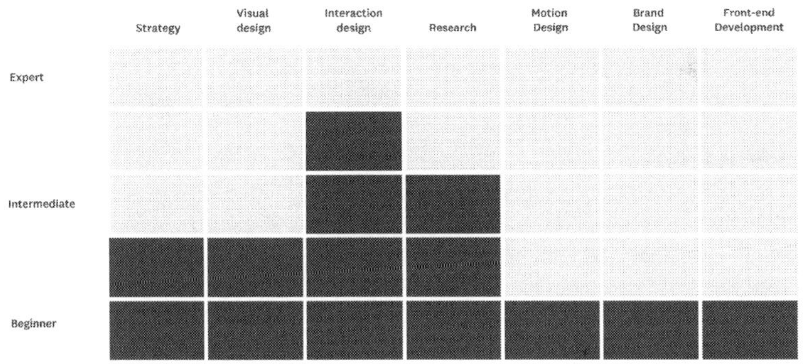

The modern designer will typically have a variety of skills at their disposal.

It's easy to progress at a skill in the beginning, but it gets harder to reach an advanced level and even harder still to become an expert. It's important to prioritize which skills are important to you. As you're going through them and thinking of specific skills, consider:

1. How important is this skill to me?
2. Where do I want it to be?
3. What skills do I want to develop next in my career journey?
4. What skills play to my strengths and interests?
5. What combination of skills will help me stand out as a designer and make an impact?

1. https://chiefexecutive.net/ideo-ceo-tim-brown-t-shaped-stars-the-backbone-of-ideoaes-collaborative-culture__trashed

Not all skills are important all the time, and your needs and industry focus will change. What's important is to be explicit about what you know, where you want to go, and what's important to you.

3.3 *Creating Value in an Organization*

Beyond understanding your own skills, you need to also think about how your skill sets translate to the needs of an organization. At the end of the day, you'll be hired to solve another company's pain point that they are not able to solve themselves. These pain points vary, but there's some consistency depending on the company's maturity.

Smaller companies, such as startups for instance, can't afford to hire many designers, so they typically bring in a senior generalist to start. Typically this designer will have a strong grasp of interaction design and research, and some visual design skills. They'll help establish a design direction for the company and ship product, while integrating design process into the product development cycle.

FIGURE: ASSESSING DESIGN TEAM SKILLS

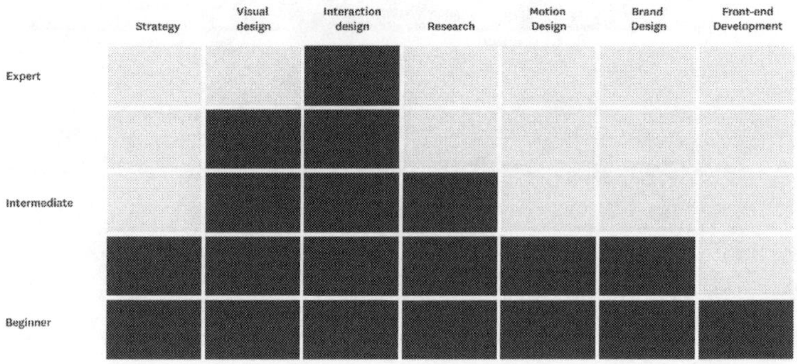

As companies grow, they start to fill out the rest of the pillars based on need.

As the company grows, specialized roles get brought on, such as brand designers, visual designers, researchers, and content strategists. As a team, their diversity and specialized talents allow them to create products that are of high quality.

If the company starts rapidly scaling, typically more and more designers get brought on with similar skill sets. At that point it's important to hire more people because there's more work than any one designer could do. Sometimes these roles might get filled by contractors if it's a temporary project or if recruiting is lagging behind. At other times, if growth is continuous, more full-time employees are brought on. By understanding where the company is in its growth cycle§4.2 and their current pain points, you can match yourself appropriately.

3.4 *Craft Skills*

To do strong design work, you have to be well versed in fundamental skills. It's a prerequisite for the job. This is the raw ability to take inputs and transform them into something meaningful based on your technical knowledge of tools and concepts.

Craft is your knowledge of the tools, methods, and techniques to get the work done. A good designer has a solid grasp of the fundamentals that are usually studied in school, but not everything will be or is expected to be mastered at an academic setting.

◇ IMPORTANT The most important skill of all? Learn how to acquire new skills or renew existing ones as the design field changes rapidly.

From a craft perspective you need to think about acquiring skills in these areas:

- Visual design.
- Interaction design.
- User research and psychology.
- Platforms and devices.
- Design tools.

This isn't a comprehensive list, so take it as a starting point. You may want to focus on some areas more than others. For example, if your work lies heavily on the content side, you might want to lean more into content strategy or copy and information architecture (a whole field in itself). Or if you're interested in doing work that spans pixels and places, you may want to understand the tools and techniques of service design.

VISUAL DESIGN

Visual design plays a vital role in the digital experience. At a visceral level it gives the user clues on what they're about to see. Is this experience serious or playful? An expert visual designer is able to come up with a pleasing composition of elements on a screen.

Today, visual designers have more power, as they play an active role in creating design systems that embed visual design and interaction rules that span multiple platforms.

Some of the core visual design skills include:

1. **Typography.** Choosing type for function and emotion, creating typographic scales that work across multiple platforms and contexts, creating your own typefaces.
2. **Grid.** Creating grids that guide the eye but knowing when to intentionally break the grid; working with baseline and vertical grids, considering the macro and micro grid interactions.
3. **Layout.** Creating pleasing layouts that come together through a combination of typography, image, illustration, and so on.
4. **Color and shape.** Choosing colors that are functional and emotional, colors that are pleasing and accessibility compliant, understanding cultural contexts of color and trends.
5. **Iconography.** Choosing icons, doing minor vector work, creating an icon family that scales across different platforms and contexts.
6. **Illustration.** Using illustration in proper contexts, understanding the nuances of colors and shapes to make changes to existing illustrations, creating your own from a sketch.
7. **Images and composition.** Using images to evoke a certain aesthetic, image manipulation and editing, creating and shooting your own photos, coming up with image and photo guidelines.
8. **Animation and motion.** Animation between screens, micro-interactions, making the customer experience feel polished, and using motion design to inform, guide, and delight.

The best way to learn visual design is to practice. Better yet, try practicing and critiquing design with other senior visual designers. Pick up on their good habits and ask them about how they think through a visual design problem. You'll save yourself a ton of time and acquire shortcuts faster.

Outside of that, make time to replicate the work of others to understand how they've made it. See if you can uncover not just the individual design elements but common patterns and think through the problem they were trying to solve.

INTERACTION DESIGN

Interaction design is about understanding true user intent and developing proper workflows to get the job done. It's the art and science of communicating to the customer in a way that makes sense for them while pushing back on technology constraints meaningfully.

1. **Sketching.** Exploring many ideas quickly on whiteboards and paper. Storyboarding to communicate key interactions. Showing rough ideas via UI thumbnails or drafts of complex multi-platform flows.
2. **Storytelling.** Creating a compelling narrative of your work, "sketching" out your user's world via succinct scenarios, writing a story that stakeholders can relate to and thus take action to make it a reality.
3. **Wireframing.** Moving quickly from low-fidelity sketches, utilizing whiteboards, paper, or digital low-fidelity diagrams.
4. **Flows and diagrams.** Distilling complex information into abstract flows, mapping existing flows of apps, knowing how to balance comprehensiveness with complexity, mapping out flows for multiple platforms and services. Synthesizing complex data and communicating abstract concepts to yourself and to other designers and stakeholders.
5. **Patterns.** Demonstrating awareness of interaction patterns and best practices that are being used right now and why they're effective. Understanding the reasoning for why certain patterns work better than others depending on the platform and context.
6. **Prototyping.** Communicating your work effectively through a series of different stages of prototypes (within a screen, across screens), focusing on prototyping the critical few interactions while leaving out the unimportant many.
7. **Copy.** Giving your product's customers "information scent," guiding them through the experience via effective copy. Providing a good way of finding clues and being consistent across screens and platforms.

There are tons of great resources out there, but if you had to read one book, then consider *About Face: The Essentials of Interaction Design,*[2] 4th ed., by Alan Cooper. It's a great handbook to refer back to as well as a primer for anyone new to design.

USER RESEARCH AND PSYCHOLOGY

As a product designer you probably don't need to be a research expert, but strong interaction design skills are complemented well with foundational research skills. Understanding your customers and their goals and being empathetic to their needs helps you focus efforts on things that truly matter.

In a large company you'll likely have access to dedicated research professionals. For smaller companies this may not be the case as they may not be able to afford both a researcher and a designer. In that case some of the research responsibilities might fall on your shoulders.

- **Heuristic review.** The easiest way to critique an interface via a list of guidelines for UI design (for example, Jakob Nielsen's 10 Usability Heuristics for User Interface Design[3]).
- **Competitive audits.** Analyzing your competitors to learn about their offerings without falling into the trap of copying them.
- **Analogous domains.** Extracting relevant patterns from a different domain and applying it in your work.
- **Usability testing.** Structuring and running unbiased usability studies that will give you proper directional data with confidence.
- **Surveying methods.** Understanding basic tenets of how to write a survey, how to take a correct sample, and how to synthesize data.
- **Contextual inquiry.** Monitoring users in context, understanding how work is actually being done (as opposed to how they say it is), and being empathetic to their needs and workarounds.
- **Research planning.** Putting the methods together in a plan that's cost effective, leading to faster feedback loops, with the right amount of rigor.

---

2. https://www.amazon.com/About-Face-Essentials-Interaction-Design/dp/1118766571
3. https://www.nngroup.com/articles/ten-usability-heuristics/

Lastly, designers should also have a basic understanding of psychology:

- **Cognitive psychology.** Limitations of human memory, how people make sense of information, and what they pay attention to.
- **Behavioral psychology.** Understanding how to influence and guide people with your product.

Need to brush up on research techniques? Check out *Observing the User Experience: A Practitioner's Guide to User Research*[4] by Elizabeth Goodman, et al. This book lays out the core fundamentals while arming you with practical tips.

PLATFORMS AND DEVICES

Understanding the advantages and constraints of platforms is a key skill for product designers. Since product design work is so closely tied to platforms, it's important to know the best practices for each platform and also how these platforms can work together (this is especially important when your company's product is multi-platform). Platform knowledge means understanding best practices and trends as well general market trends, recency, and adoption of a platform.

1. **Responsive web.** Creating a system that works well across multiple sizes and deals with different platform nuances (touch versus point interfaces).
2. **Mobile native.** Understanding touch, mobile, and tablet affordances, being aware of guidelines for iOS (Apple's Human Interface Guidelines[5]) and Android apps (Material Design[6]).
3. **Wearables.** Unique patterns in the experience (for example, designing for bracelets, rings, watches), understanding use cases, small tap targets, managing battery life and other hardware considerations.
4. **Voice.** Designing trees, anticipating user intent and actions, providing cues, new interaction patterns.
5. **AR/VR.** Inventing new patterns or stress-testing existing ones, guiding users in unfamiliar settings, understanding different VR platforms—their capabilities and trade-offs.

4. https://www.amazon.com/dp/B008QWEH62/
5. https://developer.apple.com/design/human-interface-guidelines/ios/overview/themes/
6. https://material.io/design/

Between native (touch) and web (point and click) devices, you'll have your work cut out for you. But if you're in for adventure and want to explore or pioneer new methods of interaction, you're in luck! New wearable devices are emerging all the time, and the world of augmented reality and virtual reality, while maturing, still has a long way to go.

Later on, we'll get into the pros and cons of designing for existing vs emerging platforms.§4.7

DESIGN TOOLS

Product design tools are always changing. Adobe used to be the company of choice for most digital work, but these days things are changing. Sketch has come on the scene and established itself as an industry leader, but now with the emergence of Figma, its dominance is slowly fading. Who knows what the next future design tool might look like.

Some design experts say that learning tools doesn't make you a better designer—you're just a tool expert. I disagree. Knowing how to quickly use a tool efficiently or picking the right tool for the job will help you not only generate more concepts (and thus lead to a better outcome) but also help you get there faster. You certainly don't have to learn every shortcut and install every plug-in out there, but having common ones at your disposal will help you be far more effective, so it's time worth spending.

Here is how you can think about your tool stack:

1. **Low fidelity exploration.** Quick sketches on paper using pens, markers, sketching flows, and UI on whiteboards.
2. **Static UI.** Creating polished mock-ups quickly (Sketch, Adobe XD, Figma).
3. **Prototyping.** Creating interactive prototypes and communicating micro and macro interactions for developers and users (Figma, InVision, Framer, Principle, Origami).
4. **Capturing feedback.** Helping your stakeholders comment and share their feedback on your work (Google Slides, InVision).
5. **Diagrams of complex interactions.** Providing a bird's-eye view for yourself and others of how screens and information flow.
6. **Pixel perfect precision.** When you need to do retouching or pixel perfect precision, usually for photography (for example, Photoshop).

Take this list as a starting point. Depending on the role that you're seeking out you may need to pick up new applications along the way.

Think of design tools as an extension of your skills. Are there tools that can help you generate more quality ideas faster and communicate them effectively? Sometimes the best tool is the one you have close at hand—a napkin and a pen might do when you need to capture an idea quickly. Tools will always change and evolve, but great thinking is never out of style.

3.5 *Collaboration Skills*

Design is a **team sport**. A designer is powerless if they can't communicate what they've done and if they can't work well with others. Strong collaboration and communication skills are key throughout one's journey as a designer.

Initially, entry-level designers focus on smaller features and work primarily with oversight from a senior designer. As one's career progresses, the scope and complexity increase. While strong craft skills are still a prerequisite, one's focus shifts toward influencing others and working with other cross-functional senior leaders on ambiguous, long-term projects.

CROSS-FUNCTIONAL PARTNERSHIP

There are various models of how a designer fits into a company's org chart. One of the more popular models these days is the squad model, where a designer, product manager, and a technical lead all work together to establish the team's day-to-day and overall long-term vision. However, sometimes you'll also frequently work with other specialists, such as researchers and data scientists. If this is a multi-team project, you'll probably have regular syncs with the other teams and it's not uncommon to interface with non-technical counterparts such as folks in sales, legal, operations and so on. You'll be working closely with the team to get your work shipped. Unless you're also an engineer, most likely you'll need developer support to get the thing you've designed built.

Assessing yourself on your cross-functional skills is not easy. The best way to get a true assessment is to ask peers who have worked with you, but short of that, you can also reflect on how you perceive your current skills:

- How do you work with others now?
- Do you build on the ideas of others? Do you make them feel included?
- How have you elevated other designers?

- How have you improved how the team has worked in the past?
- What cross-functional stakeholder do you work best with (for example, engineers, data scientists, product managers, and executives)?
- What cross-functional stakeholder is your weak point?

This is also a testament of your leadership and influence skills:

- How quickly can you build your influence on a new team?
- Can you establish yourself well in an environment that might not be as design focused?
- Are you able to influence your peers, manage up, and potentially change the course of executive decisions for the better?

While these types of skills may not necessarily first come to mind when we think of a product design role, the more senior you are as a designer, the more important these "soft" skills become. If you're an entry level designer—these skills will help you stand out.

COMMUNICATION SKILLS

At its core, design is about communication. In addition to communicating to customers, designers also need to be masters at relaying information to stakeholders. These skills are critical in an interview setting, especially when you're presenting your portfolio. When it comes to day-to-day work, we can view communication through these lenses: public speaking, facilitation, and documentation.

Public Speaking

Whether it's presenting to a small audience of designers at a design critique or presenting to the whole company at all hands, strong communication and presentation skills are critical. These are a couple of ways you can look into assessing your skills:

- How well can you present and explain your work?
- Do other designers understand your work? How about engineers, product managers, and executive stakeholders?

Of course practicing at work helps, but you don't necessarily have to improve these skills at work as there are many public speaking clubs or coaches that can help you practice. That said, the best way to improve is to continuously seek out opportunities to speak and to get feedback.

Facilitation

Public speaking and facilitation skills go hand in hand. As a designer you'll sometimes have to step in and lead a meeting or organize and run a workshop. Back to point number one—design is a team sport, but as a designer, you can take a leadership role in getting everyone organized and excited about the work at hand and thus contribute to the vision.

Consider:

- How well can you lead meetings? Do they all have a clear agenda? Are you able to come to the right answer quickly with a list of next actions?
- Have you run workshops with large multi-disciplinary teams before? How did you get alignment on your work from stakeholders?

Documentation

Communication is not limited to speaking; writing is just as important, especially more so when working remotely. By creating mockups and prototypes, and telling a story and documenting the nuances of interaction, a designer can ensure the vision goes smoothly from concept to implementation.

Consider:

- Does your documentation account for edge cases in your work? Do you strike the right balance of documentation that's accessible to other parties without it being so comprehensive that nobody reads it?
- Are you able to document and communicate effectively to different audiences, such as engineers, product managers, researchers, and other designers?

EMOTIONAL INTELLIGENCE

Strong designers have a healthy level of self-awareness about them. They can also feel the sentiment in the room and take appropriate measures, diffusing a tense situation or rallying the group to persevere when things don't go to plan.

Design itself is a discipline that's based on persuasion, negotiation, and often getting other team members to buy into a specific world view. Of course those views are substantiated with evidence, such as research or data, but not always. Sometimes designers must rely on industry standards or heuristics when there are no resources to run a study, for example.

Here is how you can touch on some of the important aspects of emotional intelligence at work:

- **Emotional regulation.** How well can you control your emotions? Can you harness your emotion to lead and inspire others? Or do you often find yourself unable to control what you say?
- **Negotiation.** How can you effectively push back on requirements or demands without coming off as confrontational?
- **Conflict.** What's your perception of conflict? Are you conflict averse? Do you try to hide or mitigate it? Do you use it as a force for growth? Do you see it as positive? How do you navigate conflict to maximize its positive attributes while minimizing the negative?

ADDITIONAL RESOURCES

Just like with the rest of design, the best way to improve your collaboration skills is to do so in practice. Dedicating time to assess and check in with your stakeholders regularly, not just about the work but also about the process of getting the work done, will help you be a stronger leader and contributor to the organization.

Here are a few helpful guides and resources that can help you along the way:

- *Meeting Design: For Managers, Makers, and Everyone,*[7] by Kevin Hoffman. A book specifically about meetings. I know what you're thinking: what could be more boring than attending a meeting—reading a book about it. But it's a solid read that helps you reframe how you facilitate and conduct meetings, helping you ultimately save more time.
- *Designing Together,*[8] by Dan Brown. All about how to collaborate as a designer, working with different styles, and how to take work together to achieve a better outcome.
- *User Experience Management,*[9] by Arnie Lund. More applicable for managers, it's also a good read when it comes to understanding how individual designers fit into a larger company's ecosystem.

---

7. https://www.amazon.com/Meeting-Design-Managers-Makers-Everyone-ebook/dp/B0754NL9R3
8. https://www.amazon.com/Designing-Together-collaboration-management-professionals-ebook/dp/B00CXQ8KEM
9. https://www.amazon.com/User-Experience-Management-Essential-Effective/dp/0123854962/

- *Emotional Intelligence*,[10] by Daniel Goleman. A definitive book on the topic of emotional intelligence, awareness of self, and how to use emotional intelligence to connect with others (it's not just about being "nice").

3.6 *Strategic Skills*

Should designers have a seat at the table? It depends on the organization and design maturity—some already do, while in companies with low design maturity, designers are merely decorators late in the process. But what does it mean to have a seat, and what's expected of designers who create value beyond producing deliverables?

At its core, strategy is choosing what to do and what to leave out. It's about deliberately prioritizing limited resources (time, money, people) to create value.

Not all designers will engage in strategy. Typically this is the domain of product managers or senior-level designers. Some designers might even eschew strategy altogether in favor of being a master at craft. There's nothing inherently wrong with that, but if you do want to grow your influence in a company, then understanding the business, how it makes money and how design can help, will help you advance rapidly in the organization.

When you're interviewing, demonstrating that your work has led to success will make you stand out. Yes, it's hard to get crisp data and many designers struggle with showing results of their work beyond the deliverable. If you are in this situation, follow up with your team. Get the data. Get the information you need; not only will it be important for interviews—it's important as a feedback loop overall.

10. https://www.amazon.com/Emotional-Intelligence-Matter-More-Than/dp/055338371X

FIGURE: SCALE OF IMPACT

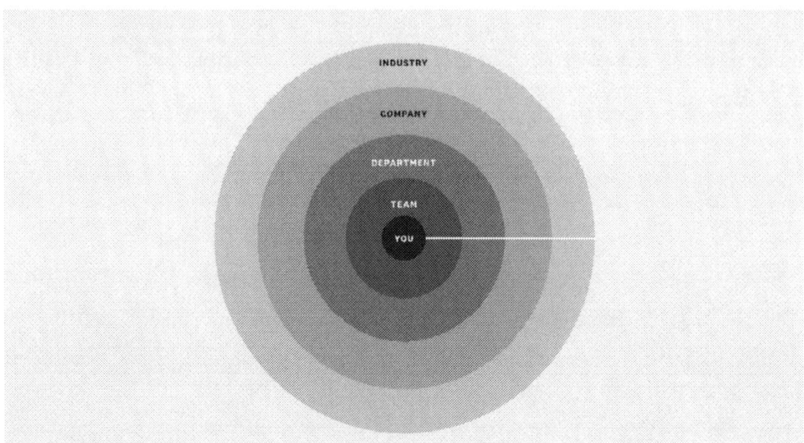

SCALE OF IMPACT

One way to determine your level of strategic prowess is to look at the scale of your impact—how effective was your work and who benefited from it?

1. **Team(s).** You made your team more efficient by bringing in new tools or by holding training that helped everyone ship new features faster.
2. **Department(s).** You shipped a feature for an internal tool that has made everyone's lives in this department easier.
3. **The company.** You created an outsize impact for the whole organization by either reducing costs or increasing revenue and profit.
4. **Industry.** Your work is known outside of the company; you're a regular speaker at conferences and have created strong brands.

The impact of scale is also relative. For example, improving a particular feature may affect a small population of a company's user base. However, if this feature dramatically improves their experience, then that impact can be still considered significant.

OUTCOMES AND MEASURING SUCCESS

Design exists to solve issues, but measuring efficacy of solutions is often fraught with complexity. It's not as simple as showing that doing Y improved a metric X by 10%. That said, ideally before engaging in any project, you have a rough sense of baseline measurement and understand how the experience is currently performing—what parts are working well and which aren't.

In your work, ask yourself:

- When and how do you define success for your projects?
- In absence of data, how did you define a baseline and success?
- What types of data do you use to measure progress—qualitative or quantitative? Are these the right measures? Why?

Sometimes it'll be impossible to get any quantitative data, or you may have already moved on from the company. If that's the case, you can reach out to the company to see how your projects have fared. Alternatively you can also find other ways to measure success, for example by including a customer testimonial or playing back clips from research participants delivering a similar message. Don't constrain yourself to quantitative feedback alone.

PROBLEM FRAMING

This one is natural to all design processes. Understanding the problem that you're trying to solve for and the opportunity that's ahead of you will help you make appropriate decisions when you're deep in the design process. Waiting too long on gathering all the problems will hinder momentum, but not taking the time up front might also cause you to solve the wrong problem and not make any progress on the underlying issue.

Consider these questions:

- Do you approach a problem from first principles?
- Based on your previous experience, did you accurately represent the problem? What did you get right? What was missing?
- How do you push back when the problem is not accurately portrayed or framed?
- How well can you prioritize problems so that the most important one is solved first or addressing one can address many of the subsequent pain points?

Problem framing is a whole exercise unto itself. Many times, it's not as simple as writing out a problem statement, agreeing on it with the team and calling it a day. Oftentimes additional problems come up, and as a designer you'll have to come back, reassess, and make calls of when to pause and when to execute on the work.

SOLUTION FRAMING AND EXPLORATION

Framing the problem is half the battle. If the solution to the problem isn't well thought out or built, then in some ways the steps that come before that were a waste.

- What type of solution are we going for? Should this be a quick-win MVP?
- How does this solution overlap with other solutions? Are we shipping the org chart, or is this a meaningful way to solve a customer's problem?
- Is this solution feasible to build? Will it take significant resources to build and launch?

In the professional world of design, as mentioned previously, quality varies depending on what you want to learn. Sometimes it's paramount to launch fast with minimum features in order to learn; other times it's important to have the final polish to stabilize the experience and potentially solve for new issues that customers may not even have encountered yet.

ADDITIONAL RESOURCES

Strategy is a big topic and resources abound. You might find these useful:

- "How to have impact as a designer."[11] An Intercom blog post by Paul Murphy that outlines the formula for impact.
- *UX Strategy: How to Devise Innovative Digital Products That People Want*,[12] by Jamie Levy. A step-by-step guidebook for how to create great products.
- *Outcomes Over Output*,[13] by Joshua Seiden. A short read on distinguishing deliverables and outcomes, with a few case study examples.

3.7 *Professional Traits*

Aside from having a well-honed skill set, designers possess traits that help them get quality work done while elevating people around them to do their best work. Strong designers raise the quality bar and are seen as lead-

11. https://www.intercom.com/blog/product-designer-impact/
12. https://www.amazon.com/UX-Strategy-Innovative-Digital-Products/dp/1449372864/
13. https://www.amazon.com/Joshua-Seiden/dp/1091173265

ers to emulate due to the positive examples they set in the workplace. Examine the following traits.

GROWTH-ORIENTED MINDSET

Design is a team sport that continues to evolve and rapidly grow over time. No one knows everything, but how you handle the lack of knowledge makes a key difference. Having a "growth mindset" (as coined by Carol Dweck[14]) as opposed to a "fixed mindset" helps you continue to push when the going gets tough and to learn from failure.

Designers with a growth mindset:

- See mistakes as a natural part of learning.
- Attribute their design skills to hard work instead of innate talent.
- Perceive others as having the ability to grow.

Although *mindset* is singular, this is not a binary switch that you flip on or off. Unlike craft and collaboration skills, we usually think of mindset as an either-or. While people do have certain preferences or attitudes and a certain inclination, a helpful mindset can be developed and cultivated.

COMFORTABLE WITH COMPLEXITY AND AMBIGUITY

There are many ways to solve a problem in design.

To understand your level of comfort with ambiguity, ask yourself:

- How have I approached complex or ill-defined ("wicked") problems in the past?
- How many complex assignments have I had in the past (for example, ones that spanned multiple teams, platforms, and initiatives, and which may not have had concrete success criteria attached to them)?
- What is the most ambiguous assignment you've faced?

As you mature as a designer, taking on larger and more undefined projects, your level of comfort with ambiguity and complexity will increase gradually.

TAKES INITIATIVE

In your approach to solving a design problem, you can choose to wait until perfect data and research come in, but oftentimes, realistically, there is not enough time and waiting too long is just as bad as moving too quickly.

---

14. https://www.amazon.com/Mindset-Psychology-Carol-S-Dweck/dp/0345472322/

As your experience increases, you'll know when to move fast and when to wait. Senior designers don't wait for problems, they seize the opportunity, create solutions for the future, and rally their team around implementation.

From a design manager's eye, this is the type of designer anyone would want to hire. Instead of having them wait for work to come in, this designer is restless and will focus on creating value and identifying the biggest gaps that they can close while delivering maximum value to the company.

TRANSPARENT IN THEIR WORK

Design work is never done, and often the first iteration of a design has missing elements and needs to evolve further. It's up to the designer to determine and seek out the type of feedback they need in specific parts of the process, while moving with quality and little supervision.

Consider:

- Are you proactive in seeking out feedback?
- How have you developed others by giving them effective feedback?
- How have you acknowledged mistakes in the past and learned from them?
- When do you ask for help?
- Have you created action plans to get yourself or the project unstuck?

This isn't about hedging or sweeping mistakes under the rug but rather admitting fault or calling for support and help when needed.

HIGH VELOCITY WITH ABILITY TO TAKE ON MULTIPLE PROJECTS

As you mature as a designer, your speed of execution will also increase. You'll be able to move quickly and get to high quality solutions faster. Of course this will vary by company and priority at the moment.

Consider:

- How often do you show your work in progress?
- How long does it take for you to go from idea to polished concept?
- How well can you context-switch, handling multiple projects in parallel while advancing the direction of all of them?
- How much are you able to take on? How good are you at juggling multiple projects? Can you only effectively work on one? Or can you pick up and run with two or more at the same time?

STRONG PLANNING AND ORGANIZATION

When the scope of your projects increases from working on features to working on things that cover multiple surface areas, planning becomes more important. At senior levels you're expected to properly set expectations for the scope of the work and meet those expectations.

Consider:

- How accurate are you in scoping projects?
- How well were you able to manage stakeholder expectations?
- How far out can you reliably plan out projects and foresee potential issues?

SETTING THE QUALITY BAR

Quality is a murky term that could mean different things to different people, and oftentimes quality is negotiable depending on where you are in the product process.

Consider:

- How innovative or ground breaking are your design proposals? Are you pushing bounds and establishing new standards?
- How well can you focus on the critical few things that matter? Can you double down on the things that are working while letting go of things that are just OK?
- How do you set and maintain a standard for "quality" work? Can you push back on constraints to maintain a higher bar for design?

Having said all that, quality doesn't always have to be a compromise. Even in projects that call for MVPs, there's always room to think more holistically and propose future versions. Thinking of quality this way can help you deliver good work in the short term while building a path toward the north star.

Quality will mean different things in the context of the company you're with. In a design agency it may mean pushing the bounds for high end, visually stunning prototypes that win over the client. For a corporate banking application, this may mean getting the details right to account for all the various edge cases while dealing while working within the confines of a legacy infrastructure.

TRAITS AND INTERVIEWS

Some of your interviews, especially behavioral and cross-functional ones, will touch on these traits. However, it's in your best interest to not just keep these traits in mind when interviewing—actively develop them so that they become second nature in your work. How well do you display these traits today? What are some key aspects of these traits that you can grow in?

ADDITIONAL RESOURCES

Carol Dweck's book *Mindset: The New Psychology of Success*[15] is an excellent read about what it means to have a growth mindset compared to a fixed mindset. This concept has been popularized in the media and may seem like old news, but I sincerely recommend the book, as the rich stories bring the ideas to life. Alternatively, you can also check out Dweck's TED Talk, "The power of believing that you can improve."[16]

3.8 *Prioritizing Career Growth*

As you can see, the modern designer possesses a tremendous amount of knowledge about various aspects of design. If you're starting out in your career, don't worry, you don't need to know everything all at once! Naturally, there will be some areas you'll gravitate toward and enjoy, and others where you may need to pay extra attention in order to improve.

If you're an entry-level designer, the core expertise and strength that you should bring to your team lies in your craft. This means you should be spending more of your time on the tactics and execution, getting stronger and faster with production. How companies determine your level of craft will vary and this is a good conversation to have with your manager. But in general you'll probably want to hone in on your interaction design and visual design skills. When you have the basics down, you should pay attention to execution and strategy. All of these things take time, so don't stress out if you don't feel like you're growing as fast as you'd like. It usually takes a couple of tries on multiple projects to improve your skills.

As a senior designer, your work will be more strategic. You may not be pushing the pixels as much day-to-day, but you'll find yourself in meetings

15. https://www.amazon.com/Mindset-Psychology-Carol-S-Dweck/dp/0345472322/
16. https://www.ted.com/talks/carol_dweck_the_power_of_believing_that_you_can_improve

and strategy sessions. You'll be responsible for leading the team toward new ideas and innovations on par with your product manager and engineering lead.

There are of course exceptions to these rules. In larger companies, for instance, there are dedicated specialist roles for visual designers, interaction designers, and motion designers If you're working at a small company or a startup, you might find yourself stepping into strategy more often than not, *and* doing the design, while also running research studies and maybe even coding some of the concepts yourself. For some designers, this can be a nightmare. Others will relish the opportunity to do multiple things at once and learn a lot. Ultimately it's up to you to decide what's the best fit.

4 Defining Your Ideal Role

Being intentional in your job search will help you find a job that's a great fit. Defining what your future role should look like will help you dismiss options that don't fit with that vision and help you make decisions that are based on values that are important to you.

If you're just starting out in your career or you've been recently laid off, it's tempting to jump at the first offer, end the search, and start doing the work. Of course everyone's circumstances vary, and if that first offer checks all the boxes for you, then definitely pursue it.

The trouble comes sometimes when we haven't taken the time to define those boxes. In those circumstances our opinion may get swayed by shiny things like the perks that companies like to advertise: happy hours on Fridays, various discounts, Ping-Pong tables, and so on. While these may sound cool, the reality is that they might not be applicable to you at all. Maybe at this stage of your career what's important to you is mentorship, guidance, access, and the ability to work with senior professionals closely so you can level up and grow quickly.

4.1 *Finding a Job That Fits*

This is why it's important to define your own criteria when looking for a job. Let's apply the jobs-to-be-done framework[17] by Clayton Christensen. Don't think about getting any job—think of **hiring a job** for your needs. This will help you identify a company that can support your growth and help you reach your potential faster with wind at your back.

Think through the company's characteristics that are important to you as if you're evaluating a candidate. What makes them great? Who would you pass and who would you hire? Not all of these characteristics will play an equal role, and you may choose to include others, so treat this list as a starting point:

- Design maturity of the company.
- Your future manager.
- Culture of the company and the team.
- In-house role or work for a design agency.
- Consumer or enterprise products.
- Platforms and devices.
- Location of the company and the surrounding ecosystem (on-site, off-site, and remote.)
- Industry specialization or breadth of expertise.
- Impact and society.

Lastly, you may notice one big thing that's missing from this list—salary. Everyone should be compensated highly based on the value and skills they provide. When you're evaluating jobs against each other, of course you'll consider compensation, and we'll dive into the nuances of it in Breaking Down Your Design Job Offer§24 so that you get the compensation you deserve.

Over time as you're searching for your dream job, you'll periodically revisit this list. It's not static. Maybe you'll learn some new info based on your interviews or by talking with people in industry. There's no penalty for adjusting your criteria; however, it does help to have it in place. Think of your job criteria§4 as your north star that can help guide you toward the right decision.

17. https://www.christenseninstitute.org/jobs-to-be-done

4.2 *How Design Maturity Impacts the Type of Work You'll Do*

A mature design company has internalized and established proven design processes that it has honed over many years. Design is not a layer sprinkled at the end of the product development cycle but an integral piece at the heart of the process, a core competency that's well funded and properly staffed.

TABLE: DESIGN MATURITY TRADEOFF

	LOW MATURITY COMPANY	HIGH MATURITY COMPANY
Opportunity to	Establish a practice of design from scratch in-line with your vision, go beyond the work and shape process and design culture.	Focus on the core work and develop strong individual contributor skills in craft and collaboration.
Best suited when...	You've been in industry for some time; you can do the work.	You're starting out and need guidance and mentorship.
You're interested in	Operations, processes, design management, policy, and governance.	Improving your core individual contributor design skills, focusing on deliverables.

High design maturity companies are great places to learn quickly and with rigor. You can continue to stay and develop your skills further to become a skilled specialist (that is, design lead) or a manager. Alternatively, you can seek a different challenge altogether by going to a low design maturity company to build the design culture there.

CAUTION Design maturity can be tricky. While it's easy to adjust in a startup, trying to instill change within a large organization can be a Sisyphean ordeal. Choose carefully.

HIGH DESIGN MATURITY LEADS TO FOCUS ON CRAFT

For a designer who's just starting out, it's best to go to a company that already has the design process established. This means you can focus on what you do best—honing in on your craft and getting your craft skills refined while at the same time expanding your collaboration skills by building relationships with your team and across departments.

You may like this environment if you:

- Like to refine your design craft skills.§3.4
- Prefer to deliver high quality work which at times may mean moving at a slower pace

- Are interested in working within an existing process that has already been advocated for and gained adoption within the company.

It's often (but not always) that higher design maturity is found in larger tech companies. If you're a designer just starting off, it's likely you'll be paired up with a mentor, a peer, and a manager, giving you the opportunity to get continuous feedback to help you quickly accelerate and grow. This is an invaluable experience and will pay dividends in the long-term. It's not unlike being back in design school, except in this case you're being paid to learn and the organization is vested in your success.

LOW DESIGN MATURITY MEANS ESTABLISHING PROCESSES

Usually companies that have low design maturity are smaller—though I've worked in companies that were tiny and had better design sensibility than some of the larger orgs. It all varies—but with low design maturity companies, you're facing the challenge of defining design.

This is more of a process and management role, which places less emphasis on craft skills. This type of challenge is perfect for designers who tend to be more senior and have their craft down, who have worked in places with developed processes before and now have the responsibility and autonomy to establish a design process at this company.

You may like this environment if you:

- Thrive in ambiguous, rapidly changing environments which may mean shipping work with less than perfect data.
- Can work on a design team but are also OK being the only designer in the company.
- Don't require guidance in your work and can lead initiatives without supervision.

During the course of your career, your requirements for design maturity may change. Designers usually start out in environments that are well structured and well defined, working on a small part of a project. Over time, as their experience evolves, they may want to stay, progress, and climb the proverbial design ladder either as an individual contributor or as a design manager going all the way to VP level.

Early on in my career I had plenty of opportunities to work in low design maturity companies, but not all of them were equal experiences. Companies that were open to change and willing to experiment with new approaches made it a breeze for design to quickly accelerate and mature as a practice. Companies, and teams really, that weren't as open continued stifling design. Ironically, sometimes these roadblocks came from existing designers who prevented others from engaging in design.

Alternatively, some designers may choose to leave and do their own thing either as an independent contractor or as the only designer at a fledgling startup. There is no "right" career path for everyone, and your desire for challenge and growth may change over time.

How do you learn where a company sits on the maturity spectrum? While you may see some telltale signs by talking with interviewers, I also recommend you ask a few questions of your own.§23

ADDITIONAL RESOURCES

The examples above are two extremes of the design maturity spectrum. The reality is that most companies don't neatly fit into those two boxes. Some may be more mature in certain characteristics than others. When you start interviewing and looking for roles, be sure to take those into account.

Here are some additional resources on design maturity:

- Level Up,[18] by Heather Phillips,[19] Design Director at Abstract. This questionnaire enables a company to assess its design maturity across multiple phases from process. Each question has four answers, corresponding to how mature a company is based on its stage (process, communication, employee development, and so on)
- Design Maturity Model,[20] a report by InVision. InVision has interviewed and conducted a large- scale study across many companies, from small startups to large corporations.
- UX Maturity Stages,[21] by Nielson Norman Group (NN/g) is a detailed two-part article on how a company evolves from design immaturity to design enlightenment. Of note is that while growth can sometimes come fast and easy in the first stages, in the last phases it takes more

18. https://designerfund.com/levelup/questionnaire/
19. https://www.linkedin.com/in/heather-phillips/
20. https://www.invisionapp.com/design-better/design-maturity-model/
21. https://www.nngroup.com/articles/ux-maturity-stages-1-4/

than a few years to reach the peak and few, if any, companies ever reach it.

- If you do find yourself being the only designer, check out Leah Buley's book *The User Experience Team of One: A Research and Design Survival Guide*.[22] It provides you the tools and methods for how to navigate your company at a low design maturity stage, advocating for resources while showing value with the tools you have at your disposal.

Lastly, another way to look at design maturity is through the lens of culture.[§4.4] Companies that have a low design maturity but a culture that's open to design and experimentation can be a great fit as well, and can accelerate your growth.

4.3 *Your Future Manager*

Your future design manager will play a key role in your career. They will have the final say about your performance. In many companies a combination of peer and manager reviews are common, but at the end of the day, the manager wields a significant amount of influence. They will ultimately decide how well you've done compared to your peers and whether your performance was satisfactory or not.

While we sometimes think of managers as omnipotent supervisors, the reality is that we still have control over who we decide to work for. In fact, during your interviews, you want to think of interviewing your manager as much as they're interviewing you. What kind of manager would you like to hire? Think about the skills that you're trying to improve and how they can help.

THE DESIGN MANAGER

Having a manager who's come from a design background can be helpful. If you're just starting out in your design career, they'll get you up to speed quickly on the craft side of things. But not all designers make great managers. Some may have turned to management reluctantly because it was difficult for them to advance otherwise. So when you are interviewing with a design manager, take note how they show up and the type of design team culture[§4.4] they've established (more on that in the next section).

22. https://www.amazon.com/User-Experience-Team-One-Research/dp/1933820187

In the later stages of your job search when you get an offer, be sure to talk with other designers[§23] who currently work with this manager or have worked with them in the past.

THE NON-DESIGN MANAGER

Occasionally your manager may come from a background other than design, usually an adjacent field like product management or engineering. That's not necessarily a bad thing. While you won't get as much craft knowledge from these folks, you can still get a lot of value from their expertise in the domain, their knowledge of the company, and their collaboration skills—all crucial for a designer to be successful.

> **STORY**
>
> One of the best managers I worked with came up as an individual contributor and was not a designer, but he did work in tech. The way he handled relationships and structured projects for the team, including stretch assignments, made it very clear what it meant to meet and exceed expectations. After nine months of working together he left, but the structures he put in place allowed me to quickly take over the work and set the team up for success, leading to a satisfactory performance review at the end.

CONSIDER YOUR MANAGER'S PERSONALITY

Another thing to watch for is a manager's personality. As you start interviewing and getting to know different types of managers, try to glean their working style and personality. Would you be able to get along well with them? How do they react under pressure? How have they handled designers like you in the past and supported their growth efforts?

It's implicit that a manager is a role model for the team. How they handle themselves, first and foremost, and other team members sets a strong precedent.

> **STORY**
>
> Early on in my career I had an interview with a well-known health tech company. Just when the portfolio review was going poorly the situation got hostile. The manager started picking apart the approach and twisting my words. Needless to say I didn't get the job, but after that interview I wasn't as enthused about the place either. Who would want to work for a manager that not only fails to

understand how you work but makes snap decisions in their mind and rips your work apart in front of others?

Usually, it's harder to understand if a manager is great but easier to see if the manager doesn't seem as friendly or welcoming. Typically, during the interview cycle most people put on an appearance of talking about how great the opportunity is and how much they want you, but sometimes little signs that things aren't as they seem slip through.

MANAGERS ARE NOT ALWAYS MENTORS

A manager's responsibility is developing their employees, but it's only a part of their job. They sometimes get pulled into messy organizational situations that can take up a majority of their time. Sometimes they may be absent due to a personal issue. Surprise, managers are people too. They don't have superpowers as much as a specialized skill set they've honed over the years.

◇ **IMPORTANT** Get into the details. When you start interviewing, it sometimes may be easy to get blindsided by a company's or a manager's prestige—for example, they worked in all the cool high-tech places and checked all the boxes. But the reality is that you'll be closely working with cross-functional engineers and other designers. Look up their backgrounds. Where else have these designers worked? What were their backgrounds? What did they achieve in their career and what work are they most proud of?

Lean on your manager for mentorship, but don't let them be your only source for professional development. For that, also consider the broader design team and their backgrounds.

ADDITIONAL RESOURCES

If you're curious about management yourself, or if you want to know what they might deal with on a day-to-day basis, in addition to what you should expect of them, check out Julie Zhuo's book *The Making of a Manager: What to Do When Everyone Looks to You.*[23] While the book is geared toward first-time managers, it's still a good read for individual contributors too, especially those reporting to a newly minted manager.

23. https://www.amazon.com/dp/B079WNPRL2/

4.4 *Assessing Company and Design Culture*

Trendy Ping-Pong tables, fun swag, cool off-sites. Some of these things may come to mind when we reference a company's culture. In reality, perks are just surface characteristics of a culture, which usually runs much deeper—it's the way things get done in an organization. Some companies may look great from the outside, but inside the reality is different. When interviewing for companies, it's important to find out the real deal (usually by interviewing the company after you've got your offer,[§23] and at the same time it helps to think about companies' characteristics that are important to you—that is, which environment aligns best with your values.

How do you determine a company's culture? One way to understand culture is by looking at how the company wants to present itself. Usually that's a company's mission statement or its list of values. But beware, what's preached is not always practiced. To ensure it performed at the highest level of ethics, one company put together a statement of human rights and espoused values, such as respect, integrity, communication, and excellence. The company, Enron, is now a popular case study in values gone wrong—the value they rewarded was the opposite of what was written.

One way to think about a company's culture is through its actions. How does it get things done?

COMPANY: MOVING FAST VERSUS APPROACHING THINGS DELIBERATELY

Some aspects of a company's culture may be defined by the industry that it operates in. For example, healthcare companies, including startups, may face a long and rigorous evaluation process before launching their consumer healthcare device to the public. Opposite on the spectrum of industries are tech companies and startups. Going too slow at a startup may be the end of it. As an example, when Facebook was rapidly growing, the common mantra was "move fast and break things." It was a rallying cry to get employees to make decisions quickly even if mistakes happened along the way.

What does this mean for design? Cultures that value a bias for action sometimes encourage a very rough, move-fast-at-all-costs type of design. This can leave you as a designer frustrated because the work is just a series of minimum viable designs that never get polished. At the other extreme is a culture that focuses too much on research and evaluation. Sometimes this leads to projects that have many hours put against them but for one reason or another were cancelled in the final stages.

> STORY
>
> In one past company, design was kept to a bare minimum. In fact, engineering sometimes would start building first and design would have to catch up. While this bias for action got features launched, many of them were later scrapped. Lack of strategy (that design could have informed) led to wasted work.

FIGURE: CHAINSAW AND CHISEL

The ideal is somewhere in the middle. Angel Steger[24] (Director of Design at Facebook) likens the product design process to carving out an ice sculpture. You'll need a chainsaw to hack away at the general shape of the work, but you'll need the chisel to get into the finer details. Doing everything with a chainsaw will get the job done, but that's about it. At the same time, doing too much chiseling may end up wasting precious time as the ice melts. Striking the balance between the two creates a ripe opportunity for you as a designer to create with speed while learning and filling out the details as the general design takes shape.

24. https://www.linkedin.com/in/angelsteger/

COMPANY: RISK TOLERANCE

This characteristic is usually tied to a company's growth stage. Unless they are in dire straits, it's rare for a large, successful company to make big bets that could potentially bankrupt the whole company. Early-stage startups, on the other hand, are always in dire straits; they have to swing for the fences otherwise it's very likely they'll go out of business. As companies mature they gain more shareholders. The IPO brings a whole new level of responsibilities and sometimes a myopic view focusing solely on quarterly numbers.

CONFUSION Playing it safe in a startup? You may be surprised to see *risk averse* and *startup* together in the same sentence. But it can happen. Startups that are data-driven (as opposed to data-informed) usually make good decisions (raising the floor of the experience), but they rarely break lead in the industry (by breaking through the ceiling).

Generally, risk averse companies tend to place a premium on shipping work that's more "buttoned up." The final product has gone through multiple rounds of iterations, reviews, and so on, and every pixel has been interrogated. If the company's design maturity is high, this might push designers to create their best work. However, if the company lacks design vision or is in the low design maturity§4.2 stage, this may feel like a "swoop and poop" where an executive comes up at the last minute and completely discards or discredits the work.

What about companies that encourage risk taking—what's their relationship with design? In the case of an early stage startup§4.5 your work may be more conceptual, focusing on finding the right product market fit. Usually this means lots of divergent explorations, iterations, and experiments, all to find a few promising ideas to build. From a company perspective, it's critical to evaluate multiple options quickly without settling on a subpar solution. Designers can play a major role at this stage, helping the company find its customers and potentially take off in a big way. However, the road there is not without bumps and setbacks. Ultimately, it depends on your appetite and level of risk-taking.

TEAM CULTURE

Within the company's culture—and perhaps the most important part—is the culture of the team you'll be working on. In smaller companies this means you'll have a close relationship with your cross-functional peers:

product managers, engineering, and so on. Be sure to get to know these folks, as you'll be working with them more closely than with other designers.

CONFUSION The industry sometimes uses the term *three-legged stool* to describe a team made up of a designer, product manager, and lead engineer. I use the term *squad,* because modern teams usually have additional contributors, such as research, operations, data scientists, and so forth, depending on the company.

DESIGN CULTURE

In some companies there may not be a design team—in fact, you may be it. As more design hires get brought on, a design culture starts to form organically. The organization will splinter into a matrix: you'll work closely with your squad, but you may also report to a design manager or designers may report to you. Depending on the work, designers may start working on multiple squads and projects. This is similar to an internal agency model where designers are called in ad-hoc as requests come in through the org. As the design team grows, designers get allocated to their individual squads where they build deeper context and relationships with their teams.

So what does all of this have to do with design culture? The short of it is that design has its own unique perspective on the product. Fostering a design culture is about team-bonding but also translating that culture to the rest of the company.

Designers will establish their own rituals to improve product quality.[§3.7] Sometimes these rituals, such as the design critique or design reviews, may be in opposition to a company that values moving quickly. This is where team cultures may start to clash—the PM demands to get something done now while the design manager is pushing for a better customer experience. Conflict is an inevitable part of collaboration,[§3.5] but how it gets reconciled makes all the difference.

As you're interviewing different companies, it's important to see how design shows up:

- Are designers respected as equal value partners on par with an engineering lead and the product manager, or are they merely tolerated?
- How do the various cross-functional stakeholders talk about design and the design team?

- Does design have enough time to get work done, or are designers spread thin across multiple projects and told to hurry up to not block engineering?

These are some of the things to watch for as you get a sense of cultures at different places.

CLOSING THOUGHTS ON CULTURE

In summary, if you've done your homework and researched the company, you'll be able to weed out the companies that have "bad" cultures (toxic environments with high turnover). They are few, but they exist. The most important thing is to find a culture that resonates with your personal values.

- How do you like to get work done? Do you prefer a more laid-back environment (slower growth but at a reasonable pace) or something more intense (potentially leading to faster growth)?
- Do you crave structure and organization (such as in a large company), or are you fine operating in environments where things change every day and the problems are far more ambiguous (a tiny startup)?

Beyond a company's culture, what kind of team do you like to work with? If the team you join gets disbanded, would you still be interested in working with those people (who might now be in a different company) or do you believe in the mission of the company more?

Usually it's hard to fully understand culture when you're interviewing from the outside. Yes, you should still read and familiarize yourself with the company's mission statement and values, but until you actually work there, you won't know all the details. One way you can get a better sense of the culture is by interviewing a member of the design team when you're in the early stages of your application process to see what it's actually like. And you should definitely set up additional time to talk with the team once you get to an offer.[§23]

ADDITIONAL RESOURCES

- Although it's more engineering focused, Key Values[25] is a useful resource for getting a sense of product culture at startups. Sites like

25. https://www.keyvalues.com/

Comparably and Glassdoor are also good resources, but take the feedback with a grain of salt as most reviews tend to skew negatively.

- Kim Goodwin, a design consultant, defines four types of cultures:[26] adhocracy, clan, hierarchy, and market. Kim defines each and provides recommendations for how to gain credibility and influence for each culture. Another way of looking at these types is through your own lens—which culture resonates with you more.
- More on Angel Streger's philosophy of design and Growth Design[27] from First Round.
- Katie Dill, VP of Design at Lyft, shares 8 Principles on Scaling a Design Team,[28] a good read on what makes a design team successful in an organization.

4.5 *Designing at a Large Company, Agency, or Startup*

In-house (big company or startup) and agency roles offer different advantages. This is a simplified model, but it should give you a rough idea of the work you'd be doing at those types of companies.

TABLE: TYPES OF COMPANIES

NAME	BIG COMPANY	AGENCY	EARLY STAGE STARTUP
Industry	You'll gain deep expertise and, depending on the company, may work within a limited subset of industries.	At an agency (unless they're specialized) you'll work with a variety of clients who come from different industries.	You'll become the in-house design expert, knowing the ins and outs of your industry and how it relates to the company.
Variety of design projects	In a large company this will be highly dependent on the team. However, the benefit of large companies is that you have many teams to choose from.	You'll be exposed to different clients and organizations. Some engagements last a week and others may last months, but variety is usually the norm.	As the only designer or as part of a small team, you'll have your hands full in a variety of design projects for the company from product, to brand, to marketing, and so on.

26. https://www.creativebloq.com/netmag/kim-goodwin-designing-culture-8135475
27. https://firstround.com/review/defining-growth-design-the-guide-to-the-role-most-startups-are-missing/
28. https://www.behance.net/blog/lyfts-vp-of-design-8-principles-on-scaling-a-design-team/

NAME	BIG COMPANY	AGENCY	EARLY STAGE STARTUP
Salary	Tends to be higher as large companies are sustainably profitable.	Usually runs lower as service businesses aren't easy to scale and most of the cost is due to human resources.	Most of your compensation here will be derived from equity, not so much cash.
Risk and longevity	Usually highly stable, less risk for the company to go under.	As a service business, agencies are inherently risky in that they depend on a continuous stream of clients.	Not many startups survive beyond their first year, and many don't turn in a profit.
Structure	Usually highly structured, defined processes, much slower than a startup.	Depends on the agency, newer agencies typically don't have as much structure.	Usually no structure, the primary focus is on getting the company off the ground.
You'll learn	Specialized individual contributor skills with an opportunity to get into design management.	Similar to the big company, you'll develop specialized craft skills, and you may also choose to advance in the client-relationship track.	You'll wear multiple hats and may cross over domains (marketing, front-end, and so on). If the company grows and starts hiring, there may also be an opportunity to manage incoming designers.

BIG COMPANIES

As an in-house designer at a big company, you'll have the opportunity to master the industry the company is operating in. You'll be responsible for seeing how a project gets built all the way to the end and then track it afterward. Your work may never be cleanly finished (compared to an agency), but that's OK because you'll develop a deeper understanding of your company and the market.

Another way to think about in-house is this: Which domain do you want to operate in? In large tech companies (think Google) you could work on a variety of different projects. In non-tech companies you'll still have project variety, but you'll likely be focused on a specific industry vertical.

In a larger company you'll have the advantage of learning from other designers. You'll also most likely have horizontal mobility to try out different teams and roles and the vertical mobility to climb the corporate ladder, either as an individual contributor or into management.

STARTUPS

Usually, in small to mid-size startups a designer will take on a generalist role. You'll have lots of autonomy, and if you're the only designer, you'll be running the show. This could prove a double-edged sword, as you'll have to continuously learn how to triage and prioritize your time to ship work quickly and sometimes compromise on quality. Most likely the design won't be perfect and corners will be cut to get things out fast.

If you're starting off new, this could be a sink-or-swim type of environment. It's helpful to get perspective and mentorship outside of the company. Startups also typically offer lower pay and are a high-risk but high-reward environment. However, that's not a bad thing (even if you do end up in one that's going through a downturn), and if you're comfortable with ambiguity, this could be a great way to learn and make an impact on large projects.

With startups there are also a few important distinctions to keep in mind:

- **Early-stage (pre-market validation).** These companies change rapidly in search of customers. Your work will change at a similar clip as well. There's a lot of uncertainty, and if you're comfortable with high risk and ambiguity, this would be a good fit.
- **Mid-stage (market validated but far from profitability).** Startups at this stage still feel relatively tame, at least in comparison to early-stage. At this phase you'll be focusing on growth and helping the company scale while lowering costs with the goal of reaching profitability.
- **Late-stage (close to a liquidity event).** These types of startups are closer to a big company; there isn't as much change and the business will do OK in the long run. The design focus will be on optimization and growing existing products.

At a startup, you'll be deep in the work and may develop strong professional relationships as a result. If this company goes well, these connections can last for decades to come—maybe you'll even launch your own startup together someday. Even if things go completely south, you'll have a mutual bond of going through this experience together.

Unlike a large company though, you won't be able to easily move around if you don't end up getting along with your workers. Startups also face the challenge of being selective in hiring the right person—they're desperate for help but usually have little to offer in cash (thus the higher compensation in equity).

WHAT IF YOU ONLY GET OFFERS FROM STARTUPS?

If you are just starting out in the design industry, you may not get the opportunity to work at a large company with established design processes. But you may find certain startups more than happy to take a chance on you.

Some industry veterans argue against newcomers joining startups. They believe that the designer is going to "lock" the company into a cycle of bad decisions and the lack of formal mentorship will stifle one's growth. I disagree. If you've taken the initiative and done your homework, you can still provide a ton of value and learn in the process. While startups typically have low design maturity,[§4.2] as long as their culture is open to design and experimentation, scaling the maturity curve won't be a problem.

Product design isn't etched in stone; things change quickly, and in startups rapid pivots are usually the norm, so no product is too precious to change. As for finding mentorship, you can supplement that from online resources outside the company. Many special groups exist out there, for new designers or for designers within a company.

AGENCIES

At an agency, you'll be surrounded by top designers—it's another great place to start to hone your craft. You'll learn quickly from diverse peers and experienced mentors. In most agencies, design itself is the product.

A downside of agencies is that they usually pay lower (compared to more established companies or larger tech companies). The hours can be long, too, but that depends largely on the company and its culture.[§4.4] As a result, few designers stay in agencies long-term; many choose to pursue more lucrative roles in-house after their agency stint. The ones who do choose to continue typically end up in client management roles, which are less craft focused and require collaboration and business savvy.

◇ IMPORTANT Aside from deeply focusing on design craft, agencies require designers to present and to interact with clients. This opportunity is a great way to get an inside peek into some of the company's inner workings, politics, and team dynamics—without actually joining the company.

The focus of the agencies varies, but in general they offer a variety of projects, which can be a great way to expand your design skill set quickly. One day you might be working for a project on transportation, another on healthcare, and the next day could be something completely different.

You probably won't be able to go very deep and grasp the nuances of each domain, but that's OK because you'll have a broad skill set that you could (in theory) apply anywhere else you feel most passionate about. If you're not committed to a specific industry,§4.10 agencies are a great way to test out the waters and make the jump.

In closing, agencies are in an interesting transition time these days. Over the last couple of years, large consulting (like McKinsey) and tech companies (like Facebook) have been buying up agencies left and right. According to John Maeda's Design In Tech Report 2019,[29] there were 19 agencies bought in that year. So if you do end up at a large company, you may find yourself working for an agency inside the company or working closely with them. Or if you start your work at an agency, don't be surprised if you become part of acquihire.

ADDITIONAL RESOURCES

Looking to learn more about different types of agencies? Take a look at SoDA, a membership organization that has a list of agencies[30] known for their high-quality work.

If startups are more your jam, I recommend starting with a resource such as AngelList[31]—think of it as a LinkedIn for startups. Many jobs listed there are of high quality and usually come with a salary range attached (unlike many job postings online).

4.6 *Designing Consumer or Enterprise Products*

If you're going in-house, two more factors to consider are enterprise or consumer. If you're going the agency route, most specialize in consumer products, but some exclusively focus on complex enterprise apps.

---

29. https://design.co/design-in-tech-report-2019-no-track/#17
30. https://www.sodaspeaks.com/members
31. https://angel.co/

TABLE: CONSUMER VERSUS ENTERPRISE

NAME	CONSUMER COMPANY	ENTERPRISE COMPANY
Places a premium on	Simplicity, high polish, solid craft, aesthetics.	Solving for complex interactions, extensibility.
Who do these companies serve?	Usually many every-day individual consumers.	Usually fewer buyers, who get the product on behalf of a company.
Watch out for	Flurry of activity that leads nowhere.	Sales-driven culture that doesn't value design's input.
Update cycle	Typically moves faster with limitations driven by platforms (for example, mobile slightly behind web).	Slower, sometimes determined by sales cycles or mandated updates that happen a few times a year.

CONSUMER COMPANIES

By the nature of their business, consumer companies are more aligned with their customers. This means that they have to provide an amazing experience right out of the gate that can't be covered up by sales or marketing. Usually these companies tend to favor designers with a high visual design acumen, but that's not always the case. Some consumer companies might have stronger service design and interaction design components, especially if those companies bridge the digital and physical realms (for example, Eventbrite, Getaround).

Consumer companies are usually the ones that are in the news since they try to appeal to a broad segment of consumers. At the end of the day a consumer company can't rely on great product experience alone—it has to make money. Usually they can do this a couple of ways:

- **Charging the consumer for a product.** This is usually rare for consumer companies, as it puts significant barriers to customers and the industry expectation of "free" is hard to overcome.
- **Charging a subset of the customer population.** This is most common with the "freemium" model where the majority of customers use a scaled-down version of the app for free and a small amount of customers pay for more advanced features, subsidizing the overall product.
- **Generating revenue through ads.** Allowing other partners to put ads on their service.

Sometimes companies experiment with a blend of different methods. Giving away the product for free is, of course, the easiest way for a company to grow, but at some point they will have to come up with a sustainable business model that doesn't rely on venture capital dollars. Usually this means relying on advertising. For design, this is an opportunity to find the right sweet spot of driving ad engagement with customers without making everything an ad.

Early-stage consumer startups[§4.5.3] sometimes may struggle to get off the ground. Because the barrier to entry for these companies is low, this may lead to high competition. This can be the right challenge for you if you're OK with a moderate to high level of risk and you're interested in getting in on the ground floor. As a designer, you'll have the opportunity to shape and define the vision for the company with the founding team by working through many conceptual designs. You'll also bring some of the promising directions to life—a rewarding experience to take the process from beginning to end.

Mature consumer companies that are already profitable, like Instagram or Pinterest for instance, offer a different type of challenge. You'll primarily work with an existing product that you will seek to optimize. Sometimes these may be small feature tweaks or they might be brand-new products or features. You'll learn lots about growth design from an experienced team, and you'll get to understand what makes the customers tick at a nuanced level.

ENTERPRISE COMPANIES

Enterprise companies operate differently from a consumer business. From a purely economic perspective, enterprise companies make money by selling their product to other companies. Although the customer base for their product is lower compared to consumer companies, the amount of revenue they make per customer is much higher.

The business model for enterprise designers can be sometimes a blessing or a curse. It can be positive because it will allow designers to focus strictly on helping the customer get the job done without detracting or distracting them with ads. However, depending on the company's design maturity[§4.2] and its culture,[§4.4] you may also run into some challenges. Companies that are sales driven may over-optimize on the client, leading to a fragmented design experience. Design may also be continuously relegated to the back seat as sales people try to "protect" their clients by blocking design from interviewing them.

Another thing to watch out for when joining an enterprise company is its **sales cycle**, which is closely tied to software updates. Due to high product complexity or just older software practices, some companies push out changes to their software only a few times a year. This can be a big challenge for designers, as it usually means fewer learning opportunities. Of course there are workarounds for slower releases, but nothing beats real-world learning once the product is out.

Selling enterprise software used to be heavily driven by relationships. An app was designed essentially to a spec sheet. Frequently this would amount to a complex, hard-to-use interface, which conveniently enough would allow the company to charge more for its services, such as training the employees who would ultimately use the software.

With the "consumerization" of enterprise products, most companies are now moving away from this outdated business model. Some companies are also flipping the top-down sales cycle on its head. Instead of appealing to key decision-makers in the company, they market to new hires who are more likely to try out new products that help them get the job done faster. The business incentive here is aligned with design, creating products that work with minimum friction and little to no training.

As a designer for enterprise, you'll frequently work on complex interaction flows and customer workflows. Every domain (insurance, healthcare, tech, and so on) has its own context and rules that you'll pick up on. If you're interested in tackling big, sprawling problems, this direction may be right for you.

WHICH ONE SHOULD YOU PICK?

In the past, the stereotype was that consumer design is glitzy, flashy, and the most coveted place to work. On the other hand, enterprise design would always get a bad reputation with its awkward looking UIs. It was usually unheard of for enterprise designers to transition into consumer. But now the lines are much more blurred. Both enterprise and consumer companies offer complex challenges for design to solve; both now require strong, quality design output.

Designers in the consumer space can help simplify complex enterprise products. Designers working on enterprise products can tackle complex flows in consumer apps as well. Design skills do transfer over, so at the end of the day it's more about personal preference and the type of challenge that excites you most.

ADDITIONAL RESOURCES

Interested in learning more about enterprise design? Check out the Enterprise Experience conference[32] by Rosenfeld Media which brings in many well-known speakers in the field.

4.7 *Designing for Platforms and Devices*

Over the last two decades the world of product design and its potential applications has exploded. Previously, desktop computers, slow connections, and basic-feature phones used to dominate the digital landscape. Now with more powerful computers and ubiquitous connectivity, new platforms have emerged on the scene. Mobile is no longer the hot new trend but is a mainstream, mature platform with guidelines that have been refined over time. Emerging platforms like virtual or augmented reality are not brand-new either, but the best practices for them are still evolving.

So what does this all mean for design? In part, it depends on where you want to take your career. Working on a mature platform will offer you a safe space to leverage existing patterns and to quickly shape new features that can help solve user and business problems. Emerging platforms, on the other hand, offer an exciting opportunity to define and pioneer the space since there are no set best practices and standards yet.

TABLE: MATURE VERSUS EMERGING PLATFORMS

	MATURE PLATFORMS	EMERGING PLATFORMS
Examples	Web, mobile.	Virtual reality, augmented reality, wearables, autonomous vehicles.
Design patterns	Established and concrete, evolving slowly.	Fluid and changing, opportunity to pioneer and set the precent.
Risk level	None, these platforms are here to stay.	High, these platforms may not be the right solution or may not be economically feasible.

32. https://rosenfeldmedia.com/enterprise2020/

	MATURE PLATFORMS	EMERGING PLATFORMS
Adoption	High across enterprise and consumer markets.	Varies, for example, the use of autonomous vehicles is restricted to certain regions.

MATURE PLATFORMS

Mature platforms have been around for a long time and offer designers the ultimate safety net. These are the devices and platforms that we use in our daily lives, such as:

- Desktop applications and operating systems, like Windows, Mac, or Linux.
- Mobile and tablet apps, such as those running on iOS or Android.
- Web, usually running inside a browser and utilizing a common practice today such as responsive web design to present the experience differently depending on the device.

One advantage of working in this space is near-term job security. Say you were working for a company that was doing native design but this company went out of business, it would be easy to transfer over the native design acumen to another company.

The interaction patterns for mature platforms are well defined, but there's still room for some innovation and optimization as platforms continue to evolve. As an example, new ways of interacting in iOS 14 offer designers new ways to present their content. However, the innovation here is incremental as opposed to groundbreaking when iOS was first launched during the era of feature phones.

EMERGING PLATFORMS

I consider emerging platforms to be those that are not yet fully mainstream and where the best practices are still in flux. Some examples include:

- **Wearables devices.** Smartwatches and fitness devices.
- **Augmented reality.** These could be dedicated headsets, like Microsoft's Hololens, or technologies that you can run on your phone, such as Apple's AR Kit.
- **Virtual reality.** Headsets such as Oculus and HTC.
- **Voice Interfaces.** Google's home, Amazon's Alexa, Siri, and many others.

- **Autonomous vehicles.** Companies like Tesla, Cruise, Uber, and Nuro.

For designers who are interested in exploring new territories and pioneering new interactions, the emerging platforms may offer a safe haven to play with conceptual, blue-sky ideas. By definition, there are usually fewer opportunities available to work in this space; usually these opportunities are found in larger, mature companies that can sustain investment into unproven technologies that may not pan out. For design, this also means many conceptual directions and ideas may never get implemented.

IMPORTANT Not sure if you're passionate about one platform or another? One way you can get a sense of these technologies is by joining an agency[§4.5] that does work across these platforms.

The hardware of these emerging platforms may also be a limiting factor. Since the technology is experimental, you may encounter glitches and issues along the way—the hardware may not work as you expect it to and the platform itself may be rife with problems. However, this is also an opportunity. By experimenting with concepts and patching together workarounds, you may be able to pioneer a new standard not just for a product but for the industry as a whole.

> STORY
>
> During my stint designing healthcare experiences for Google Glass, I quickly ramped up to speed by leaning in on my traditional design skills. When I was interviewing for companies doing work on more mainstream platforms, I was able to show how much of the design and process is easily transferable between the platforms. So if you're worried about boxing yourself in by going the emerging platform route—don't be. At the end of the day, it's how you tell your story that matters.

A few years ago I connected with a well-known designer who was a voice expert in his field. He started before voice interface became a thing, and because there were so few people operating in the space, he quickly made a name for himself as a recognized expert in the field.

WHICH PLATFORM IS THE BEST?

In the end, deciding between emerging or mature platforms is largely a personal choice. Emerging platforms can be high risk but also carry a high reward. Mature platforms have established practices that are important to study and become adept on. Ultimately, at some point emerging platforms cross over the new threshold and become mainstream. By at least having some knowledge of them and keeping track of where these technologies are headed, as designers we can stay ahead of the curve and jump into the new opportunity where it presents itself.

4.8 *Company Location and Surrounding Ecosystem*

In today's largely digitized world, the physical environment still matters to a degree. Living in a city that has a vibrant tech ecosystem confers a number of advantages. Take for example the San Francisco Bay Area. The venture capital industry creates an opportunity for many new companies to kick start growing. A few of these companies go public and become your regular big high-tech company like Google or Facebook, thus creating even more opportunity. Even in the case for startups that don't make it, and that's usually the case for many of them, the ecosystem makes it easier for employees to transition to another company. Because tech opportunities are abundant, the risk of being unemployed for a long period of time is significantly less compared to places that don't have a tech ecosystem.

Aside from employment opportunities, there's a higher chance to run into other like-minded folks and to strike new connections. San Francisco, for instance, has no shortage of tech- and design-related events happening every day. Every summer, San Francisco Design Week allows companies to open up their doors, giving eager designers a sneak peek into the space. Aside from connecting with other designers, there are courses and training for product managers, bootcamps for new engineers, and overall a vibrant ecosystem that supports professional development.

STORY

When I first moved to San Francisco, I found one of my jobs by waiting in line for a product management event. Outside the venue, in the uncharacteristic San Francisco rain, I struck up a conversation with a couple of folks behind me. One of them happened to be a data scientist who was looking for a designer for her startup. I applied and a few months later got the job. This is the power of serendipitous connections and being in the right place at the right time.

Of course the Bay Area is a well-known place, but it does have its challenges, such as rising costs of living that promotes a transient population, making the Bay less of a destination and more of a spring board. According to Hired's 2018 report[33] in the U.S.: Seattle, Austin, and Denver are some of the top cities for relocation for tech workers. New York City boasts its own tech hub, while having far more diversity than the Bay Area. Boston's high student population and medical focus create a unique culture of health tech innovation.

When looking at companies, it helps to shop for a good ecosystem that will not only support you in your current job but for many jobs to come. Of course, depending on where you are in your career (and life), it's not as simple as packing your bags and leaving. An ecosystem that's growing and evolving is helpful for career prospects. Research your geographical locations closely and think not just of the company but also of the surrounding environment.

4.9 *Remote Work and Location*

In the wake of COVID-19 many companies have gone fully remote. Some, like Facebook, Twitter, and Coinbase allow at least employees to permanently work from home. While not all companies are following this trend yet, it's highly likely that in the future more opportunities will be geographically distributed.

If you are interviewing for a remote role, it's important to dig into the details of the remote arrangement. Has the company done remote work before, or is this a first-time experiment? It's not necessarily a red flag if you're the first remote employee. That said, you should learn more about how the company will support you if you are the sole remote pioneer. Holloway's guide on Remote Work[34] is a good resource for anyone figuring out how to navigate the remote work experience.

33. https://hired.com/state-of-salaries-2018

34. https://www.holloway.com/g/remote-work/about

4.10 *Considering Industry Specialization as a Designer*

One decision to consider when you're looking for your next job is whether you want to specialize in a particular industry or domain. For example, you may want to specialize in the healthcare sector because you think that's an area where you'll make the most impact[§4.11] and you may already have some prior industry knowledge that can put you at an advantage. As an industry specialist, you'll be able to get up to speed quickly on new projects and command a premium for your salary. Typically designers choose to specialize later in their careers, but there is no right approach as it's largely a personal choice.

You can also consider remaining an industry generalist. This may be a good choice when you're not yet sure if there's a particular industry you want to focus on and if you still want to double down on your design skills. Your lack of context sometimes may also be an advantage as it may lead to breakthrough solutions that a specialist may have missed.

SPECIALIZING IN AN INDUSTRY

As a designer specializing in an industry, you'll understand the domain deeply and will be able to make a faster impact to the company that hired you. If you're coming to the design from another role (education, for instance), this could be a good way to get an in. For example, new designers who have worked in your field (let's say as a nurse practitioner) will have a domain knowledge advantage over designers who have never done work in this space.

Another benefit of focusing on a specific industry is the accrued domain knowledge. Aside from understanding the context, you'll also be able to build deeper connections with industry peers, potentially raising your profile as an industry expert.

What does a profile of an industry specialist look like? Stacy La[35] started her career as a front-end engineer, later becoming a design lead at Yammer, a company specializing in enterprise software. It wasn't until a few years later that she joined Clover, where she became a lead designer and later a director of design. Around that time she also founded Design for Healthcare SF[36] meetup group, which now boasts 2,000+ members. She didn't stop there but continues to give countless talks and interviews,

35. https://www.linkedin.com/in/stacyla/
36. https://www.meetup.com/design-for-healthcare-sf/

not just about healthcare but also about her role in building a design team from the ground up.

Making a jump into a specific industry may feel overwhelming, especially if you don't know which one to pick. If you're not sure which is right for you, one way to go about this decision is to join a design agency,[§4.5] which will typically allow you to work on projects from companies in different industries.

INDUSTRY AGNOSTIC

You can also choose not to specialize. Many designers choose that route, and it offers the ultimate flexibility. Agencies such as IDEO, while specializing in specific verticals, pride themselves in placing designers who are not familiar with an industry to uncover new insights through a fresh perspective. Big tech companies are not dissimilar—you'll have a variety of projects to work on, potentially with multiple teams.

As an example, Zarla Ludin'[37]s work was primarily in the agency space. She spent a significant amount of time working at Essential before transitioning to Motivate Design. In the end, she co-founded a design agency called twig+fish while also continuing to freelance as an experience researcher. Aside from her stint as an interaction design intern at Autodesk early on in her career, she primarily chose to work in the agency space.

CREATING YOUR OWN PATH

While the distinction of becoming specialist or remaining agnostic may seem binary, the truth is that most designers don't start out in one camp and remain in it forever. As an example, Nastasha Tan[38] started her career working in-house with notable companies like Salesforce and Samsung. She joined IDEO a few years later, where she rose up the ranks to a design director working on various projects in the San Francisco Bay Area office. After over five years of being there she was looking for a new challenge, which led her to a role as Head of Design at Uber's Advanced Technologies Group (ATG). There, she worked on pioneering Uber's autonomous vehicle experience.

A good way to think about this is the type of career experience you want to create for yourself—not just in the next job but over the next

37. https://www.linkedin.com/in/zarlashtahludin/

38. https://www.linkedin.com/in/nastashatan/

decade. How can you capitalize on the opportunities out there (or create them yourself) so that you look back and feel proud of what you've accomplished? What should your career portfolio look like? This brings us to the next topic—impact.

4.11 *Design Impact, Ethics, and Diversity*

PROBLEMS WORTH SOLVING

As you're considering companies and opportunities, it's helpful to also to step back and think about the type of impact you may want to create and the legacy to leave behind. Are you more comfortable working on a deep problem that impacts few but has the power to change their experience significantly? Or would you prefer to cover a smaller problem that affects millions? There isn't a right or wrong answer here, and just like the question of different cultures§4.4—some of these problems may resonate closer with you than others.

When we make decisions, we're usually well aware of our present surroundings and our current situation. While usually it's good to be present in the moment, sometimes it may deter us from taking on an opportunity that might seem risky in the near-term. One way to get over this risk is to reflect on this experience as if you're looking back at it. Jeff Bezos calls it the regret minimization framework—if you were to look back in your life as if you're 80 years old, how would this experience feel? Sometimes this additional perspective can help us see things in focus when viewed from a broader lens.

BUT FIRST, DO NO HARM

The world of design is changing. Another way to look at one's impact is through the lens of ethics. Are there certain industries that you wouldn't want to work for or projects that would go against your ethics because you think the impact would be a negative for society? If this was your last role—what would you have liked to accomplish there?

Some of these questions may seem "fluffy." It's easy to dismiss them as impractical and idealistic, especially when you've been laid off and you're trying to make ends meet. But the reality is that not all tech companies create impact that's positive for the world. Even for the companies that try to stay neutral or "not evil," the reality is far more nuanced. While discussing ethics in design is nothing new, too often these discussions fall by the wayside in practice. The people who bring up ethics in industry are sometimes termed contrarians, but eventually companies come around. In 2020, Twitter started flagging incendiary posts and allows users to filter replies to their posts.

DIVERSITY

Although design as a field is a discipline that's accessible to all, the reality of current hiring practices makes this a privileged profession. It takes skill, yes, plus a healthy dose of luck and a way of "looking the part" to get past the gate. Companies can often avoid negative impact by having a representative employee base. Unfortunately, design, like tech, has not caught up with diversity and inclusion best practices. What starts out as innocuously screening candidates for "cultural fit" ends up as a homogeneous workplace where everyone looks and acts the same. This can quickly lead to bad decisions if employees don't recognize or empathize with customers who are very different from them.

So choose carefully. When ranking the companies you want to work for, consider:

- What is the company's mission, and are its actions in line with what they do?
- How has this company benefited humanity, or has it made things worse off?
- How actively does this company engage in its community? What type of work does it do?
- How does this company treat diversity and inclusion? Is it an afterthought?
- Do they have a diverse board of directors? What does the management team look like?

These days it's hard not to find news of yet another well-known large tech company coming under fire for their lax diversity standards.

ADDITIONAL RESOURCES

Clayton Christensen is well known for his theory of jobs to be done, and one of his seminal books on the topic is *The Innovator's Dilemma*.[39] But

39. https://www.amazon.com/Innovators-Dilemma-Revolutionary-Change-Business/dp/0062060244/

did you know that he also wrote the book, *How Will You Measure Your Life*?[40] In this book, Clayton admonishes readers to think about their guiding principles when making decisions so that they stay true to themselves and not end up in jail.

More on Jeff Bezos' framework[41] in the 2010 Princeton graduating class address.

5 Mapping Your Design Futures

Now that you're familiar with the job criteria, take a step back to brainstorm what aspects of that criteria are important to you. You can use this job evaluation template[42] to get started. One way to think about your next role is in the context of your previous positions. What lessons did you learn there? What was useful and what wasn't as useful? What do you want to do more or less of?

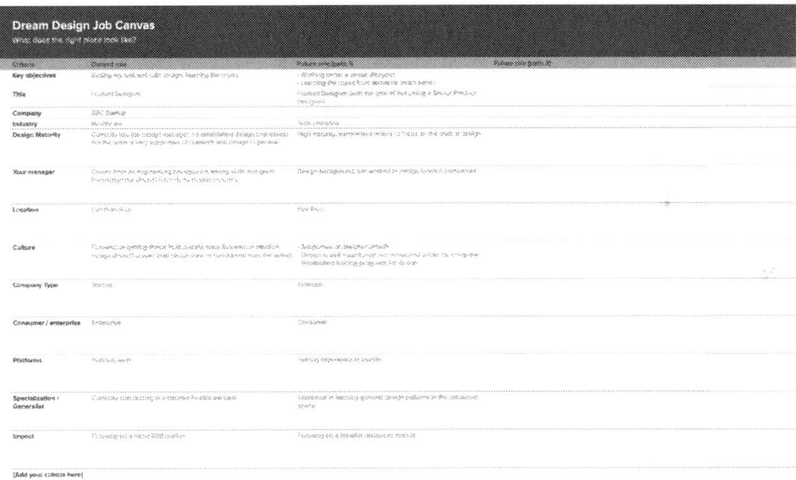

40. https://www.amazon.com/How-Will-Measure-Your-Life-ebook/dp/B006IDOCH4/

41. https://www.princeton.edu/news/2010/05/30/2010-baccalaureate-remarks

42. https://docs.google.com/spreadsheets/u/1/d/1jipbAyAOKd-Gb5slQWJH7KwUyxNVC7j2vKLzHy9BaMU/edit?usp=sharing

5.1 *Envisioning Different Futures*

When we think of career paths we might think of a linear, incremental line steadily progressing as we're improving a little bit every day. But oftentimes progress is not linear. Sometimes you hit a plateau and stagnate, other times you break through and grow fast. Imagine how your design career and your life can unfold in the next five years. You can look at this from a couple of perspectives.

Here are a few futures to experiment with:

1. What would your future look like given the current trajectory and if you stayed in the role that you're currently in over the next few years?
2. What if you specialized in a specific domain, for example healthcare or e-commerce design, over the next few years? What would your path look like?
3. Imagine everything you wanted to do in design came true. What would a day in the life look like in your wildest dreams? What would you need to make happen to get there?

In addition to these questions, add your own criteria as well. Map each scenario out over each year. How does your current trajectory look in year one, what happens in year two, and so on?

These thought exercises are useful, and as you're going through the criteria and thinking about trade-offs, it also helps to do some research to start exploring companies and roles. This will help you understand what's out there and how these opportunities could translate into your own career vision. Feel free to experiment and try out multiple scenarios to see how they fit and feel.

5.2 *Additional Resources*

If you want to learn more about applying design thinking to your life, take a look at *Designing Your Life: How to Build a Well-Lived, Joyful Life,*[43] by Bill Burnett and Dave Evans. If you're interested more in futures thinking, check out *What the Foresight,*[44] by Alida Draudt and Julia Rose West. We commonly think about the future on a linear scale, where things improve

---

43. https://www.amazon.com/Designing-Your-Life-Well-Lived-Joyful/dp/1101875321
44. https://www.amazon.com/What-Foresight-personal-explored-preferred/dp/1537424866/

gradually over time. This book challenges this notion by introducing multiple futures.

PART II: TAKING ACTION AND FINDING OPPORTUNITIES

6 Shaping Your Identity

Before diving into portfolio case studies it's important to step back and think about the type of design prowess that you bring.

6.1 *Uncover Your Superpowers*

Product designer is a generic title. In companies like Facebook, regardless of seniority, everyone is a product designer and so it's hard to understand who is senior, which level they're at, or even what their strengths and weaknesses are. That's why it's important to define the type of product designer you are—one way to do so is by highlighting your own superpowers.

When we typically think of superpowers, the first thing that usually comes to mind is the mastery of a specific skill. Obviously this superpower should be highlighted, but don't worry if you're not there yet or if you can't point to one skill that's excellent.

What skills do you have that are above average? What work using those skills are you proud of? It could be something as simple as rough illustrations and storytelling. What missing skills or perspectives can you bring to a team? What's your unique point of view? What unique experience do you have based on your previous roles?

TRANSFERABLE SKILLS AS SUPERPOWERS

Another way to get at your superpower is to look at transferable skills that you've employed at other jobs. Think about the past experiences you've had and how they've equipped you to understand the customer better, to collaborate, or to be meticulous in one's craft. For example, if you're coming to design from a different field, let's say education, then you know how to run experiments, engage a tough audience, get everyone to participate, and manage group performance over time. If you have a degree in psychology, you understand why people do things the way they do, the complexity of human interaction, and why people, as Daniel Ariely calls it, are "predictably irrational."

UNIQUE EXPERIENCES AS SUPERPOWERS

Your unique experiences can also be your superpower. No one has the same experience of the world as you do. Given your background, your environment, your circumstances, and your unique upbringing, there's something different that you bring to the table. If you can't think of a superpower—ask a friend or a colleague. The external perspective is helpful, as we sometimes don't give ourselves enough credit. Also take a look at Heather Phillips' [45]s article on how to find your design superpower.[46]

6.2 *Beyond Skills—Show Personality*

You are more than a collection of skills. When you start interviewing with employers, they also want to see who you are as a person—after all, they'll be with you and you'll be with them for eight-plus hours each workday. Now this might seem a bit like you're revealing too much, or maybe you'd rather be a chameleon and blend in with the environment to fit in. Don't.

In addition to your skills, you're hired for your opinion—your views and your unique perspective that you've been honing all your life. Of course, there's a subtle art to showing your personality strategically, as you don't want to go overboard by revealing everything all at once. Focus on things that are unique, relevant, and that people can relate to.

45. https://medium.com/u/d47df4834fef

46. https://www.fastcompany.com/3062056/how-to-find-your-design-superpower

As part of my portfolio I would sometimes include photos of dishes I made in the past to tell a more compelling story of cooking and design:

FIGURE: FOOD AS PORTFOLIO WORK

In the past I've seen designers show hobbies, such as:

- Cooking, which is a nice metaphor for design—you can be making something based on a recipe or you can create something new based on the underlying science and principles.
- Visiting museums and new exhibits.
- Sketchnoting at events and conferences.
- Drawing and illustration.

Here's an example.

> *"I love exploring real and imaginary spaces like food, alternate reality experiences, cycling, movies, and TV. In early 2013, I successfully raised Kickstarter funds for a book about ice cream around the world. The book was released January 2016. I traveled to 7 countries and interviewed over 60 ice cream shops. My favorite ice cream flavor is goat cheese ice cream with roasted cherries."*
>
> — Jennifer Ng[47]

Now that's dedication!

The point is not to start going to museums, eating ice cream, and sketchnoting tomorrow. Highlight a hobby that you're already passionate

47. http://www.think-ng.com/

about, one that will resonate with others and help them connect to you on a human level.

6.3 *Write Your Pitch*

Great! Now you have your superpowers and you have highlights of your personality. Next, put it together in an easy-to-consume narrative. If a stranger met you today, how would you introduce yourself? What impression do you want to leave behind?

By drafting a couple of versions of your statement, you'll get a better sense of the narrative you want to convey and will have a response at the ready when you're responding to emails or hitting up networking events.

As with uncovering your superpowers—don't be afraid to step away and ask for help. If you were to ask a friend or a co-worker, how would they describe you or pitch you? What would they say? Try this exercise with others or a group of friends—you might discover new qualities or some that you've taken for granted that others find valuable in you.

FIGURE: DESIGNER BIO GENERATOR

Designer Bio Generator™

Generate your next twitter or website bio.

Biker, coffee addict, music blogger, Saul Bass fan and growthhacker. Operating at the intersection of simplicity and sustainability to express ideas through design. German award-winning designer raised in Austria & currently living in New York City.

Generate another bio

Inspired greatly by Designer Bios tumblr page. Made by Taulant Sulko. Thanks to Alliy Brown for helping with the content and Ricky Miller for polishing up the code.

Tweet this bio

Share this bio on Facebook

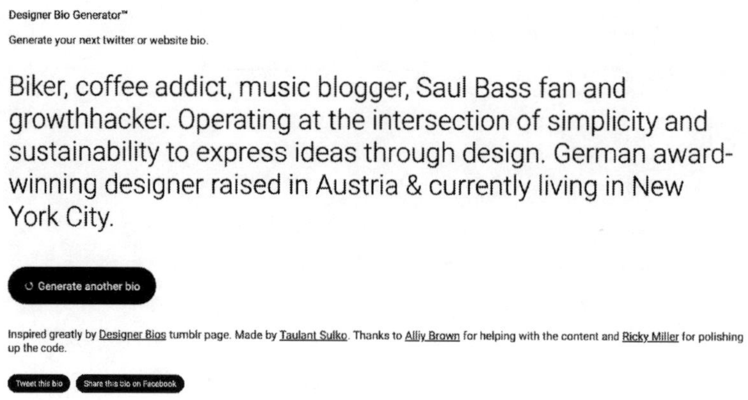

Don't write a statement that can easily end up on the Designer Bio Generator.[48]

Get specific. When you're thinking of aspects of your personality to highlight, be sure to avoid coming across as generic. Many new designers, in

48. https://web.archive.org/web/20220331054949/http://lab.sulko.co/designer-bio/#7-9-1-8-13-2-1-5-1-4-5

their statement about themselves, say that they're empathetic, customer focused, and like to drink coffee. That's not much of a differentiator. Of course as a designer you will be focused on the first two, and many people drink coffee. But not many collect coffee art or make interesting visualizations out of it.

Try it out. To start, list all of your hobbies, passions, and things you like to do. Don't limit yourself just yet and feel free to write out as many as possible. Once you have the list, think of which aspect of personality you want to emphasize—is it something creative, fun, social, or design related, or a combination of multiple things?

PITCH EXAMPLES

Sometimes writing a pitch can be daunting. Here I'll share a couple of examples from two respected design leaders in the industry that can help you refine yours. Now you may not be a design leader or have yet had the opportunity to impact many people with your design. That's OK. As these pitches demonstrate, it's not just about the content but also presentation. At senior levels of design, clear, concise communication is paramount and you can also take away great lessons in communication style.

Marissa Louie

Marissa Louie is a director of UX design at Expedia and also the founder of Animoodles. Here's how she describes herself on LinkedIn:[49]

> *Design leader with a strong product and business background. Experienced in building and coaching design teams, and leading the design of delightful products used by over 1 billion people. As a people manager, I enjoy helping grow extraordinary leaders.*
> *I started tinkering with code as a kid, and fell in love with web design while taking my first computer science course at UC Berkeley. Since then, I've enjoyed tackling really hard problems with some top notch people.*
> *In my free time, I can be found exploring visual storytelling through photography, videography, and animation, and learning about a wide range of subjects including design, business,*

49. https://www.linkedin.com/in/malouie/

leadership, and management. I am intensely curious, and in a state of constant growth.

As you may notice, the first paragraph is straight to the point and uses an inverted pyramid writing method (where you give away the punch line in the first sentence and first paragraph) in which you'll learn all the information that you need to know about Marissa. The statistic "over 1 billion people" substantiates the impact. Even though the third paragraph is about hobbies, these too inevitably intertwine with design and reinforce her current role as a founder and director.

Alissa Briggs

Alissa Briggs[50] is a design director at Autodesk, formerly head of design at PlanGrid where she managed a substantial team growing the organization. Here's her about statement from her website:[51]

I'm a strategic and energetic leader, speaker, and coach with a successful track record of scaling top-notch design, research, and writing teams. Get in touch to discuss how I can elevate your team through workshops, talks, and coaching.

At the top of her site she has an even shorter description leading with the headline "Elevate your design team," an eyebrow, "Design leader, speaker, and coach," and tying everything off with a call to action below. The pitch also links to Alissa's page showing all the different speeches and coaching she's done over the years.

PROTOTYPE YOUR PITCH

Take a moment now to draft up a version of yourself (about half a page) based on the raw ingredients of skills, superpowers, your experiences, and your personality. How does it look? Feel free to do a few more iterations. Next, see if you can get it down to a 30-second pitch that you can give to someone you meet.

Finally, see if you can compress this pitch to a one- to three-sentence summary. You'll use this line in your portfolio, online presence, social accounts, and so on. Think of it as a hook to get people interested in learning more about you.

---

50. https://www.linkedin.com/in/alissabriggs/

51. http://www.alissabriggs.com/

Your pitch will change over time as you get feedback. There's no perfect pitch out there, and making changes is part of the process. Make sure that as you do make adjustments your brand proposition stays clear. Better to turn some people away than deliver a pitch that blends in so much that it becomes unmemorable.

6.4 *Update Your Resumé*

Before diving into the portfolio, start with your resume or LinkedIn. When someone will be looking over your profile, they'll want to understand your story and have the right context when looking through your work. A lot of these initial impressions are based on quick scans of your profile.

- Where are you coming from?
- What have you done in the past?
- What impact were you able to deliver?

This is why it's important to **get the right version of your story** out there. The combination of your work history and portfolio gives the recruiter and hiring manager confidence that you'll be able to do the work and that you're a reliable hire.

Generally, a recruiter or a hiring manager will skim through your profile to learn more about:

- **You.** Who are you, how do you see yourself, what is your unique angle, and what strengths do you bring to the table? While they won't necessarily get all the information here (as usually this comes from your portfolio and subsequent interviews), this is where your pitch comes in to set the right expectations and help the viewer connect the dots between what you say you do and what you've done in the past, as well as the work that you're interested in doing in the future.
- **Work experience.** How long have you been in this industry and what is your career and background like? If you've worked with recognizable tech companies (Uber, Apple, Airbnb), it's usually a plus since they have rigorous standards and are well known. But if you haven't worked at a well-known company, that's not a minus either because, in the end, it's more about what you've done rather than where you've done it.

- **Your title.** Titles are pretty inflated, so a hiring manager might skip over that, but it should give them a rough benchmark of where you are in your career.
- **Your responsibilities.** You might have worked at Apple, but what did you actually do there? What teams did you work on? The focus is on the work that was done and the complexity that you've encountered.
- **Your impact.** What outcomes were you able to achieve?

◇ IMPORTANT You might not have worked for the big tech companies. You might not have that magical five-plus years of experience. That's all fine. What you can do is show how you were able to achieve the five years of experience in two years at a small company with outsize impact. **Outcomes are key**. What metric were you able to move? What value were you able to bring to the team? Emphasize a few key outcomes that truly moved the needle.

If you don't have concrete numbers, how else can you provide evidence of the impact you made? Perhaps there's a strong qualitative signal you got from user research that showed your work made improvements compared to the past experience. If you don't have that, ask your customers for a testimonial or a quote. You can even supplement that with an audio recording (with their permission) in your portfolio to make the story come to life.

7 Building Your Portfolio

Portfolios are a prerequisite for a design role these days. Just like with design exercises, sometimes industry experts also bemoan this point—what if the designer is too busy to make one? What if the portfolio is out of date? It's rare to get an interview without a portfolio, and even if you might get to a phone screen, you'll still be expected to present your work during the final interview. But building a portfolio needn't be a painful process.

You want to build two portfolios:

1. **Your online portfolio.** This may be private; you'll share it as part of your application. Your number one goal with this portfolio is to land the phone screen. It should pique your viewer's interest without revealing too much info (you'll talk about that during your on-site).

2. **Your on-site portfolio.** When you get to the final interview stage, you'll need to create another portfolio. This one will be less verbal and more visual. You'll typically present one or two projects in depth and may have additional slides in an appendix to go over details. The goal of this portfolio is to make a winning impression and get an offer.

In this chapter we'll cover in detail, step-by-step, how to build your online portfolio—after all, this piece is crucial to kicking off the rest of the interviewing process. If you already have a portfolio built, you might want to check out the Design Portfolio Checklist[52] to ensure you have everything covered. We'll cover the on-site portfolio[§12] in the interviews and presentations chapter, as it deserves its own treatment.

7.1 *What If You're Fresh Out of School?*

One of the common challenges that new designers face when putting together their portfolio for the first time is the lack of so-called real-world design projects. If you've just completed a bootcamp or graduated from an undergrad or graduate program, you may not have a lot of working experience. By all means, if in your school projects you worked with a client—a startup or a large company—be sure to feature that work, including any internships that you've done. But if you have none of these?

Hiring managers, especially those without a design background, sometimes don't give as much weight to candidates who don't have many real-world projects in their portfolio. Sometimes they see it as a risk to take on an entry-level candidate, thinking that they'll have to spend a significant amount of time training and developing the employee.

STORY

In a recent interview, a founder mentioned to me how he was afraid of hiring junior designers: "Yeah, we'll get them in, they'll do exactly what they're told, and that will be a complete failure. What we need is people who can push back and tell us we're wrong and come up with a better solution than we would have on our own." So don't be afraid to showcase your process and frameworks that you've used to push back on problems to come up with bet-

52. https://docs.google.com/document/d/17rCw14vFA_KKNd_4ghzGa-SHobEoIW4yaYSLqZFm3Ug/edit?usp=sharing

> ter solutions. As designers, redefining problems is our core competency—no matter the seniority.

So if you find yourself in this situation, what can you do? Generally, you can take a couple of approaches, and my recommendation is to experiment with some of these while you're still applying to your dream role.

TAILOR YOUR PORTFOLIO AND DO YOUR RESEARCH

In general, the advice of tailoring your portfolio to the job at hand still applies. You'll want to show how your projects in school can transfer to the problems your potential employer might be facing. If the company you're applying to has an experienced design manager on staff, they'll usually be able to connect the dots quickly.

However, if they don't have a design manager,[§4.3] you might want to bridge the gap for them by doing a little research and doing some work on the side, showing how in just a few hours of time you were able to take a crack at some of the challenges they're facing. Yes, this does start to look like a design exercise[§15] of sorts, but if the company isn't doing design exercises per se, a teaser of what you can do for them can work wonders to open up a more productive conversation.

ADD FREELANCING SIDE PROJECTS

While you're applying and looking to get that ideal design job, it's not a bad idea to look into design contracting or picking up a few side projects along the way. You can bolster your portfolio by attending a hackathon (which can be an intense but brief commitment for a few days). Alternatively, you can reach out to non-profits to do work pro-bono as long as they're willing to commit the time to communicate and work with you. Another source of work can be a contribution to open-source projects. Many of these are started by eager developers, but few projects have designers, so this could be an excellent way to fill in some gaps.

CONSIDER AN APPRENTICESHIP OR A DESIGN INTERNSHIP

If in your schoolwork you weren't able to do a design internship—this could be another path to consider. There's no shame in taking an internship after graduation. While usually internships don't pay much, they do provide a low-risk way for the employer to get to know you while you're working. Be sure to go above and beyond in this role if you do choose to pursue an internship. Even if things don't work out or if the employer doesn't invite you back—they can still be a strong reference for you and potentially might open doors at other places. But, of course, you also want to take matters in your own hands and continue looking while you are pursuing your internship.

7.2 *Consider Your Portfolio Personas*

The main goal of your online portfolio is to **land the phone screen.** It is not to be exhaustive in describing the rigor of your process (save that for the on-site!) but rather to start the initial conversation and continue the momentum from online, to phone screen, to an on-site interview.

Be choosy in what you show here and **focus on curating** the best representative image of your work. Because you will not present this portfolio, **your portfolio must stand on its own** when a recruiter or a hiring manager is looking through it.

RECRUITER

A recruiter's job is to source qualified candidates and to present them to the hiring manager. Good recruiters understand the design process, have worked with other designers before, and know what a hiring manager needs. Since their job is to get many qualified leads in the pipeline, they'll be scanning your portfolio and resume for signs of good work and process.

Recruiter Goals:

1. Source a variety of candidates through multiple channels.
2. Match the job requirements to the candidate.
3. Follow-up with promising candidates to see if they're a good match.
4. Present top candidates to the hiring manager.
5. Get feedback from the hiring manager and repeat the process until all positions have been filled.

Remember, the objective of the recruiter is to first and foremost **get the right candidate for the client**. You are not the client. The hiring manager is. That said, some recruiters go above and beyond to make sure both parties are satisfied.

HIRING MANAGER

This is your future manager or potentially your manager's manager. They (usually) will have a keen eye for design assuming they've been a designer themselves but sometimes they might come from another field such as engineering, data science, or product management. In that case they might also ask their fellow designer to evaluate your work.

Hiring Manager Goals:

1. Get a sense of your level, your seniority in design (based on scope, impact) and make sure your level matches the job requirements.
2. Understand how you approach design, your strengths and areas of growth and see if you have the right balance of skills for the role.
3. Watch out for any red flags or gaps in employment.
4. Get clarity on your overall career objectives and see if they align with what the opportunity and the company overall.

Imagine the manager to be busy and distracted. Their work is already cut out for them, and they're drowning in responsibilities. They need more designers! Good problem to have, but they're browsing your portfolio while running from one meeting to the next. They'll glance over it for 30 seconds. If it looks interesting, they'll give it two more minutes. If they see good things, they'll let the recruiter set up a phone call.

Sometimes another designer will be evaluating your portfolio as well. They could be a senior, junior, or a peer to you, and depending on where you're at in the company's interviewing process, they might evaluate your portfolio in the beginning or right before your final interview. Just like the hiring manager, they will have a good grasp of design. In addition, if they're a junior designer, they'll also be looking for someone they can learn from.

7.3 *Gather Your Content*

Before you begin your portfolio, it helps to have everything all in one place. It's common industry advice to "build your portfolio before you need it." But let's face it, free time can be hard to come by, and spending it on building a portfolio doesn't feel like it's time well spent. So my recommendation is to go an easier route and to develop the habit of capturing your work as it unfolds.

◇ IMPORTANT To make portfolios, build the habit of capturing key screenshots or changes in your work throughout the process.

A portfolio project often tells a compelling story of design execution from beginning to end. Having artifacts of the experience will help you substantiate your story and provide the evidence you need to come across as an expert in your craft.

FIGURE: COLLECTING ARTIFACTS OF YOUR PROCESS

Capture your design process as you go.

Here's a list of things to consider capturing. This list isn't definitive, and you definitely don't need all of these for a successful portfolio. Rather, treat this as a way to brainstorm assets that you may want to include:

- **Documentation.** Product requirements, design specifications, user research guides, research findings, and so on. You don't need to share the full documentation, but pointing to specific parts in a research finding or the user guide is helpful.
- **Photos of artifacts.** Whiteboards, a napkin, or more formal sketches—anything that has led to interesting insights.
- **Video and audio recordings.** You could use interesting interviews to pull relevant research findings.
- **Design mocks.** These can be snapshots of your work in progress but also capturing the work that got left behind on the so-called cutting

room floor. Showing what you didn't do and why you didn't do it is just as important.

- **Prototypes.** Show your work come to life. These could be recorded or live.
- **Shipped product.** This could be a series of screenshots or a recording of the live product, where you can reinforce the message of how you uphold design quality throughout the product development cycle.
- **Workshops and ideation.** Capturing photos and recordings, these could be especially great if you can show a link from a fledgling rough idea to a polished concept and connect the dots.

At the end of the day, not all of your projects will follow the same process or have the same deliverables. But rough sketches can be an interesting way to break up your presentation and introduce some variety to your portfolio.

FIGURE: ROUGH DESIGN SKETCHES

Using rough sketches can be an interesting way to break up your presentation and introduce some variety to your portfolio.

Having these raw materials handy puts you in a strong editorial position where you can pick and choose artifacts that can tell your story in a compelling way. Expect to discard 95% or more of these, and you may need to go back and find additional content to make a cohesive story. But having most of this content up-front will help you move much faster compared to trying to start completely from scratch.

7.4 *Portfolio Formats to Consider*

These days, portfolios can take on many different formats. In the past, designers would create a customer site with six thumbnails for each portfolio project. Now there are more options to choose from. Remember, the goal of your online portfolio is to get a phone interview.[§10] During that interview you'll do a light portfolio review with a hiring manager and the recruiter, so you want to show work that you're proud of and that's relevant to the job at hand.

Once you're in the final rounds, you'll have to create a different portfolio that's specifically tailored to the company and the presentation format. So don't spend so much time on building your online portfolio that you don't submit it anywhere.

TABLE: PORTFOLIO FORMAT COMPARISON

TYPE	BENEFITS	WATCH OUT FOR	LEARNING CURVE
Note-taking app (like Notion)	No technical knowledge to get started.	Navigation and organization of your case studies. Don't get stuck writing a book that has no visuals to tell your story.	None. You'll need to understand some basic mechanics of linking pages together, but it's a small time investment.
Deck (like Keynote, Figma, or Google Slides)	A deck helps you optimize for the right balance of content and visual while building interest.	By default, decks aren't as accessible on smaller devices like phones.	Some learning curve, as you may need to know the ins and outs of deck design and the app to get a good handle on your presentation.
Site building app (like Webflow)	Fastest way to get started with ability to customize and make changes rapidly as you go.	Over-indexing on layout and site design while not having strong case study content.	Some learning curve, but not as difficult as learning front-end development from scratch.
Your own site	Ultimate freedom and control; you can structure your content however you see fit.	Debugging your portfolio. You may also get unfairly judged if your site is broken.	High learning curve if you're starting out or if you're brushing up on the latest CSS/HTML.

From a hiring manager perspective, the most important part is the content itself. Creating a good-looking portfolio site is nice, but it's not as important as the work itself. Hiring managers are interested in seeing that you've worked on complex problems and shipped results. You will get bonus points if your portfolio stands out, but that's extra. The number one priority is to make sure your case studies cover complex design challenges. You'll want to get that phone call back from them, so make sure your work can stand well on its own.

STORY

Years ago I found myself on the job market with a portfolio three years out of date. I spent weeks making it look visually stunning. The irony? I never shipped it. In the meantime, while I was agonizing about the portfolio site, I created a keynote deck that I've shared with recruiters and hiring managers. In the end, the "site"

> never made it past Sketch. The deck, however, led to many interviews and several offers.

If you're having trouble deciding on the format, it's time to put your product manager hat on. Given your resources—your skill level, time, and commitment, what format can get you to a final portfolio quickly? Optimize for speed over perfection. Getting the job done to a good degree is more important than polishing up a perfect portfolio that you end up not submitting.

To help you with the portfolio, I've created folio[53]—it's free and available on Sketch, Figma, and Keynote.

FIGURE: JUMPSTART YOUR PORTFOLIO

A folio example.

If this is your first time putting together a portfolio and if you're struggling with the format, folio is optimized to follow a case study format while allowing you to expand on your process.

7.5 *Organize Your Portfolio*

Design portfolios can feel like never-ending work. Sometimes we avoid the effort altogether in favor of "research." We go online, we look at other designer portfolios, and maybe even get a little intimidated by some of the work out there. Can my portfolio be just as good?

53. http://www.getafolio.com/

Other times we dive right into design, skipping the important writing process altogether. Or we agonize about the content so much that we write a book, only to discover nobody wants to read it online.

A solid portfolio can be hard to pull off. We'll take a look at what a hiring manager looks for in a portfolio and note how to avoid mistakes. I'll use a deck format (via folio[54]—a free portfolio template deck that I've created) to illustrate these examples, but rest assured you can adapt and use any portfolio format[§7.4] as long as it communicates these key ideas.

You'll want to address these things in your portfolio:

- **Experience.** Based on your prior work, managers want to get a sense of your level and evaluate your projects accordingly. I look at the size and scope of projects. Did you initiate projects or were you mostly an order taker? Did you ship major projects across multiple quarters and teams? Let your resume and portfolio complement each other and tell a consistent story.
- **Expertise and strengths.** No product designer is the same—everyone has different strengths and areas of interest when it comes to the design process. What are your strengths? Where do you shine? This is your competitive advantage that sets you apart.
- **Craft and output.** To get the phone interview, your online portfolio must do the talking for you. Feature your best (likely recent) projects that show a breadth and depth of your skills. Show work that you're proud of—cut out projects that don't do justice to what you're capable of doing now.
- **Process.** Hiring managers are interested in your problem-solving skills. How do you approach your work? Do you have a process in place? Do you follow it too rigidly? What part of the process comes easy and which part is exciting? Hiring managers are looking for designers who can break problems down and sequence the work in a way that drives customer value while reducing engineering scope.

By the way, if you already have a portfolio and are looking to make small adjustments or if you're starting from scratch take a peek at the Design Portfolio Checklist[55] worksheet that comes with the book. It's a

54. http://getafolio.com/

55. https://docs.google.com/document/d/17rCw14vFA_KKNd_4ghzGa-SHobEolW4yaYSLqZFm3Ug/edit?usp=sharing

handy reference to ensure your portfolio covers all the basics that hiring managers are looking for.

PORTFOLIO WRITING PRINCIPLES

When it comes to writing your portfolio case study—imagine writing a magazine article. Your reader finds herself in a busy airport browsing through the newsstand. An interesting cover catches her attention, she quickly flips through the magazine pages. She finds an appealing story, and when she pauses to read it in detail she discovers the content to be well written and informative, thus making the overall experience rewarding.

- **Optimize for scanning.** Tweak the hierarchy to make your portfolio content easy to consume while enticing the reader to dig for more.
- **Support with a compelling story.** As the readers dive into the content, tell the story—give a narrative highlighting key facts that led to unexpected outcomes.

Your portfolio is an opportunity to present your version of the story. Remember your portfolio personas—**they're in a rush**, so they'll spend less than a minute scanning through your portfolio to see if there's some enticing content in there to dive deep into. It's your job as a designer to capture their attention, stop them in their tracks, and make them want you.

At a high level your portfolio should follow this structure:

1. **Intro.** Your name, date of your portfolio.
2. **Experience.** A short summary of your story, how you came to design, experiences you've had, and what makes you a strong designer.
3. **Personality.** A fun slide to show who you are as a person.§6.1
4. **Projects.** Ideally, a couple of recent projects that show the breadth and depth of your thinking and doing and that highlight your strengths as a designer.
5. **Thank you.** Closing slide (or page) with your contact information such as your email, relevant professional social networks, and phone number.

The projects are the meat of your portfolio, but **don't forget the context.** Even little things such as having a portfolio title with your name and giving a little personal background are helpful. Context makes you stand out as a designer, a person—not just a nameless portfolio deck in a stack of applicants. Don't miss this chance to make a good impression.

ABOUT YOU: SET CONTEXT WITH EXPERIENCE

In design, context is everything. For a portfolio to be successful, you'll have to set context, starting with yourself. What's your background? Who are you? What's your superpower? This is an opportunity to highlight role-relevant skills and any transferable expertise.

Think of your portfolio as an extension of your resume (or your LinkedIn profile). I'd like to understand your career path—where have you been and where are you going? The reality is that there are no clear paths or linear progressions. Circumstances change, companies go under, we get laid off. It happens.

Don't lose this opportunity to **tell your side of the story**. How did you end up where you're at currently? Why would you be a great addition to the team? Everyone has a unique story to tell.

If you can—add a personal touch. In a sea of applications, it's inadvertently easy to become just another designer. Feel free to "bring your whole self" and highlight relevant hobbies and fun facts that make you look at design differently. Play to your strengths and include things that might make you stand out as a candidate. If you've worked in smaller companies or in small and barely existing design teams—own that. If you were the only designer there, tell the story of how you stepped up to the role and went above and beyond.

SETTING UP YOUR WORK

Setting up work properly can make or break a portfolio. Think of using progressive disclosure to gradually reveal information, starting with the company, to your role, to the project, to project details.

FIGURE: ESTABLISH COMPANY CONTEXT

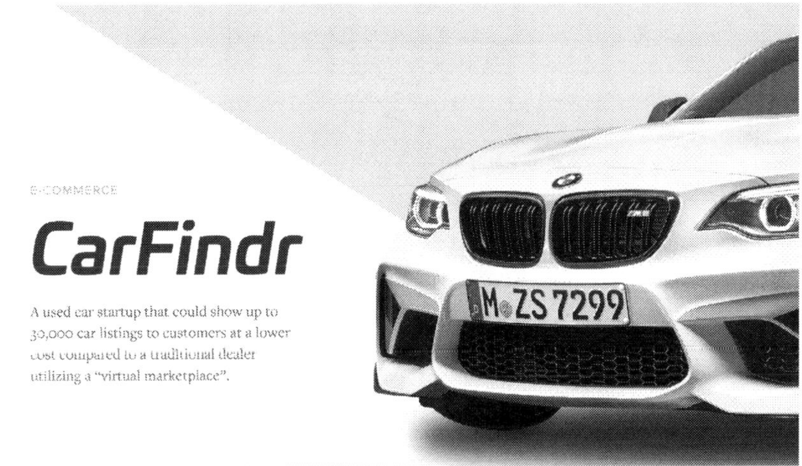

E-COMMERCE
CarFindr
A used car startup that could show up to 30,000 car listings to customers at a lower cost compared to a traditional dealer utilizing a "virtual marketplace".
M ZS 7299

COMPANY OR TEAM

If you worked at a small company, it helps to describe what the company did. Oftentimes smaller companies don't have the luxury of brand recognition, but that's OK. Summarizing what the company did in a few sentences is all it takes. Alternatively, if you did work at a larger company (like Facebook) you can specify your department or team and their area of expertise.

FIGURE: WHAT ROLES DID YOU PLAY?

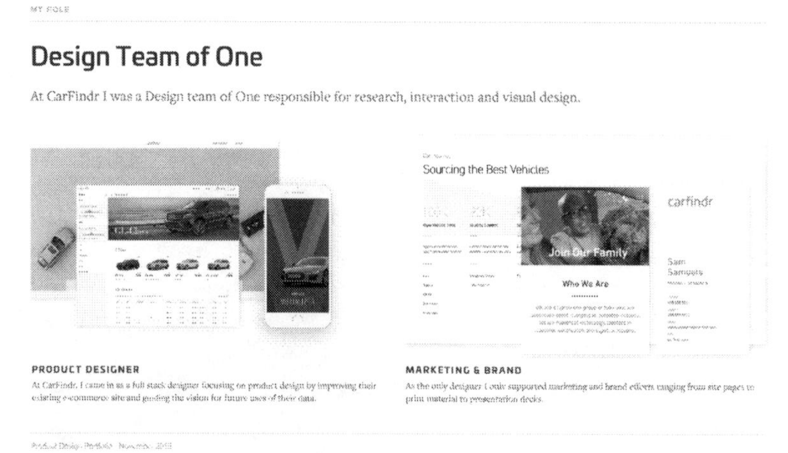

What roles did you play at this company (or team)?

YOUR ROLE AND RESPONSIBILITIES

What were you hired to do? Mention the roles you played, especially if you went above and beyond the call of duty (for example, you were hired to do product design but ended up doing that plus marketing).

FIGURE: PROJECT

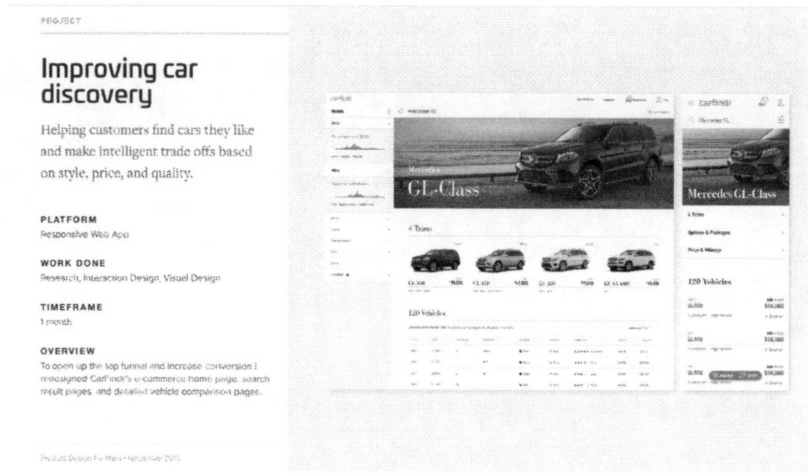

WHICH PROJECTS SHOULD I PICK?

Remember this is your high-level portfolio, so feel free to pick a couple of projects that do justice in representing your skills. Ideally this is your most recent, best work, but it's OK to include projects that aren't the latest as long as it's still work you're proud to show. If you're not proud of it, don't show it—a portfolio is meant to be a curated collection of work not an exhaustive set.

PROJECT OVERVIEW

A successful project is one that has been able to meet or exceed a goal based on measured outcomes with least amount of effort.

FIGURE: SHOWING A SUCCESSFUL PROJECT

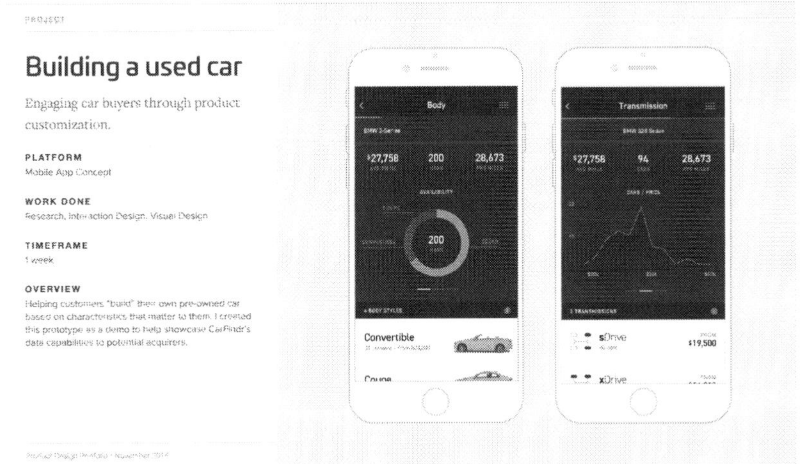

Project cover slide for a concept.

Your cover slide should include:

1. **Summary.** Project title, quick summary, platform, your role, project timespan, screenshots of key changes that capture the essence of a project.
2. **Process.** How did you approach the problem? Pull out a couple of methods that you used and explain how you used them to inform your decision-making. Use this to highlight your expertise, but don't be formulaic—show where you've bent the process to achieve outcomes.
3. **Outcomes.** What was the end result? Sometimes it makes sense to put this section at the end, but you can also put it ahead of process to entice the reader to dive in. You can highlight the metrics that were moved, the before and after, and the outcomes that were achieved.

That's it! The basic format should carry you through, but be sure to make it your own. Not providing enough project context is a common mistake that I see in portfolios. If someone who's coming into your work cold, it's highly likely they won't be familiar with your industry or product.

Design is context specific: include your project's platforms, type of work (visual design, research, or some other), team composition (you were a design lead, for instance), timelines, and so on. Think of this as building a strong foundation for the content that follows, ensuring the viewer is invested in the story. This also allows the viewer to quickly glean enough information so they can choose to either continue to read through this project or skip ahead to the next one.

Finally, include the results of your work up front—for example, "the new design led to a 20% conversion in the checkout flow." Back to the magazine example, use the inverted pyramid[56] style of writing by revealing the punchline.

PROJECT PROCESS

When structuring your process, be sure to highlight specific activities or things you've done that led to new insight. Sometimes I see two extremes:

1. **Not enough process.** Your work is purely visual and there's no explanation of how you arrived at your final outcome. You might be methodical in your approach, but if you don't show work that led up to your final deliverable, it's hard to tell.
2. **Too much process.** At the opposite end is when a designer writes out in excruciating detail all of the things they've done. It's good to see that you have a solid approach in place—but save the details for the in-person portfolio§12 interview.

Strike the right balance of using process to advance your story, pulling out unexpected and thought-provoking insights that informed your work, leading to a higher quality result. Feel free to mix and match different templates to show how your approach led to insight.

56. https://www.nngroup.com/articles/inverted-pyramid/

FIGURE: EXAMPLE PROCESS SLIDE

Feel free to mix and match different templates to show how your approach led to insight.

PROJECT OUTPUTS

Show mocks or prototypes that you've designed to test out your ideas. If you're promoting yourself as a prototype expert, you can highlight some of the nuances of your prototypes and how you were able to simulate the real thing to get the right results from your customers. Before and after shots can prove useful.

FIGURE: PROJECT OUTPUT SLIDES

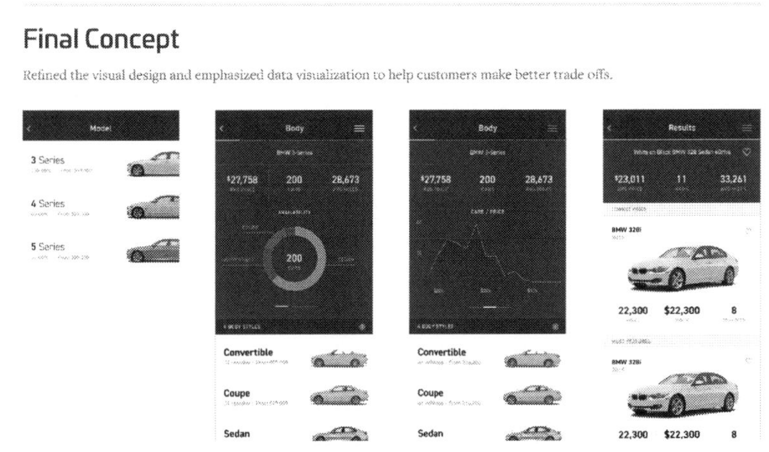

Include representative mocks or prototypes. Before and after shots can prove useful.

Projects usually aren't cut-and-dry moving from process, to prototype, to result—usually a couple rounds of iteration are involved. You'll need to shape your story and presentation accordingly to show how the work evolved.

PROJECT RESULTS

Here, we come back to the beginning—the problem statement. How did your hard work solve the problem at hand? How did you measure your impact?

You can look at it through two lenses:

1. **Qualitative.** How did customers react? Were they delighted by the change? Can you share their testimonials or other forms of feedback? Qualitative feedback can tell a powerful story but, remember, it's anecdotal; so ideally you can supplement it with quant insights to complete the story.
2. **Quantitative.** What was the impact to the metrics you were originally measuring? Were there any positive surprises? Having numbers on your side and drawing a direct link from problem, to solution, to result will help you form a stronger argument for your work.

FIGURE: BOLSTER YOUR RESULTS WITH METRICS

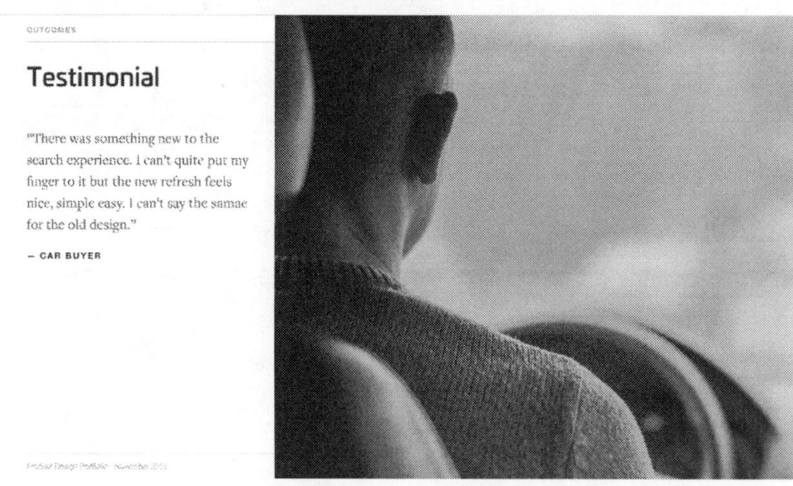

If you can get metrics, great—if not, look at other ways to show how your work led to an improvement.

Sometimes it's hard to get metrics. Even in data-driven companies it takes time to get the numbers. Or you might not even have access to this data anymore. If you can't get it, consider other ways to provide evidence showing that your project led to improvement. For example, maybe your work helped standardize components, allowing the engineering team to move faster.

CLOSE WITH A CALL TO ACTION

Lastly, don't forget the most important piece—your contact info. Include a clear call to action and **double-check that phone number**.

There are no shortcuts. The quality of your work and your thinking is what sets you apart. So don't let the hard work go to waste. Structuring your case studies in the best possible light can make a big difference in get ting that first interview. Good luck—you got this!

7.6 *Prototype Your Portfolio*

If you really want to maximize your chances, prototype your portfolio before submitting. You only get one shot when it comes to making a first impression, so make it your best one.

PLAYING HIRING MANAGER

Is there a dream job you have in mind? Print out the job description, then hand it to your friend and let them play the role of the hiring manager. As they go through your work, ask them to speak out loud. Seeing their gut reaction to your portfolio in person, as they're voicing what they see, is powerful.

If you have industry contacts, reach out to designers or design managers and get their feedback. Managers usually look at portfolios regularly, and designers, too, may sit on interviews, so they know what to expect.

> **STORY**
>
> When I was creating my portfolio I talked with one recruiter, three senior designers, and two design managers at different companies. The diversity of feedback allowed me to improve the portfolio in more ways than one and ensured I addressed all concerns. By the time I brought it to a portfolio review night, I didn't get as much feedback, and one of the portfolio mentors was interested in interviewing me for an open role.

Don't forget—you have your own circle of friends that you might fall back on now and then. Some may be looking for jobs, others have gone through this process themselves; all can give valuable feedback, provided you give them the right frame. These friends don't have to be designers either. In fact presenting your work to somebody from a non-technical background can be helpful in ensuring your content is accessible.

SIFTING THROUGH FEEDBACK

Even as you're testing your portfolio, you may get strong but sometimes conflicting feedback. One designer may say you should do X but another may think you're really better off with Y. Just like a regular design critique, it's up to you to reconcile it in the end. But when you are going through your portfolio with another designer, be sure to ask why, to get a better understanding of their feedback.

Even designers sometimes make the mistake of giving directional feedback without fully articulating their reasoning behind it. It's up to you to facilitate, to probe, to understand where they're coming from, and then either take their suggestion or leave it. Sometimes it also helps to clarify the underlying reason for why you have pursued a certain direction in order to get the most relevant feedback.

At the end of the day, though, it will be up to you to make the final decision. Remember, all the critique is advice that you may or may not follow. Some advice might not be relevant—you may purposefully try to break the rules or you may have more context on the problem than your critique giver—so don't be afraid to leave certain feedback out if you think it will not make for a stronger end product.

7.7 *Promote Your Portfolio*

As we talked about earlier, generally it helps to be very tailored and specific with your job search and your portfolio as well. But if you've already done the work, if you've created and organized your case studies, then you should also consider promoting your work in other places. Think about your online site as **a landing hub**—a place where you have fine control over what to show. Within this hub you have content about yourself, your curated work in the form of a portfolio, as well as any other side projects you're working on that make you stand out.

FIGURE: YOUR ONLINE PORTFOLIO IS A HUB

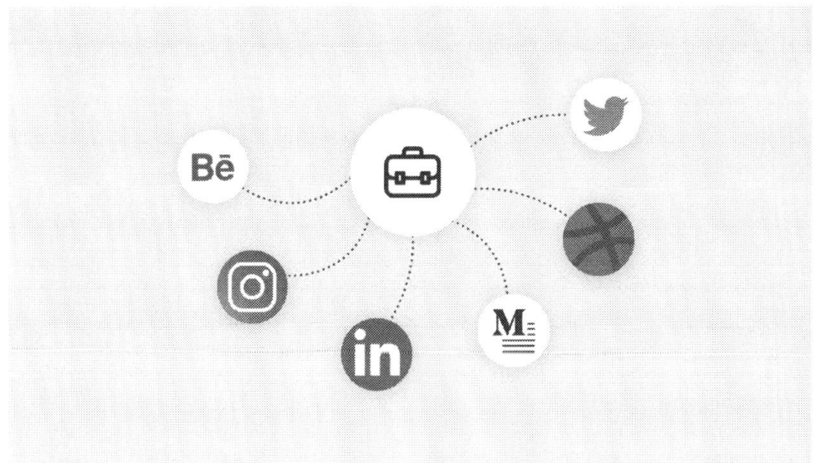

Your online portfolio as a landing hub.

To get visitors in, there are many channels that exist to promote online portfolios—Dribbble, Behance, Squarespace, LinkedIn. Consider using all of them. In the next chapter we'll talk about how you can use passive and active strategies to entice recruiters and put part of the job search on autopilot.§8.6

◇ IMPORTANT If you build it, they won't (necessarily) come. That's why promoting your work is so important. Once you've created your site and put your portfolio together, it's time to capitalize on your effort by showing it on other online platforms.

BESTFOLIOS

Bestfolios[57] curates top portfolios from recent grads and seasoned pros working at major tech companies. Oftentimes recruiters look through Bestfolios searching for talent, and I've heard a few of my friends find success with it. If you have a site that's visually compelling, submit it. If you're looking for portfolio inspiration, it's a good place to visit.

The disadvantage of Bestfolios (and other gallery sites in general) is that you'll be competing against many other qualified designers. But since this site is highly curated and generally not every portfolio gets through, it's still a good way to go, especially if it's one of many channels to feature your work.

---

57. https://www.bestfolios.com/home

DRIBBBLE AND BEHANCE

People have been talking[58] about how Dribbble[59] and Behance[60] promote a culture of posting visually stunning work without context, eliciting comments like "So cool bro!" And it's true, there's some of that. Designers view Dribbble as an exclusive club to get in, but once you're there the excitement stops. Recruiters who are looking for interaction designers, UX designers, or product designers find both platforms insufficient.

My advice is to think of these platforms as a teaser. Let recruiters get an idea of your work based on your snapshots, then substantiate these with a detailed case study on your personal site. Both platforms receive a significant amount of traffic. If you've already put your portfolio together, take advantage of this—promote it.

FIGURE: DRIBBLE AND BEHANCE

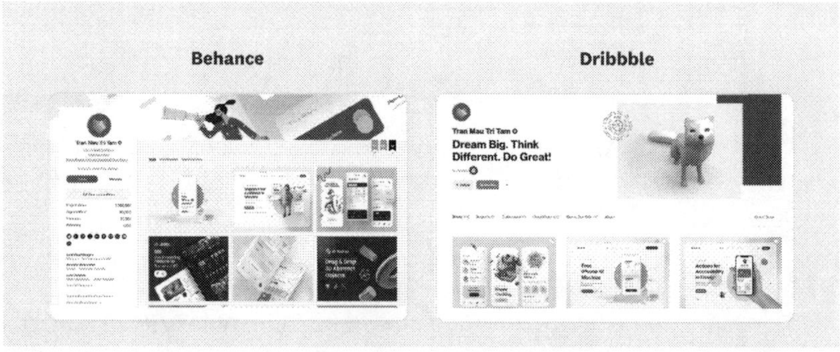

Tran Mau Tri Tam's Dribbble profile.[61]

In 2020, Dribbble launched new offerings for designers, allowing them to customize their landing page and giving advanced posting capabilities like sharing videos. While this doesn't replace a portfolio, it's a nice supplement.

MEDIUM

If you're in a hurry and need to put together a portfolio, Medium can be used as a quick way to get started. However, avoid making your portfolio look like an example from the case study factory.[62] Similar to Dribb-

58. https://www.intercom.com/blog/the-dribbblisation-of-design/
59. https://dribbble.com/
60. https://behance.net/
61. https://dribbble.com/tranmautritam
62. https://essays.uxdesign.cc/case-study-factory/

ble, Medium can be used as a teaser, it's an opportunity to also promote your profile and your work without getting into the nitty-gritty of the process—save that for your personal site.

INSTAGRAM

It might come as a surprise to see Instagram listed as one of the tools to promote your portfolio, but there have been stories of recruiters going through designers' Instagram accounts and getting an interview out of that. If you do choose to include an Instagram account on your profile, make sure you keep it professional. Some designers have a dedicated Instagram, focused specifically on design, where they share snapshots of their work a la Dribbble; but this may prove cumbersome, especially if you're not sharing actively. Either way, this could be yet another channel to drive portfolio traffic.

FIGURE: INSTAGRAM YOUR PORTFOLIO

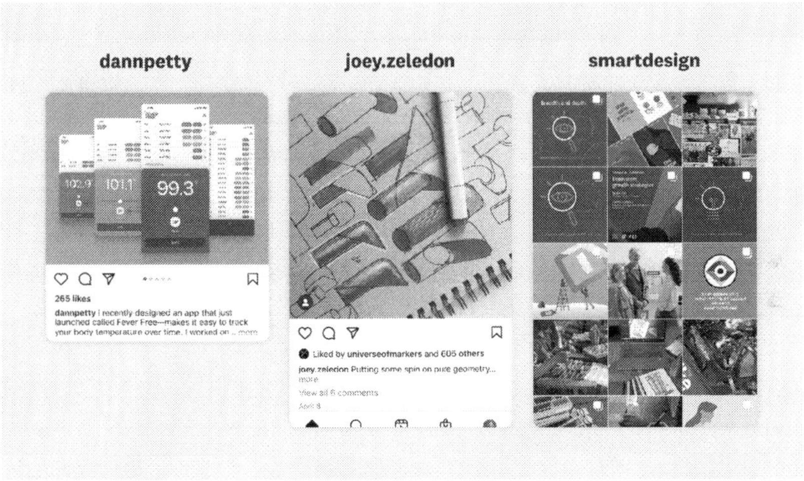

Dan Petty's Instagram feed[63] features shots of his personal life as well as recent projects he's worked on.

TWITTER

Staying active on Twitter can be a great way to engage with the community. Blatantly promoting your portfolio or case studies is frowned upon, but engaging with other designers, and recruiters, you can become an

63. https://www.instagram.com/p/CB2BByBnTfJ/

active member of the community. Beyond engagement, you can also follow UX jobs accounts and hashtags to get the latest job postings.

LINKEDIN

Think of LinkedIn as an up-to-date version of one's resume. In addition to listing out your experience, you want to also tell your side of the story. Once you have your pitch[§6.3] created, you can reuse part of it in your title and your profile description. You can also attach files—these could be either individual case studies or links to your full portfolio (which can be especially handy should you choose to make a portfolio deck).

8 Applying for Roles

What's the one unfair secret way of getting your foot in the door when applying to jobs? Easy. Connect with people first. The best strategy is not to cast a wide net by applying everywhere but to be focused on the few opportunities where you can make an outsize impact. Your future employer appreciates this effort too—they'd rather hire someone with the necessary skills, with a passion for the company's mission, and who has done their homework over someone who's just looking for whatever they can get.

When you are applying, your best bet is to use a variety of channels, from reaching out to alumni[§8.5] to promoting your portfolio[§8.6] in other channels. All of these will help you raise visibility and increase your chances. However, these tactics won't be as effective if you haven't figured out the strategy[§5] first—understanding how your skills fit with the types of jobs you're looking for.

8.1 *Two Strategies for Applying*

Broadly speaking you can apply to jobs in two ways: casting a wide net by applying to several dozen companies or targeting your search to companies and roles that fit your skills and needs best.

CASTING A WIDE NET

By casting a wide net you can reach out to several dozen companies in a short amount of time. Unfortunately, that means you're right there in the sea of resumes and portfolios, with a lower chance of standing out. You'll get some responses, but the rate will be in the low single digits.

Even if you do get a response, it's hard to tell if the role is a good fit for you. When you're desperate, it might feel like anything that looks decent enough is a good fit, but it might not be the right opportunity for you, leading to frustration when you actually start working there.

In general, I'm against this approach. It's time consuming, it has a low success rate, and it doesn't lead to much learning in the process. Too often I see heroic funnels from junior engineers and junior designers looking for an entry-level position. They list out all the companies they've submitted their application to—sometimes in the hundreds—that led to few responses and even fewer interviews.

This is why I recommend you take a more deliberate approach in your search.

IMPORTANT A close cousin to the wide-net approach is the passive autopilot[§8.6] job-searching strategy. By having your portfolio up-to-date, your social media set up, and your LinkedIn outreach preferences turned on—you'll get a trickle of recruiters reaching out. These won't always be the most relevant matches, and you'll still need to vet them, but it's a low-effort way to capitalize on the hard work that you've already done.

TARGETING YOUR SEARCH

My recommendation is to target your job search and apply to places and roles that fit your skills and needs best. This doesn't mean excluding yourself from roles that might be a stretch (that's OK!). Rather you should be picky with your job search—by doing your homework now, you'll save a lot of time later.

You'll focus your efforts and ultimately will be able to find a satisfying job with a culture[§4.4] that fits you best. It will also give you a **sense of control** and the **power to persevere** in a process that might at times feel opaque and frustrating. Being intentional in your job search will help you stay focused and lend you a sense of autonomy and ownership over a process that sometimes feels chaotic.

With a targeted job-search approach, we'll take a look at how you can use your superpowers[§6.1] and your personality to stand out.

8.2 *Using Referrals*

One effective way to apply to jobs is through an employee referral. With a contact inside the company, you shortcut the tedious part of the process and your portfolio lands squarely right in front of the eyes of a recruiter or a hiring manager. How you ask for a referral makes all the difference.

GETTING REFERRED BY PEOPLE YOU WORKED WITH BEFORE

The best referrals come from people you've developed a strong relationship with by working together. Think of these folks as people in your tight-knit inner circle.[64] These are the folks that not only can get you in the door but write a glowing review so that the interview completely flips. Instead of selling yourself, they work hard to get you in and sell the opportunity to you.

However, these are not the only referrals to act on. As a designer you're uniquely positioned to interact with people cross-functionally. This means right out of the gate you have a broad and diverse network of folks that you've worked with before, such as:

- product managers
- design managers
- engineers
- designers
- customer support specialists.

The list goes on. Eventually some of those folks join other companies, or they might know someone who works at a company you're interested in. You might not have a strong relationship here, and these folks are usually weaker ties, but that's OK. The important thing is that you still had a shared experience, which makes it easier to reconnect regarding future opportunities.

64. https://hbr.org/2018/03/why-your-inner-circle-should-stay-small-and-how-to-shrink-it?_lrsc=8a867d81-ec2f-4916-bb7e-b15f30106782

GETTING REFERRED BY PEOPLE YOU JUST MET

These are folks you might have just met, perhaps at an event or maybe you reached out to them directly on LinkedIn. For the most part, you're still strangers. Getting referred by them is harder, but like the first type of referrals, it's important to build the relationship first and make a genuine ask.

Let's imagine you were in their shoes. You're probably busy, stressed about a deadline, and somebody you just met reaches out about a job opportunity at your company—what do you do? Would you immediately submit the referral? Or would you not bother altogether, given everything else that's happening? To make sure your request doesn't fall by the wayside, make it easy for the person referring you to submit your application.

Highlight the experience and projects relevant to the job you're applying for. Show them that you've done your homework about the company, the team, and the project. Follow up by saying that you think you'd be a good fit and that you're interested in learning more. Ask yourself—**how can you make the person who's going to refer you look good?**

REFERRALS ARE NOT A PANACEA

At the end of the day, referrals are just one way to get in, and while they do increase your chance of being seen, they're not a panacea when it comes to getting the job. Any company with a strong recruiting or a hiring manager will do their due diligence and may reject your candidacy if it doesn't meet the job requirements. It's in your best interest to show why you're a good candidate and how you meet or exceed the criteria in the job post. This isn't to discourage you in applying—just think of this as one tactic out of many that you could use in your job search process.

8.3 *Reaching Out Directly*

The best way to connect with a company is by reaching out directly. Whether it's identifying the hiring manager or the recruiter, you want to initiate the conversation and start there as opposed to submitting your portfolio online and hoping for the best.

Yes, this approach does take work and it won't be easy. You may need to ask around and reach out to a couple of folks before finally reaching the hiring manager, for instance. However, because it's not easy, most people won't take this route. So this is yet another way for you to differentiate yourself and reinforce the trait of taking action and being proactive.

TALKING WITH THE HIRING MANAGER OR RECRUITER

If you know the hiring manager for the role, reach out to them directly with your application. If you don't know the manager or who's doing the recruiting, look them up. This will be harder for larger companies, but for startups or mid-size companies, usually you can poke around their site, LinkedIn, or AngelList to at least find the recruiter who posted the listing.

Reaching out to the hiring manager or the recruiter directly increases your chances of getting seen, boosting yourself directly to the top of the queue. It's kind of like that scene from the movie *The Pursuit of Happyness*, where Will Smith's character has no luck going through the gatekeepers, so he tries his luck and reaches out to the CEO directly. The call goes well and the CEO asks "Can you be here in 20 minutes?"

So if you get to this stage, have your pitch[§6.3] ready. Tailor your portfolio and show relevant work, thus making the decision to bring you on easier for them. Not only does it show that you've done your homework but it also shows that you're going to go above and beyond.

DIVERSIFY YOUR OUTREACH

Lastly, you don't necessarily have to talk to the hiring manager or a recruiter. Sometimes it's hard to find those folks on LinkedIn and it's not clear if they're the ones hiring for the role—occasionally people might still have the name of their previous company listed as current on their profile months after they've already left. So diversify your outreach. For example, you might reach out to a product manager or an engineering lead who's working on the same team.

> **STORY**
>
> A few years ago I found out about a networking event where one of the speakers was from a company I wanted to apply to. I connected with the speaker there and followed up with an email to talk about a potential design role. However, except for one email response, I never heard more. It took a second event a few months later, where I connected with the recruiter from that company, to have a more productive conversation. In the end, it takes luck, creativity, and an openness to try different methods to get to a concrete response.

SETTING UP INFORMATIONAL INTERVIEWS

A low-key way to get your foot in the door is by setting up an informational interview. This wouldn't be as high a commitment as bringing you on-site for the hiring manager or the designer you're talking with. However, you still need to fully commit to learning all you can about the company, the role, and the design culture there and come prepared with specific questions you'd like to talk about. Better yet, send these questions in advance to the person you're interviewing so they can come prepared too.

This approach works best for companies you're interested in that might not have design roles open right now but you want to start the relationship early. Be sure to follow up after the interview with a thank you, and if the right opportunity comes up, feel free to broach the discussion around jobs—if someone would be interested in a design role at the company, how might they apply to work there?

8.4 *Working with Recruiters*

Recruiters come in all shapes and sizes. To simplify things, I'm going to focus on **in-house** and **recruiting agency** recruiters. This model is not unlike that for designers. In-house recruiters have a deep understanding of the company and are sometimes embedded on the teams they're hiring for (design or engineering, for example). Agency recruiters work with multiple companies and bring the advantage of breadth—potentially placing you in a company that's a great fit for your (and their) needs.

IN-HOUSE RECRUITERS

In-house recruiters are usually your first point of contact when it comes to getting the lowdown on the company, the team, and the job itself. A good recruiter will do their best to answer your questions and make sure you're left with a good impression (even if you might not be the right fit just now). Use them as a resource to understand the role.

◇ IMPORTANT Recruiters can be your best ally. Treat them well. Focus on high-quality recruiters—equip them to succeed and they'll in turn help you.

Even if the role or you aren't a good fit, it's not a bad idea to still connect and stay in touch periodically. Sometimes things change internally and a position that was open is no longer there. But this doesn't mean that another opportunity might not come up soon after.

STORY

When one of the companies I joined was struggling, a recruiter who I connected with previously recommended me for a design role at a new company that she just joined. Be sure to keep those lines of communication open.

AGENCY RECRUITERS

With an agency recruiter, you can potentially have a lot more flexibility since they work with multiple companies. You may also develop a strong relationship with them over time. The best agency recruiters also act as mediators. They work above and beyond to not just find a good match but to give feedback to the company and you (the candidate) on what each of you thought about the other.

For example, when I was working with a recruiting agency in the past, they would usually brief me on a role and the client first to gauge my interest. If I was interested, they would then set me up with a phone call or an in-person interview. After each interview, we debriefed to understand what the client was thinking. Not every recruiter might have this process in place, but it doesn't hurt to ask.

At the end of the day, agency recruiters are usually compensated based on commission. This could be a good thing and a bad thing. It can be good in the sense that they're also motivated to get you a high salary (since they'll get a percentage cut). However, it may be bad if the recruiter gets sales-y and tries to push you toward a role that you might not be interested in at all.

Of course, not all jobs that will come your way will be a great fit with your goals. In those situations, it helps to step back and see if the opportunity resonates with you based on the future mapping[§5] exercise that you've done earlier. If you have a good relationship with your recruiter, they will try to get you a good match; but bear in mind, some opportunities will take time to surface.

BAD RECRUITERS?

Sometimes recruiters get a bad rap for reaching out to designers with UX engineering roles. It's a tough job, and many entry-level recruiters start off by spamming everyone with semi-relevant job titles. Don't worry about those but focus on the ones that have their stuff together. Recruiters who have taken the time to understand the design industry are worth their weight in gold in connecting you to the right opportunity, so use them wisely.

8.5 *Reaching Out to Alumni*

If you went to college, you have an alumni network. Universities usually do an adequate job at keeping records on their alumni—after all, who else are they going to call for more donations, though in my experience, they don't do a good job of promoting these resources to the alumni themselves. Most of the time they do exist, so it just takes a bit of time to search for them on your alma mater's website.

As an alum, you've paid a ton of money to go to school, so make sure you get the most out of your investment.

Here are some resources your school might have:

- **Official local alumni events** in your area, or see if you can find your local event organizers to potentially organize an event together.
- **Online database** of all the people who graduated from your school—great resource if you're looking to connect with someone.
- **Informal groups** that have been created and organized by your alums for professional development.
- **Identity, affinity, and interest** groups.
- **Emailing lists** informing you of (career or networking) events, latest school news, or alumni stories.

Usually there are tons of resources available for alums, and in my experience either they're not well advertised or not very well maintained, but they do exist! You never know what famous alumni went to your school. If you went to different schools for your undergraduate and graduate degrees—your potential network is bigger by default.

Same advice applies if you've recently done a design or UX bootcamp or have gone through workshops. Although those networks tend to be smaller, they also tend to be more specialized. Leave no stone unturned. It's highly likely there are resources out there at your disposal that you might not be aware of.

8.6 *Auto-Piloting Your Job Search*

Here are some low-effort online strategies to help you land the first interview. Using a blend of different methods, both offline and online, will help maximize your chances of landing the phone screen.

MAKE COMPANIES APPLY TO YOU

What if instead of applying to companies, the companies applied to you? Reverse job auction sites flip the traditional model of filling out the same form repeatedly for different companies. Instead you submit one candidate profile and companies bid on your profile over several rounds.

Although you won't find the giants like Facebook or Google here, the caliber of tech companies is high. You'll get outreach from smaller startups and mid-size companies, as well as larger and more mature organizations like big consulting companies that are building up their design teams.

Some of the sites you can check out in this category:

- Hired[65]
- Underdog.io[66]
- Woo[67]

Hired offers a personal assistant to help you navigate the job process. To my knowledge no other platform has a free service like that. That said, some designers didn't have as much luck due to being either new to design or because of applying internationally. It can be a mix, but don't let that stop you from trying these platforms out.

MAKE THE MOST OF JOB BOARDS

When applying to any job, the best approach is to establish a personal connection[§8.2] first. Without it, applying online is playing a game of numbers, and the odds are usually not in your favor since you're competing against many qualified candidates.

Yet it would be a mistake to ignore job boards altogether. Sites like LinkedIn provide advanced intelligence on companies, people, and

65. https://hired.com/
66. https://underdog.io/
67. https://woo.io/

salaries offered. If you do choose to apply through a job board, try to find out who the hiring manager is and follow up with them directly.[§8.3]

In addition to job posts on Dribbble and Behance, take a look at these other design resources too:

- Designer News[68]
- Authentic jobs[69]
- Coroflot[70]
- AIGA[71]
- CreativeGuild[72] by Creative Mornings

LINKEDIN

These days most recruiters are on LinkedIn. Usually they're given a specific criteria to find and filter candidates—for example, mobile app designer in the gaming space at a mid-stage startup. While some designers forego LinkedIn altogether, I think it's a missed opportunity, especially when you're new to the industry. With LinkedIn, you can get a summary of profiles for applicants applying to the same job.

Use LinkedIn as another channel to promote your work.[§7.7] Be sure to fill out your profile and use it as an opportunity to brand yourself. Then flip the switch on your profile to let recruiters know you're actively looking for jobs.

68. https://www.designernews.co/jobs
69. https://authenticjobs.com/
70. http://coroflot.com/
71. https://designjobs.aiga.org/
72. https://creativemornings.com/jobs

FIGURE: APPLICANT PROFILES ON LINKEDIN

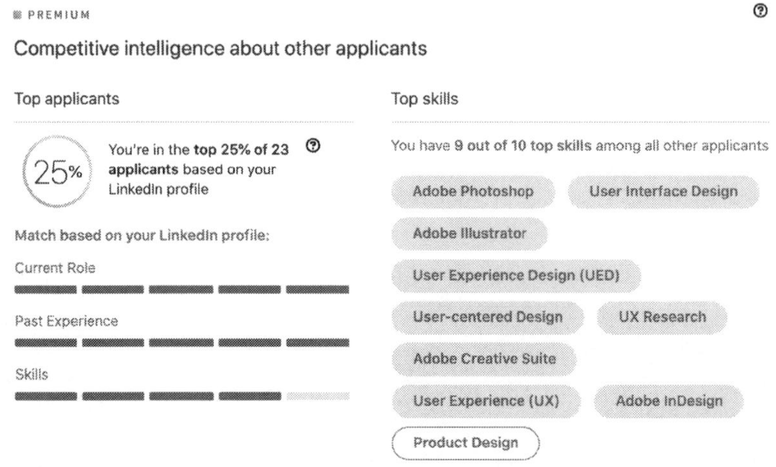

With LinkedIn you can get a summary of profiles for applicants applying to the same job.

If you haven't used it in a while, you can usually get the gold subscription for a free one-month trial. I found it helpful to get the inside scoop on jobs, profiles, and a (rough) salary estimate. LinkedIn premium now comes with LinkedIn Learning, which makes it a good value.

FIGURE: DISCOVER COMMON CONNECTIONS (AND COMPETITION) ON LINKEDIN

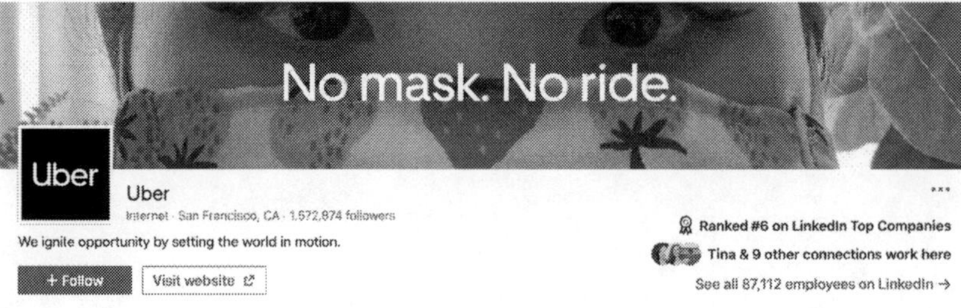

You might discover new common connections who changed jobs recently.

Check out who your competition is for the job to get a rough idea of their skill level, but don't let the job requirements or their experience deter you.

Finally, examine the company to see if there are any **common connections.** LinkedIn will also show people you went to school with who now work at this company. Use this information to get a referral—and remember, referrals can come from people you've just met.§8.2

ANGELLIST

If you're specifically interested in working with startups, AngelList[73] is a great resource—think of it as a cleaner, curated LinkedIn for applying to startup gigs while getting a transparent salary estimate.

As a side note, AngelList has one of the best newsletters and blogs for tech careers hands-down.

FIGURE: ANGELLIST DESIGN ROLES

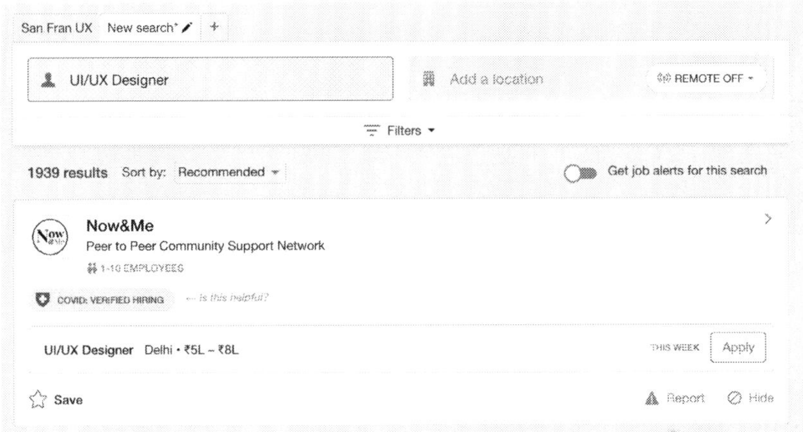

In July 2020, there were 1,939 product design roles in startups all over the world.

APPLYING TO JOBS AS SOON AS THEY'RE POSTED

Sometimes when you apply to a job through LinkedIn, the posting has been live for a few weeks and the company may have already extended an offer. You can avoid this fate by setting up job alerts and get a consolidated list of new jobs as soon as they're posted. Most job boards have this feature as well.

If you truly want to get ahead, **reach out before a job is posted**. Doing so gets you in front of the line before a line even exists. A good way to do this is by setting up an informational interview§8.2 to learn more about the company and the team.

73. https://angel.co/

FIGURE: LINKEDIN JOB ALERT PREFERENCES

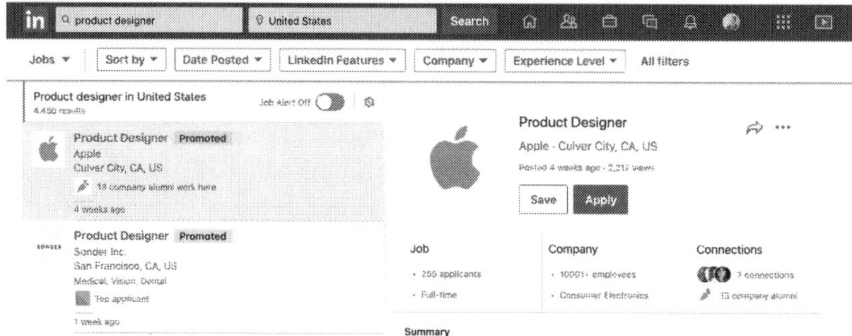

Set your job preferences.

Aside from the usual suspects like job boards and networking sites, designers are hacking together existing platforms to share job posts. Here are a couple of places I found useful.

DESIGNERS GUILD FACEBOOK GROUP

Designers Guild is a designers-only community that's managed by Marissa Louie,[74] Stedman Halliday,[75] Ivy Mukherjee,[76] David Martinez,[77] and Brad Monahan.[78] Designers Guild is a safe space for designers to ask questions and have meaningful conversations about design.

Every month there's a post on who's hiring. It's against group policy for recruiters to join, so the posts are usually made by hiring managers themselves or by designers working for those companies. Usually these posts net a significant number of responses and the caliber of tech companies is high. Most importantly, it sheds a layer of opacity since you can reach out to the person who posted the job.

TWITTER FOR #DESIGNJOBS

Twitter can be a good source for connecting with designers directly and for searching for design jobs via hashtags. Yes, this approach might be time consuming, but there are useful pockets of design gigs in the ecosystem.

---

74. https://medium.com/u/2c34f561cc81
75. https://medium.com/u/51b9f2c2c907
76. https://medium.com/u/6fe4b0908aa9
77. https://medium.com/u/80347d7b4fb1
78. https://medium.com/u/f38a4a7637e5

8.7 *Waiting Proactively*

When you've applied to jobs, there's often a delay on the other side in getting back to you. The hiring manager may be busy, reviewing other applications, or gone on vacation. That said, when you're looking for work while unemployed, every day counts. Believe it or not, you have more control over the situation. You can either continue applying to more places, or follow up with places you've applied to.

Since we already covered various strategies for the former, we'll focus primarily on the latter half—the follow-up. A big part of getting the first (phone) interview is figuring out what's happening on the other side. Did they get your application? Is the job still open?

You can get to an answer by proactively reaching out to the employer:

1. **Send a personalized email.** Reiterate your interest and let them know about your application.
2. **Call on the phone.** Potentially leave a succinct, actionable voicemail that gets them to respond.
3. **Meet in person.** At a networking event or even for coffee.

Your approach should be personable and focused. You're not looking for any job. You're interested in this specific position that this company has, and it would be their loss to not hire you.

SALES THINKING FOR DESIGNERS

What comes to mind when you think of sales? Mad men? Do you view it as a necessary evil? The truth is, promoting your work, letting people know of your achievements, is a big part of career success long after you get the job. Think of applying to jobs as a sales process with a cycle. Every application you submit is like prospecting. You're generating a qualified list of companies and roles that could be a good fit. Then you develop that relationship further through various means of contact.

An important part of sales is understanding your clients' needs. After your conversation, you might discover that this is not the right place for you after all. Or they might reveal specific requirements they're looking for that you can mention to them in your presentation.

SENDING AN EMAIL THAT GETS A RESPONSE

Here's a general format to follow. Think of this as similar to a pilot's checklist, ensuring you've got the obvious and basic things covered before take-off.

1. **Catchy title.** Grab their attention.
2. **Address by name.** This shows that you've done your homework in finding who the recruiter or the hiring manager is.
3. **Be clear.** State up front that you're inquiring about a specific role.
4. **Tell them how they know you.** You either have chatted with them on the phone or this is the first time reaching out; maybe there's a connection you have in common.
5. **Get specific.** Show them relevant projects that you've done that are in this industry or close to the work that they do.
6. **Build enthusiasm.** Get them excited by being enthusiastic in your message about this job and the value you can bring to the team.
7. **Close with the ask.** "When would be a good time for us to chat?" Suggest a couple of time frames and mention that you'll follow up with a phone call next week if you don't hear back from them.

You can use this general format for the initial outreach or incorporate parts of it in a thank you email after the conversation. If this is their first time hearing about you, you want to make sure you start off the conversation strong.

THE RESPONSE

In my experience, you will usually get three basic responses. Here are the underlying messages behind them:

- **Yes.** Come on in, we want to get to know you better. It looks like your skill is on par or slightly above average. It's possible you could be a good fit.
- **Maybe.** We're not sure about you based on what we've seen. We might be looking at other candidates. This job might not be available soon and we're unsure ourselves.
- **No.** We perceive your skill to not match the job requirements. You might be too strong or not have enough experience yet. We might not want to tell you this due to legal limitations.

If you do get an outright rejection, treat it as a gift. In today's world of recruiters ghosting candidates and candidates ghosting jobs, having some transparency is helpful so you can focus your energy on quality opportunities.

One point to remember is that a **no** is a **not now**. Take the rejection as an opportunity to follow up, thanking them for their time, and ask if you can get their feedback on areas where you can improve. Suggest that you'd like to stay in touch so that when the timing is right the next time, you'll both be on each other's radars.

Sometimes you won't hear back (yet). People are busy, emails get lost, or sometimes folks just forget to respond. Reach out again in about two weeks, or better yet follow up with a phone call (remember, you already mentioned this in your email above).

A few years ago I was applying for a product designer role at the same company but in a different department. Because it's an internal job board, you would think I'd get a response quickly after submitting the application. However, it took at least a month and a couple of follow-ups to understand that although they were actively interviewing, they never received my application to begin with.

So don't despair if you don't get an immediate response—there many reasons why that could be the case. The important thing is to get clarity on where you stand in the process and keep moving your application forward.

FOLLOWING UP WITH A PHONE CALL

Nobody calls anybody these days. That's why reaching out with a friendly phone reminder is a good tactic. It also flips the dynamic; now instead of waiting for them to interview you over the phone, you have a little bit of leverage to interview them before the official interview starts.

Your phone call should follow the same principles as your email. Get in an enthusiastic frame of mind, mention your application and how excited you are, and inquire what the next steps are. Sometimes you might even be able to get away saying you'll be in the area next week and wouldn't it be great to do a quick chat in person.

It helps to practice this conversation ahead of time. Do a quick rehearsal with a friend. Consider writing out the key points and questions before the call. You won't have a lot of time on the phone, probably two to five minutes if the conversation goes smoothly, so make that time count.

The key points are also helpful if you're leaving a message. In that case, also make sure to leave your number—repeat it slowly twice at the end of your message along with your name.

MEETING YOUR INTERVIEWER

If all else fails just show up at their office, right? That tactic of showing up unannounced might get you escorted out by security. Ideally, you've been able to move the process along so that you've sent an email, called, and now you've set up a meeting in person.

Another way you can meet your prospective employer is by looking at which networking events they're participating in and where they might be headed off to next. Usually, smaller companies announce conferences they're attending or presenting at, or if they'll have a presence such as a booth to demonstrate their services or product.

In my experience, some of the best ways that I've connected with employers was by following up with them at professional networking events. If I'd already submitted an application or even when I had already interviewed with them, it was useful to chat with them in an environment that's more relaxed.

GETTING TO YES OR NO

Hopefully this chapter gave you some new tactics to try. The key principle that helped me when I was going through this process myself a couple of times was getting clarity and feedback.

When I wasn't sure what was going on on the other side, I reached out. I got plenty of rejections along the way, but having a clear answer was more helpful than no answer at all. As you get feedback rolling in, use it as an opportunity to further improve your application, your communication skills, and the types of companies you approach. Good luck out there—and keep learning!

9 Networking Authentically

Think of networking as another powerful tool in your job-searching arsenal. Aside from the short-term benefit of finding a job by networking, it opens up the possibilities of making mutually beneficial long-term connections that can last over the course of one's career.

FIGURE: DISCOVER NEW IDEAS AND PEOPLE AT EVENTS

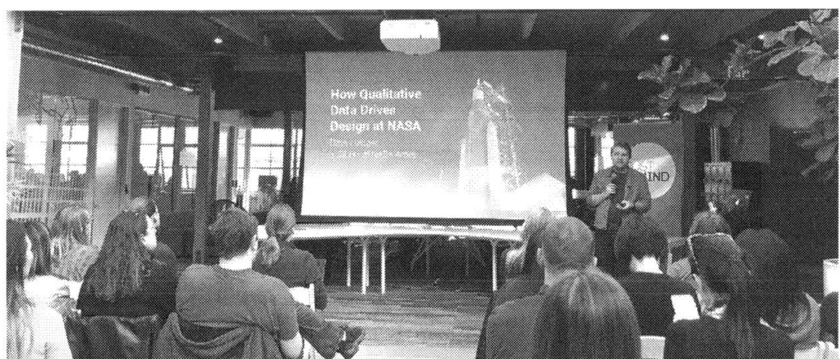

Events are great for exposing you to new ideas and people.

If you've moved to a new location, attending professional events is a good way to immerse yourself in the local community. While most talks tend to be light on details they're useful for exposing you to new ideas and, most importantly, new people to follow up with.

> **STORY**
> When I first moved to San Francisco, I found one of my jobs by waiting in line for a product management event. Outside the venue, in the uncharacteristic San Francisco rain, I struck up a conversation with a couple of folks behind me. One of them happened to be a data scientist who was looking for a designer for her startup. I applied, and a few months later got the job. You never know what might happen unless you get out there! Sometimes waiting in line can be an advantage.

9.1 *Networking During a Pandemic*

NEW Since COVID, the rules of networking have shifted. More events take place remotely, so the opportunities for a casual chat before an event are going away. But in some way, it's also an opportunity to connect with the person you're interested in talking with after the event is over. Reaching out to them via email or a LinkedIn invite and letting them know that you've both attended an event recently can help you establish common ground in addition to the topic.

FIGURE: REMOTE CONFERENCES

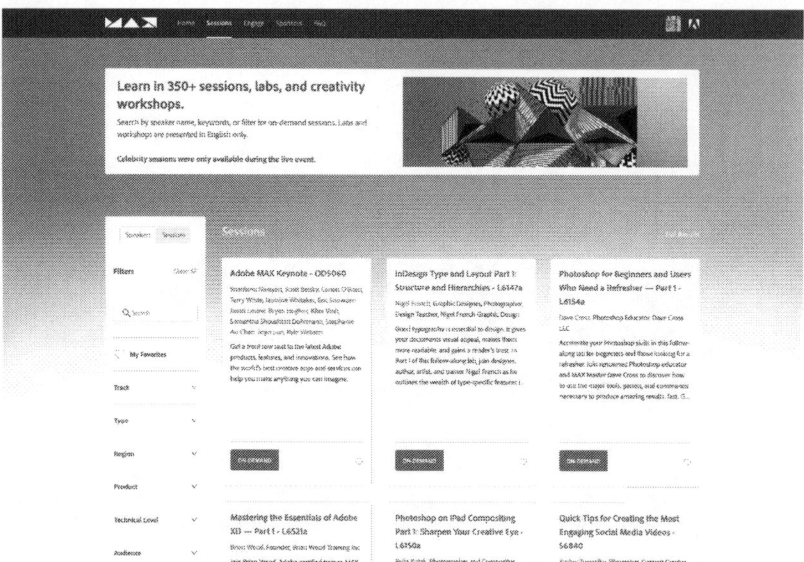

In 2020 the biggest design conferences and events primarily took place online. Adobe Max streamed hundreds of sessions across the globe from the US, Europe and Asia. Who knows, remote-only conferences might be the future.

9.2 *Tips on Talking with Strangers*

You might not feel like going out there because you're not an extrovert and prefer not to be the life of the party. That's OK. It's a common myth about networking that you need to get out there, shake hands, and hand out business cards left and right while jumping from one person to the next.

When I first started going to design events I usually froze, latched onto the first person that I met, and kept talking to them as if they were my lifeline. But over time, by attending many events, networking has become more natural. Today, I still enjoy spending my time alone, but going out is no longer a fear-inducing activity—it's fun to meet new folks and find ways to give back.

At its core, networking is about finding mutually beneficial ways to help each other. If you're new to it, here are some things you can do. If you've gone to events before, feel free to skip.

1. **Don't be afraid to be the first one to strike up a conversation.** You can start by asking what brought them to the event? What are they hoping to learn? Have they attended similar events?
2. **Be interested.** It's easier to connect with someone by letting them talk about their favorite topic—themselves. Find out what's important to them and see where you can help.
3. **Go alone.** This forces you to get out of your comfort zone (as opposed to relying on the safety net of talking to your friends).
4. **You're not obligated to keep the conversation going.** If you feel like you're not connecting, don't feel bad excusing yourself: "It was nice meeting you; I promised myself that I'd chat with more folks here."
5. **If it does go well, ask to connect.** Usually it's as simple as adding them on LinkedIn or getting their business card (do those exist still?).
6. **Follow up the next day.** Don't wait too long—suggest a time and place to meet and continue the conversation.

If you're curious to learn more, I've included a few books at the end of this chapter that I personally found useful on my networking journey.

9.3 *Deciding on a Conference*

If there aren't many events in your part of town, see if you can attend a conference that brings design professionals together, ideally for a couple of days so that you can make a couple of high-quality connections. There's no shortage of conference[79] lists[80] these days and, with talks now going remotely, attending is easier than before—no need to figure out the logistics of scheduling flights, hotels, and transportation to the venue.

ORGANIZERS AND TOPICS

Before going, it helps to familiarize yourself with the conference itself. What's the theme? Who are the organizers? Have they done this confer-

79. https://medium.com/@ariannaorland/30-design-conferences-to-attend-in-2019-de235647fbcf
80. https://www.invisionapp.com/inside-design/2019-ux-conferences/

ence before, and how were those (you can usually find reviews online). Next, look at who's going to be speaking and what their credentials are. Based on this info, start comparing conferences and earmarking the ones that look good.

◇ IMPORTANT Aside from looking at the speakers and companies that are attending, take a close look at the schedule. One major thing to watch for are the breaks between presentations. The magic happens between, not during, the talks. More breaks equal more opportunities to connect. Is this conference packed back to back with little time to spare, or is there enough time for breaks between talks? Are there also dedicated food breaks—lunch, extended coffee, and treats?

Conferences that last a couple of days offer more chances for you to connect, not just at the venue itself but also afterward over dinner or drinks.

GETTING A DISCOUNT OR VOLUNTEERING TO GET IN

In my experience **price is not a good indicator of quality**, and unfortunately most conferences tend to be pricey. If anything, price is an artificial barrier for who can attend. That said, most conferences do offer discounts, especially if you're a student or if you're in transition. You can also look for ways to volunteer. Usually, by helping organizers with setup and logistics, you get your ticket fee waived.

> STORY
>
> When I was trying to save up some money, I reached out to one of the conference organizers for a volunteering opportunity. I helped out by packing swag bags, helping out with speaker timing, and manning some tables. The effort wasn't demanding, and it was fun to build camaraderie with other volunteers along the way.

While conferences tend to be pricey and are a one-time deal, events are usually a fraction of the cost and happen more frequently.

9.4 *Picking Events to Go To*

Depending on where you live, the cadence of events varies. It's usually easier to find them in larger cities. When I used to work in a suburban area,

I would drive an hour to Boston just to attend some of the events there and stay close to the community. Here are a couple of things to consider when evaluating where to go.

INTEREST-BASED DESIGN EVENTS

One way to choose events is based on a topic or theme. Over the years I've been passionate about healthcare and design and have attended multiple events in that space, from hackathons, to quantified self meetups, to design events with a focus on healthcare. Attending these types of meetups is a great way to meet people in the broader industry and especially good if you want to focus your career on a specific vertical.[§4.10]

FIGURE: THEME-BASED EVENTS FOCUS DEEPLY ON A TOPIC

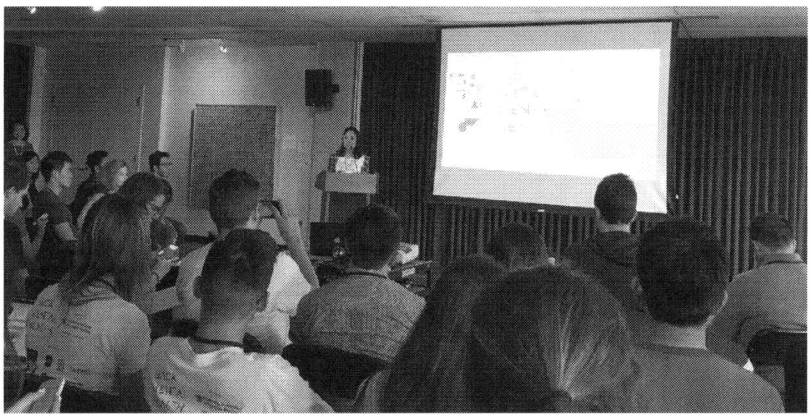

STORY

A few years ago I joined the Design for Healthcare community, where I found my next role without actively looking. It was through happenstance that I saw a designer give a talk on Google Glass for healthcare, and I knew I had to find out more. So I cornered one of the designers working on the product there and peppered him with questions. Turns out the company had a position open, but I was already happily employed at the time. We stayed in touch, and when the company I was with at the time went through a downturn, I decided to make the switch. In short, it helps to invest in relationships long-term.

WHO'S COMING TO THE EVENT?

Another way to choose an event is based on who's going to be there. Aside from connecting with speakers, certain platforms (like Meetup) allow you to check the guest list. It's not a guarantee that the person will actually be there, but it's a good signal.

If you're interested in connecting, reach out to them before the event. This way you can optimize your networking time even further once you're there. On occasion I also post on Twitter or LinkedIn, notifying peeps that I'll be going to an event in the future to see who else is interested in attending.

FIGURE: CREATIVE MORNINGS

Creative mornings are a great way to meet creators of all stripes.

9.5 *Where to Find Events*

Where can you find events? Start by searching for "design" on Eventbrite, Meetup, or even Facebook Local. It's as simple as that.

Here are a couple of well-known organizations that are good to check out:

- User Experience Professionals Association[81]
- Interaction Design Association[82]
- Service Design Network[83]
- Creative Mornings[84]
- Interaction Design Foundation[85]
- AIGA[86]

These are just a few of the big ones. Aside from hosting events, these organizations also give you access to an online community, which is great not just for jobs but also for mentorship and career advice.

9.6 *Connecting with Local Professional Communities*

In addition to the more prominent orgs such as the ones above, you can also search for local chapters or local orgs. Usually these have more clout and can better connect you to the local community. I'll list the ones that I know of in San Francisco, but even if the same ones don't exist in your city, it's possible your local organizations follow a similar format. If not, that's something you could pitch to them (for example, organizing a portfolio review event or a mentor night).

Aside from talks, mentoring and portfolio events provide opportunities to connect with people and companies you're interested in and improve your skill at showing the work itself.

Andi Galpern[87] organizes the Cascade SF events. In addition to design talks, she hosts mentor nights where attendees get to show their portfolio (or ask for career advice) with up to four mentors. I've been mentored there and provided mentorship and can't recommend this format enough.

---

81. https://uxpa.org/
82. https://ixda.org/
83. http://www.service-design-network.org/
84. http://creativemornings.com/
85. https://www.interaction-design.org/
86. https://www.aiga.org/
87. https://medium.com/u/29d8e5feab49

Julie Stanescu[88] runs Rethink,[89] which hosts informative events (you can also find recorded talks online) and they pack a big crowd. Interestingly enough, Julie started Rethink when she first moved to San Francisco as a way to build a forum for design discussion and connect with great designers here. So if you find yourself in a place that has no design communities, consider bootstrapping one yourself.

Every year SF Design Week[90] runs a series of varied events and workshops for designers of all stripes for over a week-long series of talks, workshops, and office visits to design agencies and tech companies. I also recommend checking out their studio crawls—it's when agencies and companies open up their spaces for attendees to check out, connect, and learn more about the work.

FIGURE: SF DESIGN WEEK

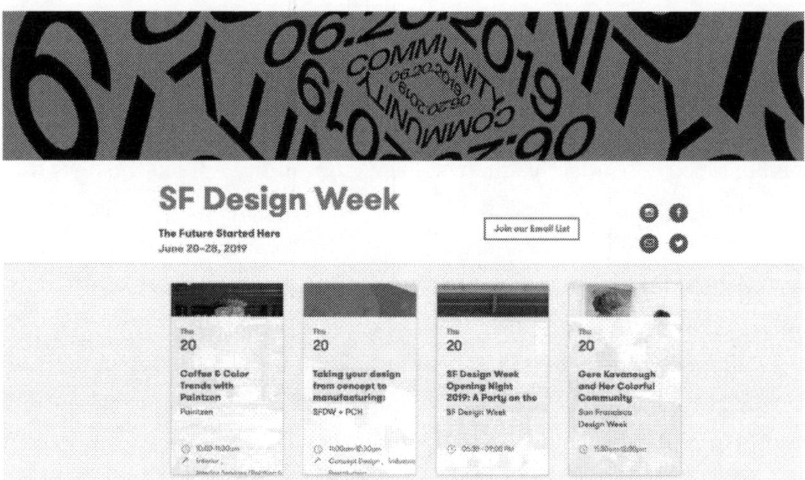

SF Design Week brings designers of all stripes together for over a week-long series of talks, workshops, and office visits to design agencies and tech companies.

9.7 *Don't Stop at Design Events*

There are many others! Once you go to an event you can ask the attendees where else they like to go. Don't limit your events to product design

88. https://medium.com/u/9088475dc405
89. https://www.rethinkhq.com/
90. https://sfdesignweek.org/

though. Here are some good ones that I've attended in the past and found useful:

- Products That Count.[91] Founded by SC Moatti, in-depth events with presentations from PMs, VCs, and other big movers and shakers in industry.
- Product School.[92] Hosts informative events from speakers of top-tier tech companies in addition to doing PM training.

So if a product management or an interesting engineering talk comes around, consider going. Not only will you learn something new but you'll have more opportunity to connect with folks who are potentially looking for design talent, and you won't be competing against other designers at the event.

9.8 *Get Started Now*

With most events going remote this year, the opportunity to connect and attend an event is becoming easier and easier. Here's how you can find some good ones:

- Search for design on EventBrite, Facebook Local, and Meetup. What's coming up?
- Sign up for one event you'll attend this month and go there. Post on your LinkedIn that you'll be attending that event and you're looking forward to meeting folks there.
- Look for conferences. Make it a point to find one or two great conferences this year and attend. If money is an issue, reach out to the organizers and ask to help out.
- Are there any community gaps that exist where you live? Considering filling that gap by organizing a meetup.

---

91. https://productsthatcount.com/

92. https://www.productschool.com/product-management-events/

9.9 *Additional Resources*

Here are three books that I think are a must-read:

- *How to Win Friends and Influence People,*[93] by Dale Carnegie. The classic in the field, still just as relevant today.
- *Never Eat Alone,*[94] by Keith Ferazzi. Although it has mixed reviews, Keith does a great job of providing tips and frameworks you can use to meet people. At the heart of it is the genuine message that we're better off connecting and sharing resources than hoarding away our contacts.
- *Networking for People Who Hate Networking,*[95] by Devora Zack. For those shy persons jumping into their first event, this is a great step-by-step guide. The book leads you through a series of exercises to make networking fun and enjoyable, especially for those of us who would actually prefer to spend our time (and eat) alone.

93. https://www.amazon.com/How-Win-Friends-Influence-People/dp/0671027034/
94. https://www.amazon.com/Never-Eat-Alone-Expanded-Updated/dp/0385346654
95. https://www.amazon.com/Networking-People-Who-Hate-Underconnected/dp/1605095222

PART III: PREPARING FOR DESIGN INTERVIEWS

In this chapter we'll dive into the various interview types that you might encounter. During the interview cycle you'll be talking primarily with a recruiter and a hiring manager. For the final interview[§11] you'll interact extensively with the cross-functional team—engineers, researchers, data scientists, product managers, and so on.

The same tips in the previous sections apply here as well. You want to know the role requirements well enough so that you can clearly sell the team on your candidacy. In the case of behavioral interviews this means thinking about the specific situations that can speak well to the desired requirements.

By knowing what to expect you can practice and prepare ahead of time. This will make your responses sound natural and you'll be able to focus more on the interviewer's questions and understand what they're ultimately trying to ask.

Lastly, it's likely that during this process you might encounter design exercises, such as the take-home design exercise,[§15] the whiteboard challenge,[§19] or the app critique.[§17] Since design exercises are a special type of interview, I've outlined them in a following chapter with a few sample solutions and practice prompts to help you get better at these types of interviews.

10 Preparing for the Phone Screen Interview

Your first interview will start with a voice call where you'll typically speak with a recruiter. This interview is usually preceded by an email—sometimes multiple emails from recruiters trying to get your attention. To be successful at this interview type, you should do your homework ahead of time, prepare your pitch, and be able to tell a compelling story demonstrating value so that you can advance to the next stage of the interview.

10.1 *Screening Calls at a Glance*

Design phone screens are usually short, about 15–30 minutes interviewing with one person. They give you an opportunity to present yourself, your work, and your interest in the company.

If this is your first phone conversation with the company, a recruiter will usually reach out. They'll talk about the role, ask some questions, and will try to gauge your interest. Aside from screening, they also want to leave you excited about the opportunity. Take advantage of that by treating the recruiter as an ally in the interview process.

◇ IMPORTANT Your 30-second intro should be punchy, specific, and short.

A call with the hiring manager is usually next. On occasion I also had these calls with peer designers. Either way, since both parties have domain expertise, they'll dig deeper on your design process and case studies.

◇ IMPORTANT Practice ahead of time. If you're feeling nervous about the conversation or you're not sure, practice with a friend ahead of time. Start by writing out your answers and reading them out loud. Then have a friend call you and have them ask you some tough questions. Let them also throw you off a bit so that you can practice how to react to questions you haven't prepared for.

The first few minutes of a phone screen are usually formulaic, so it helps to think through the questions ahead of time. Preparing by writing your answers down will help you come off as confident and even spontaneous if you rehearsed your story thoroughly. Generally, you'll be asked about your work background, your design approach, and your current work situation.

Below are examples of some of the common questions you might encounter.

YOUR STORY AND WORK HISTORY

This is an opportunity for you to set up the context of your story. Remember the pitch you've prepared.[§6.3] You want to come off as having a deliberate career path[§5] in mind.

Sample questions in this category:

- Tell me more about your career journey—how did you end up where you're currently at?
- What would you like to do next?
- Why are you interested in working with us?
- Where do you envision yourself long-term?
- What are you looking for next in your role?

These questions give the interviewer a sense of your past, your present, and where you want to be in the future.

YOUR CURRENT WORK SITUATION

Not exactly the most fun questions, but these are necessary for the interviewer to ask to make sure everyone's on the same page:

- Why are you searching now?
- Would you require visa sponsorship in the future?
- What salary are you expecting?

CAUTION Remember, in most states (in the U.S.), it's illegal for a recruiter to ask you how much you're making. But if they do, you can give a generic answer stating that you're being paid the fair market average. That said it's legal for a recruiter to ask about compensation expectations. One way you can answer this question is to ask what band[§24.2] they have for this specific role.

10.2 *Preparing for the Call*

Before the call, review what you already have about the company, the role, and the person you'll be talking to. Have your list of answers (based on anticipated questions) and your list of questions printed so you can take notes without getting distracted by typing noise.

DURING THE CALL

It goes without saying that you should be in a quiet room with strong cell phone reception. You might even consider getting a phone number from Google as a backup, but in that case make sure you have a strong wifi connection.

As the conversation wraps up, you'll usually have a few minutes for questions. Your questions should be tailored to the person who's interviewing you and the role itself. Focus on a few specific questions to open up the conversation and follow the thread from there. You can think of this as doing user research. What important questions should you ask first? What's a deal breaker? What are some nice-to-haves to follow up with?

◇ **IMPORTANT** Be sure to listen actively and take down notes during the interview.

Make sure you don't ask questions that are easy to find online. Do your homework first. With that said, here are some basic questions to get you started:

- How is the design team organized?
- What challenges are you facing today?
- What problems can I help you with?
- What excites you about working here?
- How big is the design team now?

If you've run out of questions or can't think of a good question to ask, say they've answered your current questions, but would it be OK if you could follow up in an email if more questions come up later? Ten times out of ten, they'll say yes.

ENDING THE CONVERSATION ON A HIGH NOTE

Depending on how much time is left, I usually end the conversation with a key question that I learned to use many years ago: "Is there anything I said or didn't say that would make me a bad candidate for this role?"

How they respond is just as important as what they say.

IMPORTANT Use the final closer to gauge their interest, "Is there anything I said or didn't say that would make me a bad candidate for this role?"

Finally, end the phone call with a friendly close: "It was great getting to know you and learning more about the opportunity—I can't wait until we chat again. **What would be the next step?**"

AFTER THE CALL

After the phone call, take a few moments to reflect on how it went. How did you feel? Do you imagine yourself working at that company? Are there any lingering questions left unanswered? What could you have done better? Take a breather and write your thoughts down while the information's fresh.

In my experience with phone screens, it's usually easy to tell if the company is not a good fit at this time. For example, you want to work on the consumer side of the org but they only have opportunities in enterprise this year. Remember, you're evaluating them as much as they're evaluating you.

In all cases, nothing wins an interviewer over like a good thank you note after the call. Even if this opportunity didn't seem like the right fit, you never know if a new one might come along. Genuinely, follow up with an email a couple of hours later mentioning specific things you talked about in regards to the role, the team, or the company.

WHAT TO EXPECT NEXT

Unless there are obvious mismatches between your application and the role, usually most interviews proceed to the next stage. Sometimes this means you'll talk with the hiring manager next, or you may get a take-home design exercise to complete before advancing to the next stage.

10.3 *Preparing for the Hiring Manager*

This interview usually follows a few days after the recruiter screening call. Generally you'll talk to a hiring manager, or occasionally another designer may field this call.

Similarly to the screening call, this interview should last about 15–30 minutes. By this time the recruiter should have relayed some of the information to the hiring manager so they're on the same page. But you should still expect to introduce yourself and have your pitch ready, in addition to mentioning why you're excited about this particular opportunity.

YOUR DESIGN APPROACH AND PROCESS

The interviewer is interested to see if you have a specific process when approaching problems. What framework do you use? Is your approach rigid or flexible based on the context at hand? Are you able to bend and break the process while focusing on outcomes?

Typically, they'll ask you to walk through one or two projects from your portfolio. Think of this as a portfolio presentation in condensed form.

Some questions they may ask:

- What does design mean to you?
- What is the most exciting project you worked on? Why was it exciting?
- What was the most challenging project you worked on? What made it difficult?
- Who was the most difficult stakeholder in this project?

These questions are designed to probe your design process, get some initial signals around your collaboration skills, and to get a glimpse of how you solve problems.

QUESTIONS YOU SHOULD ASK

By this time you want to have done your homework based on your previous interview—this means looking up the person who's talking to you (know whether they're a manager or a designer). Tailor your questions based on their experience.

Additionally, this is a chance to learn what it's really like to work there:

- Can you walk me through a project that you worked on recently?
- What was the most complex or largest project you worked on? What made it complex?

- How does the design team work together?
- How do you think the design team can improve?
- Where do you envision yourself as a designer in the next couple of years?
- What inspires you?

ENDING ON A HIGH NOTE

Just like with the previous interview, you should always be thinking about how this interview can set you up for success in the next one. Thank them for the interview, ask if there are any other open questions they have and, if not, ask about next steps.

11 Final Interview Preparation

The final interview is a big step in the process. Congrats on making it this far! This is an opportunity for you to arrive with confidence, be prepared for the unexpected, and, finally, leave your interviewers excited to work with you.

NEW Since COVID expanded remote work, the traditional on-site or final interview is often now conducted remotely. While the format is changed, many of the steps are similar. It's important to prepare and to test out your remote interviewing setup[§13.3] ahead of time.

So what's next? By now you should have received an email from the company with an interviewing schedule to help you prepare for the big day. If you haven't received the schedule, now's a great time to ask for it. This is a good way to communicate initiative while also properly preparing ahead of time.

11.1 *Table: On-Site Schedule*

TIME	INTERVIEW TYPE	PRESENT
1 hour	Portfolio presentation	Cross-functional team and designers
45 minutes	Whiteboard exercise	1–2 designers
30 minutes	App critique	1–2 designers
30 minutes	Product collaboration	Product manager
30 minutes	Design collaboration	Designer
30 minutes	Engineering collaboration	Engineering manager or engineer
30 minutes	Team fit	Hiring manager
30 minutes	Wrap up	Recruiter

11.2 *Learning About Your Interviewers*

After learning the schedule, now's the opportunity to learn more about your interviewers—if this company has already invested time in getting to know you, it's only fair that you should get to know them too. Start with LinkedIn and look at each interviewer's profile: their experience, common connections, and recent posts. Look for their other online social networks or sites where they were mentioned or shared their work. If you're applying to a startup or a smaller company, be sure to research the leadership team too.

This info will be useful during the interview itself, as it will help you:

- Anticipate types of questions you'll get asked.
- Address potential concerns relevant to portfolio pieces.
- Ask specific questions to each person, given their role and experience.
- Build rapport with the interviewers based on common organizations or connections.

STORY

Having a schedule isn't a guarantee the interviewer will be there. One time I was researching a product manager who had a fascinating design and search background. I agonized over which questions to ask him, only to learn the day of the interview that all PMs were having a last-minute off-site.

Even though some people may be missing due to last-minute rescheduling, in general preparing and looking folks up ahead of time will make you stand out. To the interviewers, it's a signal that you're interested in the job and the team.

This goes for all levels—from new designers to experienced design leaders. If, as a candidate, you don't have any questions or don't show curiosity when given the chance to ask questions, it's a strong red flag you're unsure. Luckily this isn't hard to do, nor is it time consuming, as you can get this info in less than half an hour of online searching.

11.3 *Creating Your Own On-Site Packet*

My deliverable at this stage is an on-site packet composed of:

- **Summary page.** This has the name of the company, schedule, street address, and point person for the interview and their phone number, in case I need to call when I arrive or get lost.
- **Pages for each interviewing event.** Covers any interesting facts and questions I want to follow up with for each person.
- **Extra pages.** Just in case, for note-taking during interviews.

This packet makes it easy to keep track of interviews, take notes, and cross reference information all in one place throughout the interview. It's also helpful as a reference afterward, if you choose to follow up on certain questions when you receive an offer.

11.4 *Day of the On-Site*

For your on-site, it's important to have the basics covered. That means eating well a few hours before and getting proper rest. Think of this as a test. You have the knowledge and skills, now it's important to demonstrate your major skills and accomplishments in one go.

GATHER YOUR BELONGINGS

If this is a full or a half day of interviews, it will probably be demanding, so be sure to bring your:

- laptop (even if you're presenting on an iPad, have it as a backup) with a charger
- notebook, sketching kit (or at the very least pen and paper)
- on-site packet
- excitement.

Now you might scoff at some of these. Getting rest? Excitement? Who cares! I've been doing design for years. While it's important to bring your whole self to the interview, it's also important to show interest—after all, you've selected this company to interview with, and if at all goes well, you'll be working with these folks everyday.

◇ IMPORTANT If you are interviewing in-person it helps to check with your company contact (usually the recruiter or a hiring manager) about dress code. Even if the dress code is informal, it helps to dress a level up to show that you're serious about the position.

SHOW YOUR EXCITEMENT

In addition to evaluating you on your skills, your potential future employers will also be looking at you from a behavioral perspective. They want to work with someone who is enthusiastic, easy to get along with—in other words, a good cultural fit.

Culture§4.4 is a loaded term. That said, it's in your interest to appear engaged and enthusiastic about the interview. The team is excited to talk with you, and they hope that you're just as excited about the opportunity.

> STORY
>
> One time, after a friendly chat with a head of product, I got passed for the role due to my lack of enthusiasm at the interview. I thought the interview went well but was later told that I came off as too professional. I took that lesson in stride and applied it to all of my on-sites since. I knew I mastered it when a founder at another company sympathized at the end of my on-site interview, "I can see how excited you are about design and this opportunity; it must be draining at the end of the day, so please take some time to rest afterward."

RETHINK STRESS

Lastly, if you're starting to feel stressed out—you're actually excited. As professor Jamie Jamieson's research on stress suggests (recounted in Kelly McGonigal's book *The Upside of Stress*[96]), it's not that high performers don't feel stress, it's that they ascribe this stress to be a positive force that helps them reach peak-level performance.

In one study, participants were asked to give a speech. Those who thought of stress as a positive force were rated higher and appeared more confident compared to those who were asked to ignore their stress response. So take that lesson to heart—if you're starting to feel overly stressed, take a deep breath and reframe your mindset as an exciting and positive force.

GET THERE ON TIME

When it's time for the interview, I usually figure out my transportation options so that I can get there at a comfortable time, about 30 minutes before the start. This leaves you a ten-minute buffer in case something goes wrong, ten minutes to sign in, with ten minutes to settle in or get a quick office tour before you start. You definitely want to leave yourself enough buffer so as not to shortchange yourself by being late.

HAVE A BACKUP PLAN READY

Finally, it helps to have a backup plan in case technology fails—maybe your laptop dies, maybe there's no internet connection. It's surprising how often simple things that should work fail during moments that matter. To prepare, aside from having your portfolio downloaded locally to your laptop, have it as a backup on a thumb drive or a private online link that you can access.

GOOD LUCK AND ENJOY THE PROCESS!

Interviews can be grueling, but if you've done all this work up-front, you'll thank yourself later. With prep done, you'll arrive with confidence, on time, and will have a process in place when facing the unexpected.

12 Presenting Your Portfolio: Crafting a

96. https://www.amazon.com/Upside-Stress-Why-Good-You/dp/1101982934

Compelling Story

As part of your final interview you'll be asked to present your portfolio. Out of all interviews, this one is priority number one. See this as an opportunity to show the great work that you've done, reinforcing the fact that you can do it and more again.

◇ IMPORTANT The in-person portfolio is different from your online portfolio,[§7] which the interviewers have already seen. This is an opportunity to **feature one to three best projects** and go in-depth on how you've achieved and exceeded objectives given the constraints.

Here's how you can create a gripping narrative that gets your interviewers excited to work with you.

12.1 *How Your Portfolio Will Be Evaluated*

Your portfolio presentation will be evaluated from multiple angles. The criteria here are broader than the design exercise since you'll be showing work you've done as part of a team. Your interviewers will be interested in seeing the following:

- **Problem scope.** How complex were the problems you were addressing? This in part determines your seniority—did you lead multiple projects in parallel, with ambiguous goals, across various channels?
- **Collaboration.** How did you work with your team? What conflict did you encounter and how was it resolved? Were you able to inspire and bring out the best in your teammates?
- **Adaptability.** What approaches did you try? What failed and how did you iterate on the process to keep things moving?
- **Quality.** What is the quality bar for your work? How fast and to what degree of quality did you work? Were you able to explore many options, prioritize low-effort solutions, while leading toward a north star design?
- **Outcome.** What was the result? What did the customers say? What was the impact on engineering? What metrics shifted?

Aside from the work, you'll be evaluated on your **delivery**. Are you able to communicate clearly, present an intriguing story, and keep folks engaged during your hour (this is your time)? In the next section, we'll cover techniques to make your speech sparkle.

12.2 *Your Audience*

A variety of folks will see your presentation, each with a different focus:

- **Design manager.** Craft skills, quality, process, and style.
- **Product manager.** Prioritization, business outcomes, impact.
- **Engineering.** Productive collaboration with engineering.
- **UX research.** Methods you've used, how you've partnered with research.
- **Data science.** Formulating initial questions and area of inquiry.

Keep this audience in mind when you're practicing. It's very likely you'll see this cast of folks again during your one-on-one behavioral and cross-functional interviews.

12.3 *Building Your Deck*

The number one person you're building this deck for is yourself. You'll want to create a modular portfolio that you can remix at a moment's notice if you're called in for an interview with another company. To help you get there, I recommend you start an assessment of your recent work.

STACKING YOUR PROJECTS

What were your **recent** projects that you consider to be your **best work** that show a **variety of skills**? Highlight projects that played to your unique identity as a designer—your combination of skills, point of view, and process that led to a result no other designer could have achieved.

One way to put together a project stack is to evaluate each project individually on your craft skills,[§3.4] such as user research, interaction design, visual design, and affected platforms.

FIGURE: PROJECT 1, INTERACTION AND RESEARCH FOCUS

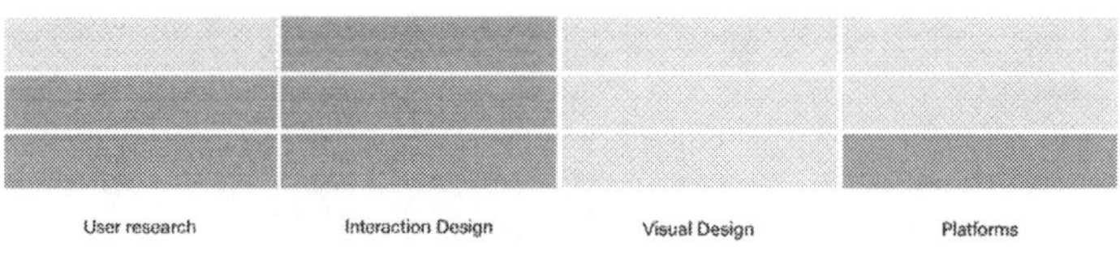

An example project with a heavy interaction and research component.

As an example, you might have a project where you were heavily involved with customer interviews, solving a complex interaction problem for a desktop app, but you were operating within an existing design system, so there wasn't much visual design work.

FIGURE: PROJECT 2, VISUAL DESIGN FOCUS

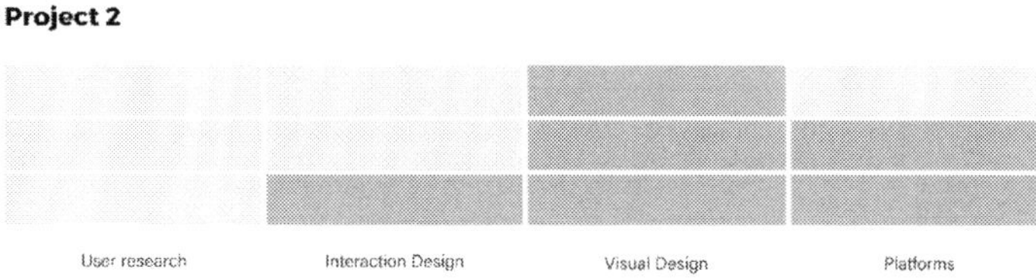

An example project with a visual design focus.

FIGURE: BREADTH AND DEPTH OF SKILLS

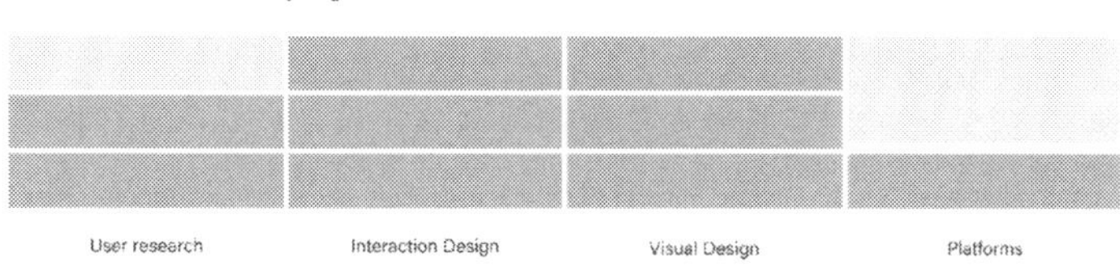

Combining different projects to show your breadth and depth of skills.

Combining these projects in your portfolio demonstrates that you have strong skills in many areas. These graphs were inspired by Irene Au'[97]s article, Writing a Job Description for UX People.[98]

You might also consider other project dimensions:

- **Project complexity.** Simpler projects can span a few weeks, others might take months or years.
- **Visionary projects.** Projects that were in a completely brand-new space without a precedent, going from 0 to 1.
- **Optimization projects.** Mature platforms that you were optimizing, going from 1 to 10.
- **Operational projects.** Initiatives you worked on to improve a team's impact—for example, design systems or design process.

---

97. https://medium.com/u/6d23645ba40b
98. https://medium.com/design-your-life/writing-a-job-description-for-ux-people-bcad01be93b0

When you're interviewing for multiple roles, I recommend building a deck composed of about six projects. You'll present two or three projects during your portfolio review and have the other few in your back pocket in case interviewers have additional questions during one-on-ones.

TAILORING YOUR PROJECTS FOR THE ROLE

After evaluation, it's time to tailor the portfolio to the role. You'll get a good sense of what to include (or exclude), what to show first, and what to put in the appendix based on the job description. Ideally you get a sense of their underlying needs from the phone interview. Not sure what to show? The recruiter (or a dedicated contact at the company) is your best ally in this process. Don't guess—reach out and ask them to describe their ideal candidate and what work they'd like to see.

12.4 *Storytelling for Success*

To make an impactful presentation, turn it into a story. You're the hero of your own script. What trials on your path gave way to triumphs? Let's break this down into three parts: **presentation**, **project**, and **process**.

FIGURE: PRESENTATION, PROJECTS, AND PROCESS

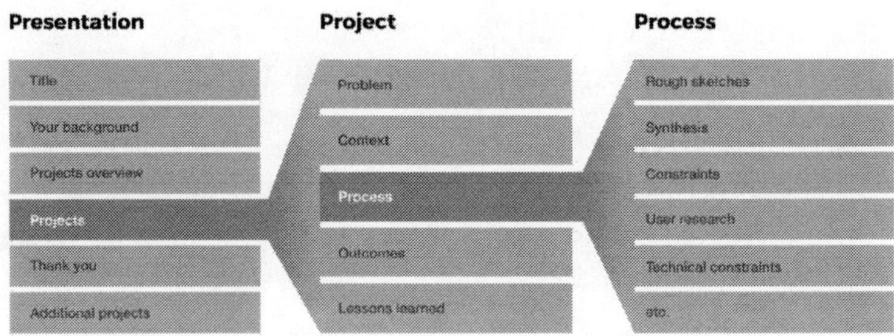

The majority of your presentation will be spent on process, but don't skip context.

PRESENTATION OUTLINE

Your overall in-person portfolio outline will be similar to this:

1. **Title.** Your name and interview date.
2. **Background.** A snapshot of your education, skills, and experience.

3. **Projects overview.** A snapshot of the projects you'll be presenting.
4. **Projects.** Detailed case studies of two or three projects.
5. **Thank you.** The last slide and cue for interviewers to ask more questions.
6. **Additional projects.** A few projects you might want to show to provide detail. These can come handy during one-to-one interviews.

Don't skip the intro! Introducing yourself, your background, and the projects you'll be showing sets the tone for the rest of the presentation.

PROJECT OUTLINE

Unlike a scannable online portfolio, you'll want to keep your audience in some suspense and excitement. A mix of problem setting and storytelling is helpful:

1. **Problem.** What was the issue that was identified; who raised it?
2. **Context.** What was the company, the team, and the time frame, and what role did you play?
3. **Process.** How did you do the work from initial discovery through to concepts, iteration, research, and collaboration with cross-functional partners?
4. **Outcomes.** What was the result?
5. **Lessons learned.** What would you have done differently given everything you know now?

You'll spend the most of your presentation on process, showing your approach, how you framed the problem and moved the project forward while overcoming obstacles along the way. This is an excellent place to think of a narrative arc for each project.

The hero's journey is one framework you can use to add a layer of excitement to your case study.

FIGURE: THE HERO'S JOURNEY

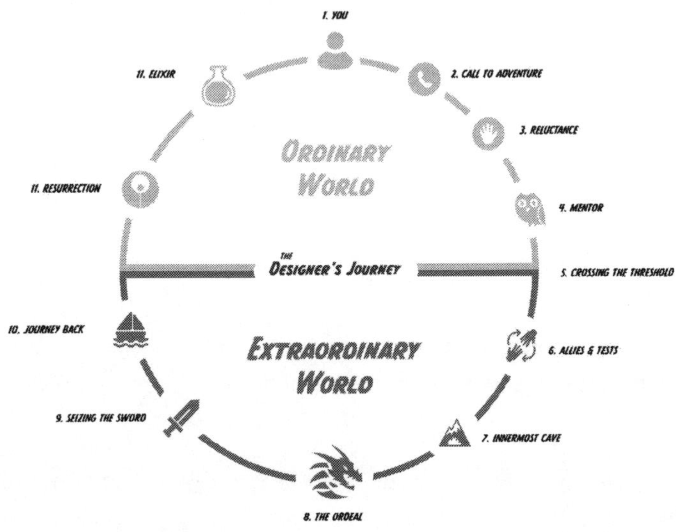

The hero's journey is a popular framework for effective storytelling.

Here's how the framework can be translated for design:

1. **You.** About you and your background.
2. **Call to adventure.** You found a big problem that no one saw.
3. **Refusal.** But you already had many projects at the time.
4. **Mentor.** A former manager encouraged you to take the first step.
5. **Crossing the threshold.** You decided to re-prioritize your projects.
6. **Allies.** As you embarked on your journey, you found support from engineering and research teams.
7. **Innermost cave.** You created different concepts to address the problem.
8. **Ordeal.** You tested your concepts and many of them failed...
9. **Seizing the sword.** But you found solutions that worked and developed stronger bonds with your researcher counterpart.
10. **Journey back.** As you started implementing the solution and working closely with the team, new challenges emerged.
11. **Resurrection.** Finally, you were able to overcome these challenges and emerge with a new solution that no one had thought of before.
12. **Elixir.** You obtained new knowledge, moved metrics, and acquired customer love.

Don't force yourself to use all the elements, as it might make your case study formulaic and rigid. Instead, take a few that lend themselves well to your project already and build them out.

PROCESS INGREDIENTS

Talking about process lets interviewers peek behind the curtain on how you approach the work. This is an opportunity to show what matters most to you and what methods you use to inform and evolve your work at each stage.

FIGURE: PROCESS INGREDIENTS

You choose the process ingredients for the best result. *Photo by Calum Lewis*[99]

Here are some process ideas worth considering for your slides:

1. **Problem framing.** How did you reframe the problem you were given?
2. **Synthesis.** How did you synthesize data from different sources to understand the problem at hand?
3. **Constraints.** How did you overcome the constraints of a project (lack of money, time, and so on)?
4. **Data science.** What did the quantitative analysis tell you?
5. **Compromise.** When did you have to lose a battle to win the war? How did you navigate tough decisions?

99. https://unsplash.com/photos/vA1L1jRTM70

6. **Rough sketches, whiteboards, sticky notes.** Don't just include the sticky notes, but tell a story why a rough sketch helped you move forward in the design process.
7. **User research.** What validation have you done? Did you survey, interview customers, or test out the competition?
8. **Changing requirements.** Did the requirements change on you mid-project? Take that opportunity to highlight your adaptability.
9. **Technical constraints.** What system issues did you encounter? How did you collaborate with engineering to come to a great solution together?
10. **Conflict with co-workers.** You wanted to zig but they wanted to zag—how did you resolve differences?
11. **Ideas left behind.** You had to move fast and not everything got implemented. What was left out and what would you take forward?

Presenting a compelling (**not comprehensive**) narrative is your main goal, so don't be afraid to leave things out.

◇ IMPORTANT Put extra work in the appendix. It may be tempting to add a lot of context and describe your process from beginning to end. If your deck is starting to get over 60 slides however, watch out for timing. If there are additional details that don't significantly alter your story, include those in the appendix. If questions come up, you can always pull from that section. This will also free you up in delivering a strong presentation from the beginning since you're not worried about going over time.

WRITE A SCRIPT

Now that you have all the key ingredients, it's time to write a script. This may sound like extra work, and you may even wonder, isn't a script going to make me sound stiff and predictable? Nothing could be further from the truth. A script allows you to see a bird's-eye view of the presentation and ensures that you don't lose sight of key points you want to communicate.

As you're writing out your script, take note of your presentation's flow. When you're done, present your portfolio in the mirror as if you're interviewing yourself. Time it. Inevitably you'll need to pause and make adjustments to the script. After doing a couple of run-throughs with it, not only will you improve your content but you'll by then have it memorized to the point of it becoming second nature.

Next, present your work to friends. Lure them in with snacks, but get them hooked with the story. When you start interviewing, don't stop improving the presentation deck. If you get confused looks, yawns, or people checking their phones, that's a sign.

13 Portfolio Presentation: Public Speaking Tips

Amplify your message and engage your audience. Your speech will be part script, part improv. Here we'll cover presentation basics from where to sit to how to end on a high note. These days many companies are shifting in-person portfolios to online conference calls. While the context is different, many of the same tips still apply.

13.1 *Your Content on a Silver Platter*

Think about the last time you went out to a restaurant. What did you order? Where did you eat? If it was a high-end restaurant—the light (or the lack thereof), the ambience, the music, and the way your dish was presented all played into a delectable experience at first bite.

Now think of the time you got a similar dish for takeout. Most likely it came in cheap, disposable packaging. The food might have come in different packets that you had to mix yourself. Same basic ingredients—completely different experience. The way you frame your presentation is the difference between fast food and fine dining.

13.2 *Setting up the Environment to Your Advantage*

Aside from getting the following basics covered, remember, this is **your time to shine, not shy away**. Carry a leadership mindset with an executive presence to your on-site interview. The goal is to tell your story, show the work, and connect with your audience.

Practicing ahead of time by yourself or with your friends will make a big difference. If you really want to get into it, I recommend joining a local public speaking group or taking an improv class. Both will give you structure and frameworks for scripted or spontaneous scenarios.

BUILD RAPPORT WHILE SETTING UP

Hopefully before you start your presentation, you'll have time to set up your laptop and project on screen. But if you walk into a room full of expecting looks, fear not, now's the time to say hello and ask questions about how to get your laptop to project with whatever setup they have. This usually takes a while, so get ready to troubleshoot.

SILENCE NOTIFICATIONS

"Hey bae, what u up 2 tonight?" Whoops, you forgot to disable your notifications. Make sure the do not disturb mode is on. In fact I sometimes go so far as creating a new user account with only my presentation and backup portfolio work on it—no distractions, no messages. If it's an emergency, it can wait until the end of the interview.

FIND YOUR STAGE

Since table, chair, and monitor configurations vary, a good rule of thumb is to position yourself where you can see your portfolio and your interviewers. This helps you see what you're presenting so you can point out specific things, and connect with your audience while observing the room.

Ideally, you're sitting side by side or slightly behind the interviewers to give the impression that you're leading the group through a journey together.

At times you may also have to present in-person and on a remote video chat. In that case, it'll help to turn on your laptop's camera to put yourself on equal footing and build rapport with the folks who are off-site.

13.3 *Setting up Your Remote Environment to Your Advantage*

Since COVID has made remote interviews common, it helps to set up your space in advance and to get familiar with the conferencing software.

PRESENTING WITH MULTIPLE SCREENS

Depending on how your home setup works, you may have one or two extra monitors in addition to your laptop. Usually the laptop will have a camera but the displays will not. Since you'll want to face your interviewers, my recommendation is to project your presentation on your display in front of you, while having your presentation notes (if you're presenting in a note-style format) in front of you on the laptop.

CAMERA SETUP

Although there's plenty of advice out there about how you can buy a better camera or even link up a DSLR to a computer, the truth is most of the interview will be focused on your presentation. Even in your behavioral interviews, it's likely that you'll have to pop back into your portfolio to show an example or two. So it's OK to use the standard camera on your laptop. Just make sure the lens is clean and you're in a place that has plenty of natural light so that people can clearly see you and your face.

TEST EVERYTHING BEFORE THE PRESENTATION

As you may know by now, I'm a huge fan prototyping, whether it's your pitch or your portfolio. So it should be no surprise that you need to prototype your remote setup as well. Hop on a conference call with a friend (or even with yourself from another device, like your mobile phone). Try to simulate the real interviewing setup as much as possible. Use the conferencing tool that the company you're interviewing with will be using. You want to make sure everything is properly installed and you have the right permissions enabled so that you don't run into any issues while presenting, thus avoiding wasting precious time during the interview. Lastly, this will also help you develop that muscle memory for how to quickly share your screen.

13.4 *Speaking Tips for Success*

Now that you have all the technical hurdles behind you, it's time to dive in. One way to kick off is to let the people in the room introduce themselves first. This allows for a nice segue into your own intro via the presentation deck.

Your intro is your unique frame of your identity as a designer. Use this opportunity to weave a story about your education, background, interests, and your unique perspective, ending with why you're excited to be interviewing with the company today.

As an interviewer evaluating a candidate—this intro is critical. You want to confidently communicate your story to send a clear signal to interviewers that you're deliberate and intentional in your career path. Don't shy away from revealing relevant hobbies; this is an opportunity for you to come across as a whole person, not just as a designer who consumes coffee and produces pixels. As an interviewer I want to know what makes you tick, what are your strong areas, and what aspects of design excite you the most.

As I mentioned, if you're really interested in getting better at presenting, I recommend taking a public speaking workshop. Many years ago I signed up with Toastmasters, a public speaking club that would meet weekly. The basic course alone was inexpensive and provided a good step-by-step foundation to practice various speech techniques in a safe space.

The following tips could prove useful in your presentation.

INVOLVE YOUR AUDIENCE

As you're presenting your work, be sure to **talk to your audience**, not your screen. This sounds obvious, but I'll guarantee that you might get nervous, you might forget, and—without consciously paying attention—you just might spend most of your time talking at your screen instead of connecting with your listeners.

One way to combat this is to use notes. A simple cue can help you remember your message so you can focus on the audience instead of the screen.

I would also recommend you go a step above and **engage your interviewers**. An easy way to do this is by asking questions or doing a poll. This can be especially memorable if you have an insight to present that flies in the face of what your interviewers might expect. Instead of saying what it is, you can let your audience guess first, and then you can reveal who's right and why that insight was important.

STRIKE A COMFORTABLE PACE

As you get into your presentation, you want to keep a good rhythm going. Sometimes nerves will get the better of you and you might speak too fast, trying to cover a lot of ground. Alternatively, you might get bogged down in slowly explaining the details.

Sometimes you'll have to accelerate or slow down to make sure your interviewers are with you. Be mindful of how much time you have, though. Most presentations have an automatic timer, and having practiced before you'll likely be aware of when to check yourself.

Usually, good moments for a time check are at the end of your intro (first ten minutes), your first case study (middle of the presentation), and your last or second case study (with ten minutes to spare at the end for questions). Time checks help you keep pace and be deliberate in presenting or skipping content if you do end up running short on time.

PROJECT YOUR VOICE AND USE VOCAL VARIETY

Although you won't be speaking on stage, you still want to project your voice and speak clearly. You can also use vocal variety by altering your tone or volume to build interest when appropriate.

To try this out, I recommend recording your speech. Yeah, I know, it sounds weird to hear yourself talk at first, but it's a good baseline for how people actually hear you (as opposed to how you think they do). You might even find yourself a bit bored and disinterested when you play back the recording—a good sign to cut your speech and clarify your message.

TAKE A DEEP BREATH, PAUSE FOR QUESTIONS

Great speakers use silence to their advantage. When you get to the end of the project, it's a good time to pause and ask for questions. Since you've been monitoring and reading the room, you'll also know when to deliberately slow down to give enough time for your listeners to process and follow up with critical questions.

By default, people won't be in rapt attention of your presentation, and if they have a burning question, they might even actively block new information from coming in.

Ultimately, you'll have to practice your facilitation skills here—how much time you give interviewers for questions now or later.

END WITH TIME TO SPARE

Lastly, you want to end your presentation with time to spare for questions, for you and the audience. This is the final opportunity for your interviewers to ask questions about the work and dive into the specifics. Most importantly, have questions for them too—this is something you can include in your own on-site packet.

STORY

I once interviewed a senior design manager who came from a well-known company to present his work. The portfolio was solid and he was able to talk about his past experience and how he helped designers grow in their careers. In the end, he did good on time and had 15 minutes for questions. We asked him questions and then gave him the opportunity to ask us questions—he didn't have any. Don't make the same mistake.

13.5 *Practice, Practice, Practice*

When you're heads down, operating on your presentation, it's hard to step back and do a practice run. I get it. But I do hope that this will encourage you to think hard about how you frame your message, not just what you choose to present. Ultimately, a combination of strong content and engaging presentation will lead to a memorable experience in the eyes of your audience that will separate you from other designers.

◇ IMPORTANT If you give speeches regularly (and most folks don't) then you can get away with less practice. But if you don't and are feeling rusty, a general rule of thumb is to spend about ten times as much time practicing a speech as giving it. Now this might seem like a lot—a one-hour presentation would equate to ten hours. But if you're presenting your portfolio to multiple companies and you're interviewing in several places, this number becomes much more reasonable.

14 Behavioral Design Interviews

Behavioral interviews usually follow soon after your design presentation and the various design exercises. I'll break this interview format down by function: outside of design, you'll learn how to build rapport with product management, engineering, and research. You'll want to build rapport and get people excited to work with you. I'll also share best practices with stories of success and failures along the way.

14.1 *Behavioral Interview Format at a Glance*

The goal of cross-functional interviews is to get a 360-degree view of how you approach your work and collaborate with others. Typically these will be one-on-one interviews about 30 minutes each or one-hour pair interviews.

If you're applying for an in-house role[§4.5] (either at a startup or a large company), you'll talk with cross-functional peers in product and engineering. You might also have a researcher or a data scientist sit in. For agency roles, you'll be primarily speaking with designers.

The best way to prepare for your final interview is by actively working with your recruiter. Find out what to expect, the schedule, and the people you'll be speaking with. Lastly, many companies are starting to do behavioral interviews over the phone or a video conference. While the format is different, many of the same principles apply.

◇ IMPORTANT When you're presenting your portfolio, you usually get into the details of the situation and provide specific examples because no projects are alike. Same with behavioral interviews—get specific[§14.5.1] and answer the question succinctly. Aim to respond to the question in about two to three minutes. Hypothetical responses that err on how one should or in theory might do things aren't good responses as they don't give the interviewer a clear signal of how you actually handled things in the past.

The behavioral interview format might also vary. Some companies, for instance, have a "lunch social" interview. While the goal of this interview is to give candidates a breather and not get barraged by interview questions—you'll still want to be on your best behavior[§14] and treat this casual format as just another type of interview.

14.2 *Peer Design Interview*

Usually, right after your portfolio presentation you'll be slated for a peer design interview. If that's the case, expect some detailed follow-up questions on your work. They'll also dig into:

- **Your past experience.** Anything that was mentioned in your portfolio, resume, LinkedIn, and so on.
- **Design collaboration.** How you work with other designers.
- **Your working style.** Preferences in process and your approach to work.
- **Design focus.** Areas of design that you find interesting.

Sample questions you may get asked:

- How do you keep up-to-date on the latest trends in design?

- Why are you interested in working here?
- The PM wanted the design to go a certain way that you thought wasn't right. How did you defend your rationale?
- Tell me about a conflict you had with another designer. How did you handle it?

In my experience interviewing candidates, some folks fail to provide an adequate answer to why they're interested in the position in the first place. It doesn't have to be anything out of the ordinary. Talking about the team, the role, or specific aspects that you're hoping to develop are all good starters. Employers want to see people who are interested in the opportunity as opposed to fishing for whatever they can get.

Interviewing with a peer designer also gives you a glimpse of what the design process and design culture[§4.4] is really like. See how they approach their work. What barriers do they encounter? What's an exciting project they've recently worked on? What are they looking to learn next? Get them to open up to learn more about the culture and process.

14.3 *Hiring Manager Interview*

Most of the time the hiring manager[§4.3] for a design role will come from a design background, but in smaller startups they might be an engineer or a PM looking to establish a design team. Depending on who you get, the questions will vary slightly but the objectives are similar.

Usually you'll talk to them at the end—by this time the other interviewers have submitted feedback or flagged additional things to probe on. In addition to these, the hiring manager will try to assess your:

- **Professionalism.** How you carry yourself and how you come across.
- **Career aspirations.** Where do you expect to be in the next few years.
- **Team fit.** What team would serve you and the company best.

If this is a seasoned manager, they'll get straight to the point and will ask you the hard questions. Since the final decision rests on them and the consequences of a bad hire are high, they'll want to make sure there are no remaining red flags. But it's not all bad cop—they'll also sell you on the role and the team.

Sample questions you may get asked:

- What aspect of design is exciting to you? Why?
- What's your area of strength?
- What's your area of growth?
- Where do you see yourself in the next few years?

Use this time to learn about your manager§4.3 as well. Are they growth oriented? Do you feel like you can get along with them? How have they supported designers previously?

14.4 *Cross-Functional Interviews*

After interviewing with the designers, you'll talk with your cross-functional peers: product managers, engineers, and researchers. The primary goal of these interviews is to understand how well you work with others and measure your level of empathy and consideration of others.

PRODUCT MANAGER

In many cross-functional teams, you'll work with the PM closely on a daily basis. They'll want to know:

- How you've worked with PMs and any conflicts you've encountered.
- Your ability to work on multiple projects with different timelines.
- How you balance different constraints in your work.

Sample questions you may get asked:

- What is your design process like?
- You're given a project that you need to execute on in one week to meet a deadline. How will you approach it?
- How often do you like to share work? How do you share work with the team for feedback?
- What types of conflicts have you encountered with product managers? How did you resolve them?
- How will you let me know if you're going to miss a deadline?

Take the time in this interview to understand what kind of PM they are. Just like product design, product management has many aspects to it. What gets the PM excited to go to work every morning? What part of the process do they enjoy the most? How do they see design contributing to the product development process? Have they done design before? These are all good questions to keep in your back pocket.

ENGINEERING

Engineers have the final say on what gets built, as they're the last persons to touch the artifact. Similar to a PM, they'll be interested in how you partner with their kind. They'll examine:

- Collaboration with engineering and empathy for constraints.
- Handling conflict in design and engineering situations.

Sample questions you may get asked:

- How do you prefer to work with engineering?
- How did you successfully partner with engineering?
- What's the worst part of working with engineers?
- How do you assess a design's technical feasibility? When do you consider it in your process?

If you're new to design or have never worked with engineers before, you might not know how to proceed or how to find common ground with your engineering counterpart. One way you can address this gap is by selling the engineer on your collaborative skills and your ability to learn quickly.

If lack of collaboration skills is a big barrier, you can invest some time by participating in a hackathon or contributing to an open-source project. Many of these are engineering-led and don't have a design contributor. Find interesting projects and reach out to the engineers there.

UX RESEARCHER

Sometimes you might get interviewed by a UX researcher. If you do, consider yourself lucky—great design rests on solid research, and knowing how research is treated will give you deeper insight into the company's design culture. Researchers won't expect you to know the ins and outs of doing research, but they will ask you how you've engaged with their function:

- Your preferences working with research.
- Conflicts you've encountered when working with research.

Sample questions:

- How have you worked with researchers in the past?
- Tell me a time when you successfully collaborated with research. What made the collaboration successful?
- Was there a time when your design failed in a research study? Can you tell me why it failed and what happened next?

If you have time left over, use this to learn about the company's design maturity.[100] A couple of ways you can get at that question is by asking when researchers are included in the product planning process (if at all). Ask them about what pain points they've encountered in their role and how they prefer to work with design.

WRAP-UP

At the end of your interviews you'll meet either with the hiring manager or the recruiter. This is another opportunity to reinforce your enthusiasm for the role. They'll let you know what happens next and the time frame for the final decision on your candidacy.

For another list of interview questions, check out BuzzFeed's design interview questions.[101]

14.5 *Behavioral Interview Tips*

Even when you have your answers prepared, your delivery still matters. Here are a few best practices to consider.

USE A STORY FORMAT

Many behavioral interviews will ask you about a situation in the past to assess how you handled it. It's not unlike the methods we use in user research. We don't ask participants to predict what they'll do in the future—we ask them what they actually did. In an interview setting, you'll also have to get specific and use your storytelling skills to give an example and provide concrete learnings.

100. https://www.invisionapp.com/design-better/design-maturity-model/

101. https://github.com/buzzfeed/design/blob/master/recruiting/interview-questions.md

As an example, here's how the structure might look like when you're asked "Tell me about a time when your design failed":

1. **Summary of the situation.** I was working on a design for a photo sharing feature which failed in usability testing.
2. **Set up the context.** I was in the middle of this project when I briefly chatted with my researcher. We decided to do a quick study to validate the idea, as the problem wasn't well defined.
3. **Your actions.** After seeing the fourth participant struggle through a prototype I built, I understood that we had a bigger problem to solve.
4. **Outcome.** I met with my PM and researcher to scope down the initial feature so we could focus on learning and buy us more time to understand the problem. This did cause some delays, but it also helped us learn faster and iterate on a solution that helped people to more easily share their photos with their loved ones.
5. **Lessons learned.** This situation helped me build the case for defining problems with product up-front. I also built a stronger relationship with my researcher, and we keep each other regularly informed about new work.

While this example is somewhat simplistic, as you can see the format is not unlike that of a portfolio case study. You can practice by brainstorming a few notable scenarios that you might want to bring up. Once you have your list of situations, you can break these out based on the outline above.

You can go even further by recording your responses on video as practice. This is a good way to see yourself and how you come off. It will also help you check your responses for filler words (uh, uhm), brevity, and clarity. The point isn't to memorize these verbatim, but a little practice does make it easier to jog your memory when you're in the middle of the interview.

BRING EXCITEMENT AND ENERGY INTO YOUR INTERVIEW

Sometimes when you're been interviewing for a while without much progress you may feel absolutely down. It's OK to feel that, but don't bring it to the interview. You only have one chance to make an impression, so make sure it's good. Do what you need to do to get yourself centered.

◇ IMPORTANT Interviews are a time to put your best foot forward. It's not a time to relax and to spill the beans or reveal your struggles, even if it feels like the interviewer feels nice and considerate. You want to be operating from a place of strength and centeredness and not get caught up in the negative, such as by bad-mouthing your previous employers or co-workers.

Ultimately, your goal is to leave your interviewers excited to work with you so that once you leave, they'll be sure to mention you to other colleagues and will fight to get you in. This might not be possible to do all the time—it's a good north star to keep in mind. Aside from doing the work, interviewers also want to know if they can get along with you and, ideally, if they'd be excited to work with you.

CONNECT ON A PERSONAL LEVEL

Unlike a formal presentation where you're talking to a group of people, one-on-one interviews offer a more intimate environment to learn about someone. Don't miss this opportunity to ask specific questions regarding their recent work or projects. Ideally, you can also connect based on common interests (for example, that same volunteering group you saw on their LinkedIn).

> **STORY**
>
> When I was interviewing with a product manager at a big financial company, I searched for her name to learn more about her work. When I brought up a blog post that her team did on a project she recently completed, she was pleasantly surprised; she didn't think the post was online. Sometimes you can be more informed on the outside than you think.

CLARIFY AND REPHRASE QUESTIONS

Sometimes your interviewers are new to interviews. Maybe you're that lucky candidate they're talking to. In these types of high-stakes situations, it helps to take a step back and rephrase the question.

> **STORY**
>
> One time I was scheduled for an onsite interview at a design agency. The interview was only an hour, and about halfway through the chat, one of the designers asks, why don't you show us something cool you worked on? So I decided to talk about a recent school project. Unfortunately, this got me a rejection. The kicker? My work wasn't strategic enough.

WATCH OUT FOR CULTURE TELLS

Although usually you and the interviewer are on best appearances during interviews, sometimes people let their guards down. Remember when we talked about culture?§4.4 Now that you know what you're looking for, it's time to take note.

> **STORY**
>
> During one interview I was asked "off the record" about what I would do to convince a co-worker to work over the weekend? And what if "it was their kid's birthday that weekend"? These "off the record" questions are more telling of the underlying culture than a list of values on the company's website.

You can read all the Glassdoor reviews, but you won't really know what it's truly like on the inside. Take the time to observe the environment in between your interviews. How do people behave—do they look happy or stressed? What do they say "off the record?" Spend time getting to know the person who's giving you that office tour, chat with folks at reception. Lastly, to truly understand the culture of a place, you'll need to do a little more digging§23 for further information once you get that offer.

14.6 *Additional Resources*

If you're applying to a large company, it's highly likely that some of those questions have already been documented somewhere. These questions may not be as easy to find for smaller startups but it helps to look around. You should consider using resources such as LinkedIn and Glassdoor. Note, these questions will change so don't expect the exact question in your interview, instead treat these questions as practice.

PART IV: ACING DESIGN EXERCISES

Design exercises are one of the most controversial interview types and are not without fault.[102] It's not uncommon for many designers to bemoan them, and with good reason. These interviews sometimes inadvertently screen high-quality candidates out. After all, not everyone can dedicate hours outside of work on a take-home design exercise. Sometimes the criteria for success can be confusing for interview candidates, and this is often exacerbated by the people who are conducting the interview when they don't have a clear idea of what they're looking for.

So why do companies do them?

The short of it is that design has become a competitive landscape with many candidates applying for design jobs. A portfolio, the strongest indicator of one's skill as a designer, sometimes doesn't tell the full story. Usually most design projects are team projects, so it can be hard to tell who did which part. So when you are presenting your portfolio, be sure to reinforce the role that you've played and the specific work that you've done.

For certain companies—those who cannot afford a design manager or who may just need a strong individual contributor from the outset—they may not know exactly what to look for. They frequently see designers as having nontransferable skills between industries; for example, if you worked in design for enterprise products, you may not flourish at a fast-paced startup. These are just some of the common misconceptions that you may encounter at a company that has a low design maturity.[§4.2]

That said, sometimes you may find yourself in a situation where doing a design exercise is a matter of getting a job. The goal of this section is to arm you with framework and techniques so that you can pass these interviews with flying colors.

---

102. https://orgdesignfordesignorgs.com/2018/05/15/design-exercises-are-a-bad-interviewing-practice/

Here are the most common exercises you'll encounter during the design interview process:

- **The take-home design exercise.**§15 Typically you'll get it in your early interview stages. Companies use the exercise as a qualifier to advance you to the next round. You'll have a few days to work on it before submitting and presenting it to an interview panel.
- **App critique.**§17 Usually you'll be paired with another designer or two to evaluate an app, giving sound reasons for your critique.
- **Whiteboard challenge.**§19 One of the more challenging exercises, you'll uncover your design process as you're sketching out your thinking and reacting to curve balls that your interviewers throw at you during the process.

Take heart. Design exercises aren't easy. I've seen some candidates fail the whiteboard challenge and still get an offer. At other times, certain design exercises elevated a candidate's design level, which led to a higher compensation package. So if you decide to take on a design exercise, make the most out of it and come out on top, stronger.

15 The Take-Home Design Exercise

As I mentioned previously, design exercises are not without fault, and as a candidate you always have a choice whether or not to accept one. Sometimes companies allow you to swap one design exercise for another—for example, instead of the take-home exercise, doing a whiteboard challenge.

Or you can choose to forego the design exercise altogether and end the interview—sometimes this is an option if you're interviewing at other places and this one isn't worth your time, and they're not budging on pushing back the timeline.

CAUTION Beware of companies that try to get free work out of you via a design exercise. The design exercise should be different from their business and the deliverable shouldn't be a fully coded concept that can be implemented. That said, the companies who have challenges that are similar to their business aren't necessarily trying to get free work out of you. Sometimes they don't know how to evaluate designers and therefore they create a challenge similar to their business because they're the domain experts.

At the end of the day if you have concerns or suggestions—these are all great points to bring up with you recruiter. Try to better understand why the company is doing a take home exercise and what they're trying to achieve. Some companies are also starting to compensate their candidates for the design challenge thus making this interview type a little more palatable.

If you do choose to accept this challenge, you can play to your strengths by **highlighting your potential in practice**—that is, if you weren't encumbered by constraints, what would your work look like? Maybe your current job didn't offer you the right environment to prove yourself, or you think your portfolio isn't an accurate representation of what you can do now. It happens. Now's your chance to show off those skills.

15.1 *Design Exercise Format and Criteria*

Typically, candidates are given a few days to a week to complete the take-home assignment. Usually recruiters warn candidates not to spend more than "a few hours on it," but in reality many candidates spend a fairly significant amount of time. After all, if you really want to differentiate yourself, you have to put in the work.

So you've got a design exercise on your hands and the clock is ticking. To make sure your solution is adequate, you'll need to make sure you understand the evaluation criteria. Every company will vary, but typically they look for:

1. **Process.** How you approach and solve ambiguous problems.
2. **Craft.** Strong interaction design and visual design work delivered in a short amount of time.
3. **Creativity.** Generating divergent and out-of-the-ordinary ideas quickly.
4. **Prioritization.** Converging on critical concepts that lead to impact.

Sometimes companies also use different types of design exercise formats when they want to zero in on a particular skill. For example, some may focus heavily on visual design aspects, while others may want you to focus more on interaction design. Typically this will be specified in the design exercise prompt.

And yet some companies may not have a rigorous process established (usually in startups) and they may not really know what they're looking for in an answer. These can be the toughest take-homes to crack, but usually, following the design process to a tee and showing how your process has yielded new and interesting solutions helps put them at ease.

15.2 *Nine Principles for a Successful Design Exercise*

There are no shortcuts, but you can increase your chances by:

1. **Practicing.** If you've never done a design exercise, practice by finding a problem you're interested in. Give yourself a deadline, write a prompt, do it in the allotted time, and give yourself an objective evaluation.
2. **Understanding context and questions.** Get to know the constraints and how your work will be evaluated.
3. **Going above and beyond.** After understanding the baseline requirements, see how you can exceed expectations. As Paul Graham[103] says, "The best protection is always working on hard problems."
4. **Letting the narrative guide your presentation.** It's not about the technology or the process—it's about how all the work you've done helps the customer lead a better life.
5. **Showing and curating process.** Generate lots of ideas and be deliberate in what you focus on. If it doesn't make your narrative stronger, leave it.
6. **Talking to customers.** Actually talk to people. Yes, this will be a biased convenience sample, but having rough customer feedback is better than none at all. Scrappiness is a virtue.
7. **Synthesizing findings.** Show the meaning you've extracted from disparate data sources to frame the problem accurately.
8. **Treating it like work.** Imagine you're already working at this company. How would you approach this challenge?
9. **Delighting the client.** When your foundation is solid, can you add a cherry on top that leaves interviewers in awe? Or in the words of Ueno,

103. http://www.paulgraham.com/hs.html

"When someone asks you for a coffee, bring the best one you can, but always add a piece of chocolate."

15.3 *Start with Context*

OK, you have your design exercise prompt. What should you do first? Since this is a high-stakes project, it's important to get context up-front to save time by executing in the right direction.

WHAT IS THE FINAL DELIVERABLE?

What are they looking for? Is this a mobile app, a sitemap, a research brief, or a desktop app? Are they looking for you to show your skills in interaction design, information architecture, research, visual design? This should be clear from the prompt.

◇ **IMPORTANT** When you're working through a design exercise, know when to take shortcuts and know when to go bespoke. Creating every asset from scratch may take a long time and may not be necessary.

WHAT'S UNCLEAR?

Even with clear prompts you're still bound to have questions. That's a good sign. Generate a list—reread the prompt and think how the answers can help you move faster when you're heads down on a challenge.

HOW COLLABORATIVE DO THEY WANT TO BE?

Interviewers might be willing or expect to provide feedback during the course of your work. You should both be on the same page as to how often you can reach out, to whom, and what feedback you will get and when.

WHEN IS THE DELIVERABLE DUE?

Structure the deadline to your advantage. When I had a lull in work, it was easy for me to focus intensely on the design exercise to get it done. Other times I've taken a day off or pushed back on the start date of the exercise so I could work on it over the weekend.

◇ **IMPORTANT** You only get to do the design exercise once, so make sure your submission is the best it can be given the timeline. If you are employed but don't feel like you have enough mental energy to take on a design challenge, take a day or two off. Design exercises are already hard; don't put yourself in an impossible position of running out of time.

WHAT ARE YOUR OPTIONS?

Design exercises are time intensive—some companies offer the choice of a whiteboard challenge instead. I took this option when I was already doing two design exercises. This saved me time—while delivering high-quality work for the other two, the third interviewers felt they got everything that they needed from the whiteboard.

HOW WILL YOU PRESENT YOUR WORK?

Usually, at the end of the design exercise you'll present at their office. Typically, to save time your presentation will be part of your final interview.[§11] If possible, try to get a sense of what you'll be working with: their room set up, monitor, seating, and so on. It's always good to know your context and be prepared with backup in case their tech fails.

16 Real-World Take-Home Design Exercise Solution

Here is a sample design exercise solution that I completed a few years ago. This presentation (as well as the rest of the interview) helped not only secure my offer but led to a higher design level than I anticipated and a higher salary as well. The prompt asked to design a car dashboard for an autonomous vehicle. For this exercise I didn't have that much time (about five days) so I had to skip my usual approach of asking many questions upfront and started working right away.

As is usual with any design briefs, I began by reframing the problem. Instead of "designing a car dashboard," I wanted to think about the experience broadly—from the car's interior to its exterior and how the car can be part of a larger ecosystem. I sketched a few different directions before settling on one, which I fully fleshed out, and lastly, I sneaked in a surprise at the end of my presentation.

16.1 *Looking at Analogous Domains for Inspiration*

To start this exercise, while riding the train to my next interview, I began typing some thoughts on my phone in the notes app on how to approach the task. The train itself was an inspiration—could public transit be the answer? I pursued the mass transit idea further by looking into Emirates airlines and other luxury transit services, including the new luxury Japanese train.[104] The luxurious interiors looked nice, but what about everyday mass commuters? What are their existing activities and habits when taking the train to work?

FIGURE: YOUR OWN PRIVATE AUTONOMOUS VEHICLE

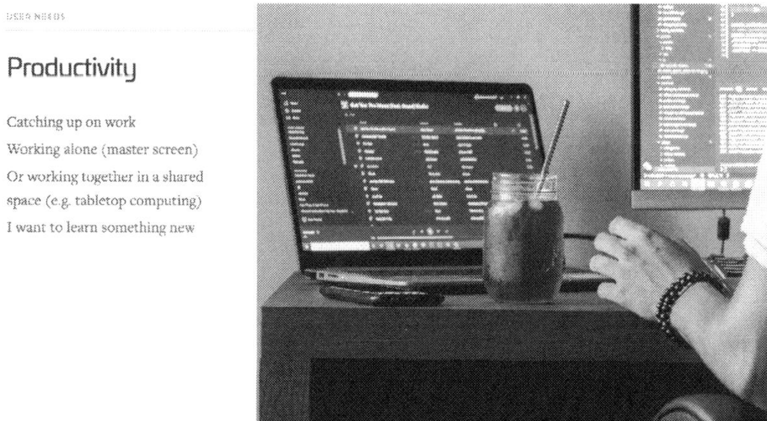

Productivity
Catching up on work
Working alone (master screen)
Or working together in a shared space (e.g. tabletop computing)
I want to learn something new

I didn't have time to set up a proper study, so I relied on three 12-minute interviews with friends and asked them about their experience with riding trains, buses, ferries, and so on. From searching online and from the conversations, I identified four major categories of activities on mass transit: productivity, relaxation, social, and health.

16.2 *Questioning Assumptions*

When you're going deep on the design exercise, it helps to periodically step back and remind yourself about the problem you're trying to solve. In my case the prompt was asking for an in-car UI design for a self-driving car. I decided to take a slightly different approach because many car man-

104. https://www.express.co.uk/travel/articles/788774/japanese-train-luxury-Shiki-Shima-glass

ufacturers have been addressing this problem for decades. Redesigning the car display would be optimizing for local maxima prematurely.

FIGURE: INTERIOR DISPLAY VS EXTERIOR

Manufacturers have spent their attention on the interior display taking eyes away from the road.

What if we could expand the display from a small tablet to include the windshield? And what if the car was smart enough to capture inputs from the outside world and provide contextual info. Technology without an explicit need is like a solution looking for a problem. As designers, it's our responsibility to take technology's raw potential, intersect it with customer needs, and build a solution that drives results for the business.

Augmented reality (AR) is a potential solution, but it can also get out of hand. As designer Keiichi Matsuda[105] shows in his explorations, an AR that bombards a city resident with visual noise promotes anxiety. I included this in my presentation as an extreme example to steer away from.

I also considered voice assistants. After all, even Ironman's advanced AR suit still had an omnipresent assistant. To see how these technologies could work (or collide) together in the customer's space when they're taking transportation, I started doing some light synthesis with some simplified diagramming.

105. https://vimeo.com/chocobaby

FIGURE: START SYNTHESIZING YOUR FINDINGS

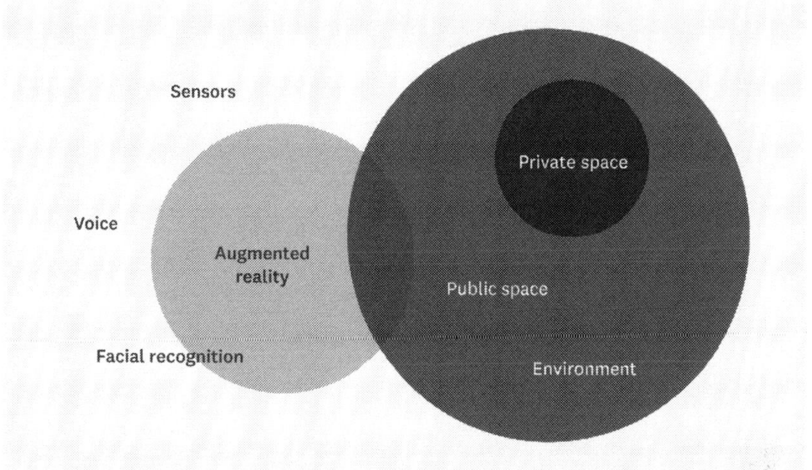

Simple diagrams to start synthesizing and modeling how various trends come together.

This led me to a few core principles to evaluate my work against:

- **Personalized.** The assistant should deeply understand the person(s) in the car.
- **Unobtrusive.** The technology should let the customer be in the driver's seat.
- **Context aware.** It should provide relevant suggestions based on context and customers' interests.

Although I didn't explicitly mention these anywhere in my presentation, having these explicitly documented held me accountable by enforcing constraints, which led to a streamlined concept.

16.3 *Exploring Solutions with Storyboards*

With problem discovery done, I did some rough explorations via storyboard sketches showing how a car interior could transform to a suitable activity from an interactive gym inside a car, to a productivity station, to an experience that connects two strangers by showing activities and people they have in common.

FIGURE: BRINGING PEOPLE TOGETHER

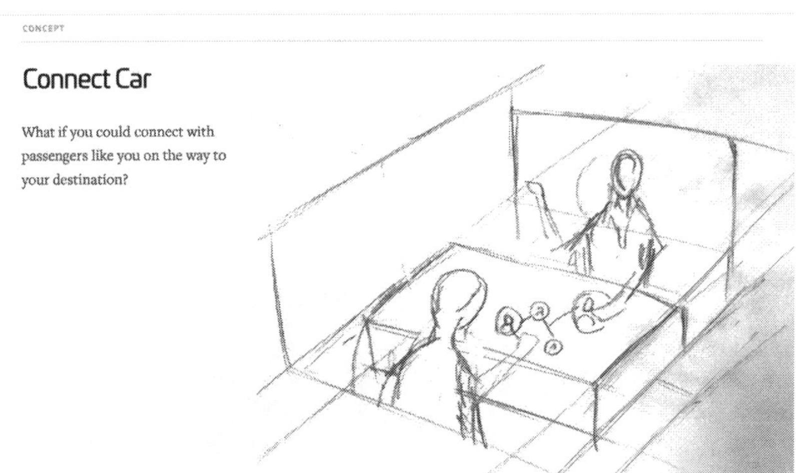

CONCEPT
Connect Car
What if you could connect with passengers like you on the way to your destination?

Bringing people together based on shared connections and activities.

In the end I converged on an idea I thought was most exciting—tourism; imagine an Airbnb experience guide but in a car. This concept hit on many things from my diagram—interacting with public and private spaces, using sensors, voice, AR, even facial recognition to do complex computation in order to provide the right answer. Here's an example wireframe of what a smart social table may look like.

FIGURE: SMART TABLE

Sample wireframe of what a smart social table may look like.

16.4 *Using Storytelling to Make the Concept Come to Life*

To make the concept come to life, I wrote a story about a fictitious solo business traveler, Sarah, who has a few hours to kill in the evening in San Francisco by doing a tour of the city. The solution is an assistant in an autonomous car that understands Sarah and anticipates her needs. It also has a bit of snark to its personality, something Sarah appreciates.

FIGURE: MEET SARAH

PERSONA

Sarah

Persona

Business traveler

Visiting SF for the first time

Interested in sightseeing and exploring over the weekend before heading back to Australia

Scenario

Sarah is interested in a quick 6-hour tour that can give her some of the highlights of the city.

Meet Sarah.

Writing and rewriting a story is a quick way to prototype. I usually start out almost all of my design work by writing first. I went through a couple of drafts first and later sketched a few screens on paper before quickly turning to mocking up screens (at that time) in Sketch. The digital work in turn helped me refine the story further and add some elements of amusement and delight.

16.5 *Showing, Not Telling Sarah's Journey*

Here are a couple of highlights from the narrative that I've put together. Her journey starts on her phone near the place she's staying.

FIGURE: THE JOURNEY BEGINS

The journey starts on the phone...

She lets the app know what she's in the mood for, and as a car arrives the experience seamlessly transitions to her car dashboard.

FIGURE: AN OVERVIEW OF THE TRIP

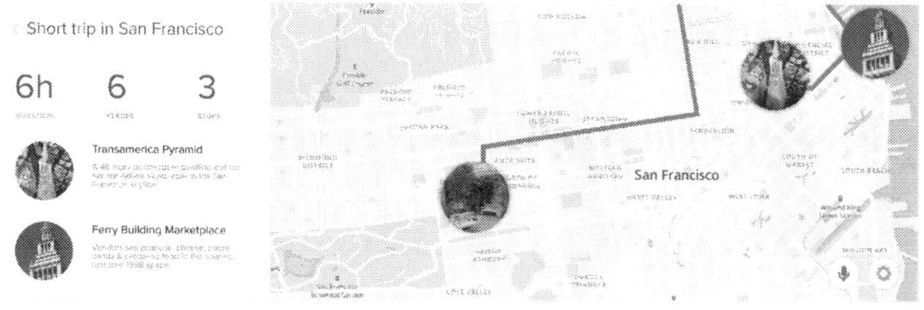

The car dashboard shows an overview of the trip and destinations.

But the main action is in the tour that Sarah experiences through an AR windshield with a voice-assisted guide.

FIGURE: SPACE AND CONTEXT

The windshield takes advantage of the large space and provides the right context.

The assistant is smart enough to make personal recommendations and get out of the way. It gives Sarah enough time to explore the Ferry building on foot so she can find her favorite chocolates there. The car goes to park itself, but the assistant is available a tap away on her phone.

FIGURE: ASSISTANT AT THE READY

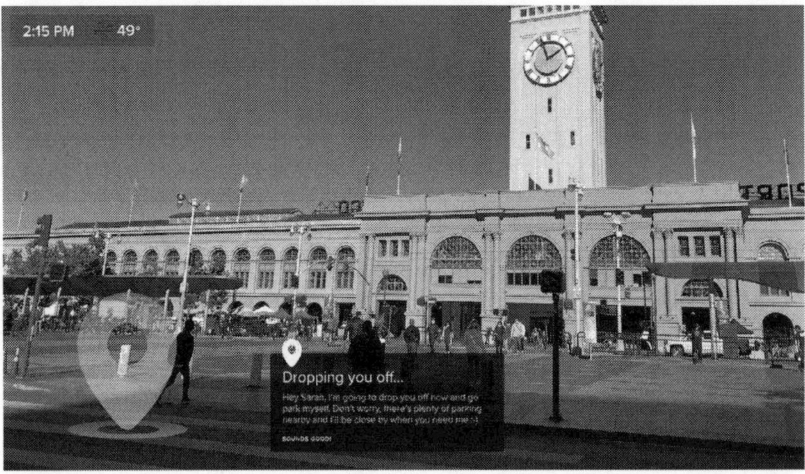

Throughout the journey in the car, the assistant is intelligent enough to anticipate how Sarah feels (like if she's falling asleep) and provide an appropriate remedy (coffee) with minimal input.

FIGURE: HOW ABOUT AN AMERICANO?

Would you like me to order a $20 Americano for you?

16.6 *Putting It Together*

The final presentation came down to 40+ slides in four chapters:

1. **Technology trends.** In AR, VUI, and automotive, showing how there's potential for customer value but also danger in going overboard.
2. **Research synthesis.** Show already-existing behaviors of people in relation to semi-autonomous and autonomous vehicles.
3. **Contextual scenarios.** Show storyboards highlighting divergent exploration, ultimately converging on the final segment of the presentation.
4. **Sarah's story.** Illustrates how technology and people's needs come together and solve a customer's problem.

The context of tech and research made the audience understand what solutions are possible, and Sarah's story illustrated a specific use case.

A couple of years ago I went to an AIGA event where I met the fine folks at Ueno. One of the designers mentioned how if a client asks for coffee, don't just bring excellent coffee but bring chocolate.[106] Understanding the **underlying but unspoken** need is key. In my case chocolate was a box.

106. https://loremipsum.ueno.co/designers-should-always-bring-the-chocolate-7eb597300215

FIGURE: PHYSICAL PROTOTYPES

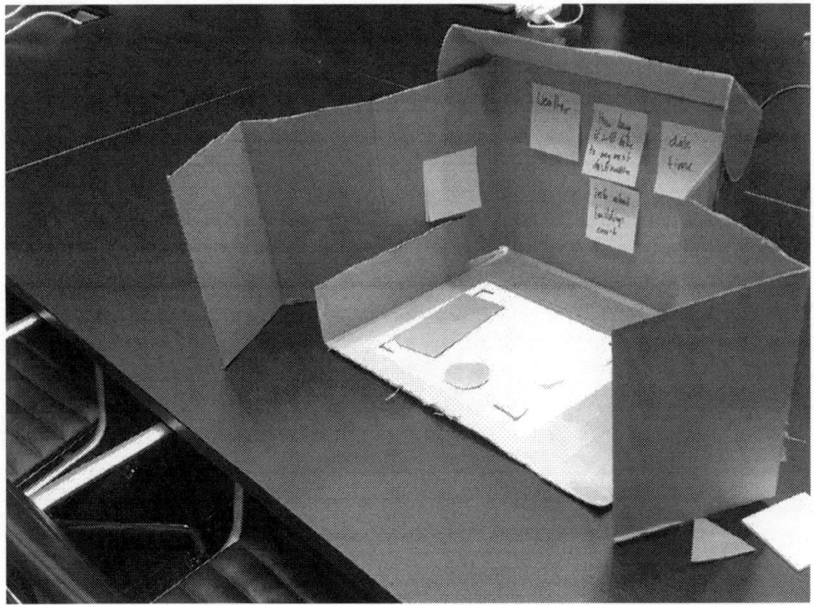

Sometimes to think outside the box you have to think inside the box.

At the last minute, a few hours before the interview, since I'd already sent the deck for a pre-read, I decided to build a physical prototype of an autonomous vehicle. I spent about an hour cutting up boxes and gluing cardboard together. What if we could have customers co-design the experience by interacting with the physical prototype?

16.7 *Outcome*

The on-site presentation of this exercise was my third to last interview. I lucked out on the presentation space, as Sarah's story came to life on a beautiful large display. The box and the rough sketches surprised and delighted the interviewers, as they had never seen anything like it.

This is **one way** to solve a design exercise but **not the only way**. I do hope that by showing some of my process behind the work and the deliverables, you can see how I've followed (or ignored) the design exercise principles (they're not set in stone) based on the situation at hand.

The design exercise is an opportunity to leave your personal mark on the work. Take it and have fun with it. Find out what the evaluation criteria will be and use your unique perspective, experience, and knowledge to stand out.

16.8 *Additional Resources*

Coming up with a new design proposal from nothing can be a lot of work. Usually, when you're joining a company you have frameworks already set up for you, be they design systems, brand assets, or just existing processes that can help you stand up a new concept quickly.

◇ IMPORTANT When you are using outside resources for your design exercise be sure to properly attribute and credit the work.

Many of the assets that I've used for design exercises (including this one) came from popular, free-shared libraries. Here are some I recommend for the raw materials for your design exercise.

- **Photography**
  - Pexels.[107] Bills itself as a free and *inclusive* photo and video library.
  - Unsplash.[108] One of my favorites, and the go-to resource for high quality photography.
  - Pixabay.[109] Over a million images and videos shared, free for personal or commercial use.
- **Illustrations**
  - Humaaans.[110] A customizable illustration library by Pablo Stanley. Use is free for personal and commercial use.
  - Blush.[111] Founded by Pablo Stanley, it's a customizable illustration resource that allows you to remix, change colors, and find illustrations for different occasions.
  - Undraw.[112] Similar to illustration libraries already listed but with less focus on the character and more emphasis on staging.

---

107. https://www.pexels.com/
108. https://unsplash.com/
109. https://pixabay.com/
110. https://www.humaaans.com/
111. https://blush.design/
112. https://undraw.co/illustrations

- **Maps**
  - Your project may not require maps, but if it does, spending a little time customizing a map could be another way you can differentiate your design.
  - Mapbox.[113] Probably one of the most robust APIs out there. With Mapbox studio you can customize tons of things (you have to create an account). The learning curve may be a little steep at the beginning, so I recommend you take a couple of pre-existing Mapbox maps and customize those first to get a feel for it.
  - Google map styles.[114] You can select a theme or you can come up with a brand-new style, customizing things like buildings, landscapes, points of interest, roads, transit lines, and water.

17 Acing the App Critique

The app critique is one of the easier interviews you'll encounter when interviewing for a product design role. Unlike the take-home design exercise or the whiteboard interview, you don't have to create something from scratch.

Unlike a critique of an app that you're designing, you're not encumbered by any internal constraints (tech, business, and so on), giving you an immense amount of freedom. The challenge then lies in how to come up with reasonable constraints to help you navigate the critique.

◇ IMPORTANT As you're facilitating the app critique, ask yourself—can I work with this team if I was hired? Do they seem like people I can bounce ideas off freely?

We'll cover different techniques that you can mix and match to come up with evaluation criteria for your app.

113. https://studio.mapbox.com/

114. https://mapstyle.withgoogle.com/

17.1 *Interview Format and Criteria*

App critiques usually last 30–45 minutes. Typically, you'll interview with one or two designers. Either you'll be asked to bring an app for critique (based on interviewer criteria) or the interviewers will pick one for you.

Your interviewers will assess you on:

- **Collaboration.** How receptive are you to feedback? How do you react to different opinions? How effectively can you facilitate the critique?
- **Craft.** How well can you reverse engineer an app, breaking it down to its first principles?

The craft component will vary depending on the specific role you're applying for. For visual design, you'll zero in on the UI. UX design roles will focus on information architecture and interaction design. Product design roles tend to be generalist, so expect a mix of both.

Based on how you approach the problem and how you respond to questions, your interviewers will also try to gauge which part of the design process is exciting to you.

Don't forget the interviewer's perspective. As they're watching you critique the app, they're also evaluating if they can work with you day-to-day. How you show up matters. Same goes for you—use this opportunity to see if the culture of this team resonates with you.

◇ IMPORTANT If you're critiquing an app remotely, instead of trying to hold up your phone to the camera, it's a better experience to dial into the meeting with your phone and share your phone screen. I definitely recommend you practice dialing in and setting up your phone permissions ahead of time as the setup can get tricky and you don't want to be wasting precious time during the interview fiddling with settings.

17.2 *Establishing App Critique Objectives*

Before diving into the app critique, it's important to understand how the critique will be carried out. Your interviewers might give you a general prompt like "critique app X" or get specific: "how can app X maximize revenue from its existing customer base?"

In either case, start with high-level objectives:

- **Context.** If you're bringing in an app yourself, let the interviewers know why you've selected it. If an app has been picked for you, you can set the context based on what you know about it.
- **Goals.** If the prompt is open ended, narrow the scope by establishing goals. What's the business objective? What is the user trying to achieve? What are we trying to get at in the next 20 minutes?

With these established, you can start to take the app apart. These don't have to be fully fleshed out, but it does help to have at least some explicit objectives defined up-front. But be ready to adapt. Even though you'll come prepared, your interviewers will likely change objectives midstream. Think of the app critique like improv—you're building on top of interviewer feedback.

17.3 *Six Frameworks for Critiquing Apps*

Now the fun part. Here are six frameworks to help you examine the app:

1. **Jobs to be done.** Uncovering the core objective.
2. **Personas.** Goals, motivations, scenarios.
3. **User familiarity.** New users, intermediate users, and experts.
4. **Expert evaluation.** Using best practices and industry standards.
5. **Inclusivity.** How accessible is this app?
6. **Zooming in and out.** Aesthetic, functional, and strategic layers.

Many of these frameworks complement each other, and you'll use a combination of them in your critique.

JOBS TO BE DONE: UNCOVERING THE CORE OBJECTIVE

Do you know what job a milkshake is hired to do? In his famous example, Clayton Christensen recounts the story of a struggling milkshake company trying to increase revenue. They try everything—making milkshakes thicker, larger, but nothing works. Only after observing customers buying milkshakes do they come to a realization.

In the morning, customers prefer milkshakes because they're a portable source of energy when commuting to work. The milkshake fills them up, it's easy to hold in the car, and it doesn't leave a mess. In the evening parents swing by with their kids to treat them to the shake. But kids struggle. The straw is difficult to use, and the packaging is clumsy at best for small hands.

As you can see, the job varies depending on the context. Uncovering the jobs-to-be-done, or JTBD, will provide you objective criteria to critique the app against.

- What is the customer trying to accomplish?
- If the app didn't exist, what would the customer do?
- Is the alternative better or worse than the app? Why?

A JTBD might be enough context to start getting into app flows and the UI.

PERSONAS: GOALS, ATTITUDES, AND BEHAVIORS

While JTBD provides an objective high-level framework, personas can give you an extra layer of empathy with details. They're especially helpful when you're addressing users who are very different from you and the interviewer.

In the app critique context, you won't have research handy, so you'll need to make these up as you go. One way of organizing this info is through proto-personas, as coined by Jeff Gothelf.[115] If you have a whiteboard handy, jot down your assumed persona characteristics:

- **Goals.** What objective(s) are they trying to accomplish?
- **Motivation.** Why are they motivated to use the app?
- **Attitudes.** How do they feel about the task they're trying to accomplish?
- **Behaviors.** Where in the context of a user's life does the app fit in? Where do they use it—home, work, or on their commute? How do they use it? What else is happening in the background?

Pairing personas with a scenario (think mini customer journey) will help you make the most of them by putting yourself in their shoes and imagining how they would use the app to accomplish a task.

NEW USERS, INTERMEDIATES, AND EXPERTS

You can segment your prototypical persona further, based on how familiar they are with the app.

115. https://medium.com/u/94a2a063be85

1. **Welcoming newcomers.** New users offer a different type of challenge compared to your everyday users who are already bought in. The app will need to communicate quickly to entice the user to continue. Depending on how much time you have, consider stepping all the way back to the initial app discovery phase. How do the users find the app? What gets them to download and try it out?

   As a new user who downloaded the app:

   - What is the value proposition? Can I easily find it? Does it resonate with my needs?
   - Do I need to sign up or can I try it out without commitment?
   - How much effort do I need to make in the beginning?
   - What barriers or friction do I encounter during onboarding?
   - Is it clear what I need to do next?
   - How much guidance do I need in the onboarding process?
   - How does this app incentivize me to use it more?

   The new-user perspective might be easiest to take during the app critique. It doesn't assume prior app knowledge and it gets you and the interviewer on the same page by starting out fresh.
2. **Becoming a regular user.** With continued use of the app, the customer gains experience and becomes an intermediate user. Tasks that took a long time are a snap to complete. For an app critique, this provides a rich exploration area—how do I as a new user become a repeat customer?

   - How does the app guide me?
   - Where can I find shortcuts? What accelerators exist to improve my workflow?
   - How does the experience grow with my needs?
   - How can the experience be more personalized?

   This approach works well with popular apps like Facebook that you and the interviewer use frequently. Be sure to establish some common ground first, though, as they might be proficient on parts of the app that you don't use.

3. **Expert users.** Depending on the application, experts have taken the time to squeeze every last bit of efficiency out of the tool. Similar to intermediate users, you can think about evaluating the experience from a transition perspective:

    - How does the app level up intermediate users?
    - Where can you find advanced functionality?
    - What tools are missing that might be helpful for an expert?

    For the app critique, this might be the hardest perspective to take, but it might be worthwhile for tools that are highly task oriented. Usually these tend to be enterprise apps like Photoshop or Visual Studio. Taking this perspective shows that you know the user well and that you've developed a point of view on how to meet your user's needs.

EXPERT APP EVALUATION: INDUSTRY BEST PRACTICES

JTBD, personas, and different user types will help you define a critical path that can help you stay focused in the limited time that you have. As you're putting yourself in the shoes of your prototypical user and thinking out loud, you want to also overlay your design-expert commentary.

One way to communicate your expertise is by referring to existing popular guides, such as Nielsen's 10 Usability Heuristics,[116] which can be applied for different platforms. Depending on the app that you're evaluating, you can also lean in on official recommendations, such as Apple's Human Interface Guidelines[117] or Google's Material Design.[118]

As an expert, your knowledge doesn't have to stop at these guidelines of course. This is an opportunity for you to demonstrate your knowledge based on experience. What patterns have you seen hold up over time? What patterns work well for this industry or this audience segment? What have you seen fail or work in practice when testing concepts?

INCLUSIVITY AND ACCESSIBILITY

So far, we've talked about ideal user journeys and expert evaluation techniques with no mention of edge cases or customer impairments. If you want to step up in the critique, consider accessibility. Ensuring apps don't exclude users is not a nice-to-have—in many parts of the world it's the law.

---

116. https://www.nngroup.com/articles/ten-usability-heuristics/

117. https://developer.apple.com/design/human-interface-guidelines/

118. https://material.io/

The Google Design team created an accessibility card deck to generate different scenarios.

FIGURE: GOOGLE'S ACCESSIBILITY CARD DECK

The Google Design team created an accessibility card deck to generate different scenarios.

I won't be able to do justice to accessibility here, but for the purpose of the app critique you can think about the following impairments:

- **Vision.** What affordances does the app make for users with low vision, color blindness, or blindness? Think size, color, contrast, or environmental factors like screen glare.
- **Hearing.** How does the app make use of sound? Does it provide backup cues? Does it have alternative text or captions? Think about the app's use in a busy environment—for example, a busy train station.
- **Motor.** Does the app require intricate touch gestures? Are tap targets large and easy to discover? Think about using the app while walking.
- **Cognitive.** How much cognitive load does the app require of the user? Does the user need to memorize instructions or remember complicated operations?

For more info, take a look at Inclusive Design[119] by Microsoft.

ZOOMING IN AND OUT ON THE EXPERIENCE

As you're going through the customer journey, you'll at times be going back to the strategic goals of the critique to make a point, diving into app functionality or zooming all the way in to a particular micro-interaction.

119. https://www.microsoft.com/design/inclusive/

FIGURE: COVER FUNCTIONAL AND STRATEGIC ELEMENTS

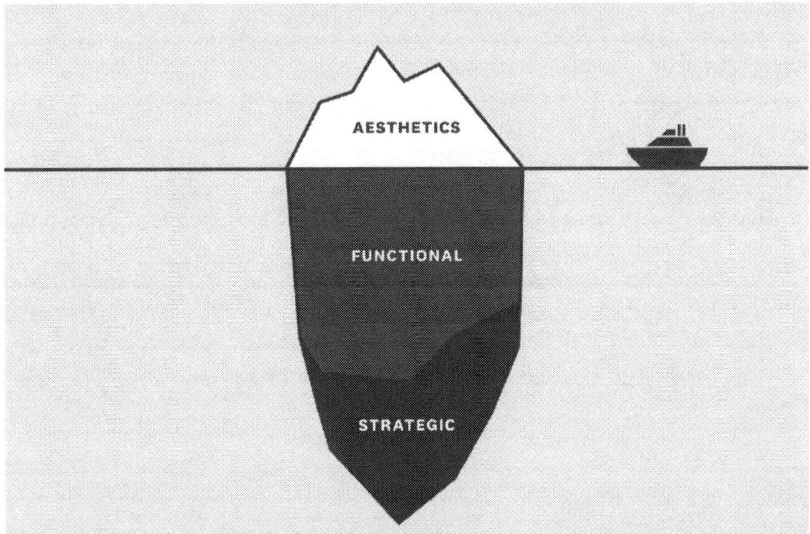

Consider both visible and invisible layers.

One way to think about this is a top-down structure that encompasses **visible** (aesthetic) **and invisible** (functional and strategic) layers:

1. **Aesthetic.** How it looks. Domain of visual design, motion, sound, touch.
2. **Functional.** How it works. Domain of information architecture and interaction design.
3. **Strategic.** Why it exists. Domain of value props and business strategy.

Aesthetic Layer

This layer is a summation of all the parts that you experience when you open up the app. How does this application achieve visual design and consistency?

- **Brand.** What message is the app trying to convey?
- **Visual.** How does the app use the visual language (color, shape, type, and so on) to reinforce its identity? What is the aesthetic experience like?
- **Motion.** How does animation help orient the user? Are there any signature moments?
- **Sound.** How does the app use sound to inform or entertain?

- **Touch.** What gestures exist and are they easily discoverable?

Pairing this layer with personas will be helpful. This is also a prime layer to think about accessibility and inclusivity.

Functional Layer

Below aesthetics lies functionality—these are core mechanics that help the user accomplish their goal.

- **Information architecture.** How is the information labeled and organized? What paths exist to browse or search?
- **Interaction design.** How does the app work? What macro and micro flows exist? What patterns are being used, what are the trade-offs?

This layer pairs well with personas and expert evaluation.

Strategic Layer

In this layer you'll find problem framing and value proposition.

- **App.** Why does this app exist? For whom? What problem is it solving?
- **Business.** What problem is the company trying to solve? What are the values that we believe in? How does the company want to portray itself? How does it make money? What's the company's mission? What values does it abide by?

The strategy layer overlaps significantly with JTBD, so you'll probably be going back and forth between the two.

17.4 *Avoiding Common App Critique Mistakes*

From my time as an interviewer, I've seen a couple of mistakes that designers make when doing critiques for interviews.

- **Stopping at aesthetics.** Sometimes it's tempting to dive right in and point out all the things that look off on the UI. Don't get stuck on aesthetics. None of that will matter if the app doesn't help the user achieve its core goal in the first place. Establish your first principles based on the frameworks above and work forward.
- **Stuck on one approach.** If you have an app that you've already picked yourself, then you've already come prepared with how you're going to

critique it. But be ready to adapt your approach and consider different methods when prompted. Doing so also allows you to show off other tools at your disposal, and handling ambiguity is a sign of maturity[§3.7.1] as a designer.

- **All praise, no substance.** I've encountered situations where instead of critiquing, the designer lavishes praise on the app. As an interviewer, this tells me that you can't reflect critically on the work and you assume that whatever's been launched is best.
- **Spending too much time describing the UI.** Don't get stuck explaining what you see or what the app does. If you're not actively sharing your mobile app screen where the interviewer can see it, it's ok to give some context but make sure you focus more on the critique itself. Interviews want to know your thinking, they don't want you to to recite the UI.

◇ IMPORTANT Always ask why. Why does this work well—what makes it good? Why does this not work—what things make it less effective? A critique framework helps you stay objective and avoid this pitfall. I also recommend looking at similar apps and comparing them against a user's job to be done.

17.5 *Getting Better at Critique*

Like any activity, you'll get better at critique with practice. To make the most of your practice, I recommend critiquing an app with a group, isolating your weaknesses, and comparing and contrasting similar apps.

CRITIQUE IN DIVERSE GROUPS

Practice critique with a partner or two. Get a group of designers who have different strengths and feel free to include other disciplines, such as engineering. Practicing together with a diverse group will widen your perspective significantly, compared to practicing alone.

ISOLATE AND FOCUS ON AN AREA OF GROWTH

If you've already evaluated your craft skills, you probably uncovered one or two areas of opportunity. Let's say you're interested in motion design. Look at the app strictly through that lens—how does it use motion to communicate? Try replicating the interaction in your favorite prototyping tool. Copying work will help you learn more through practice and see the finer details.

FIGURE: CRITIQUE APPS IN THE SAME CATEGORY

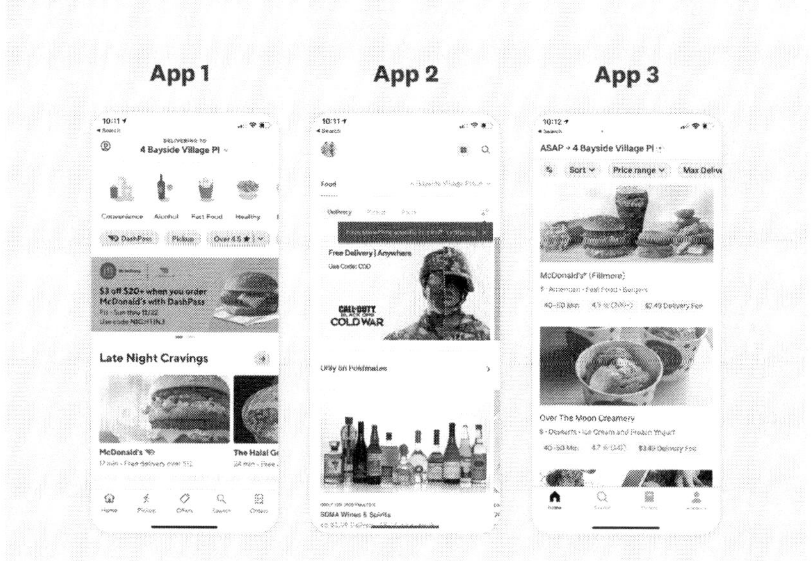

COMPARING SIMILAR APPS WITH JTBD FRAMEWORK

Look at similar apps through the lens of a JTBD statement. How's one app better than the other? What does "better" mean? For example, a tourist visiting a city wants to go from point A to point B. You can start from a narrow app lens and zoom out from there:

1. Getting a rideshare (Lyft, Uber).
2. Renting a car and driving yourself (for example, Getaround—how does it compare to rideshare?).
3. Taking public transit (Transit app, for instance—how does it compare to Uber?).
4. Walking (how does the city help me understand my current location and my proximity to the destination?).

You can do similar types of exercises in other industries like sports (training for a marathon), social interaction (Facebook), or finance (Mint). Remember the customer's objective—while there's an app for that, it doesn't mean that the alternatives don't exist or aren't better.

GO BEYOND THE APP

If you're really interested in diving into strategy and product positioning, go beyond the app. Look into how the app presents itself in the App Store, Play Store, on web (even if the web site is just a glorified ad for the native app download). When you have the app, look at how it tries to pull you in via non-app channels such as e-mails, pushes, etc.

17.6 *Additional Resources*

If you're interested in growing your critique skills, here are some hand-picked resources to help improve:

- Personas vs. Jobs-to-Be-Done,[120] by NN/g. A short read on how to use both methods effectively.
- *Discussing Design,*[121] by Adam Connor and Aaron Irizarry. A book on the mechanics and the nitty-gritty of critique facilitation.
- How to Make Sense of Any Mes,[122] by Abby Covert. A short book that arms you with basic information architecture tools and techniques.
- *The Elements of User Experience,*[123] by Jesse James Garrett. A quick read that breaks down a design problem into multiple layers: visual, skeleton, structure, scope, and strategy.
- *About Face,*[124] 4th ed., by Alan Cooper, et al. A hefty volume of nearly 700 pages, it's a solid reference for all things interaction design.

18 App Critique in Action

In this example, we'll go through Yelp's iOS app, evaluating the app in a couple of ways. We'll make our first impressions by examining the home page, and then get a sense of its structure by navigating to different pages.

---

120. https://www.nngroup.com/articles/personas-jobs-be-done/
121. https://www.amazon.com/Discussing-Design-Improving-Communication-Collaboration/dp/149190240X
122. http://www.howtomakesenseofanymess.com/
123. https://www.amazon.com/Elements-User-Experience-User-Centered-Design-ebook/dp/B004JLMDOC
124. https://www.amazon.com/About-Face-Essentials-Interaction-Design/dp/1118766571

We'll look into personalization and go through one of the core flows by looking for a nearby restaurant.

We'll evaluate the app based on its visual and interaction design. We'll also consider strategy, also known as "product thinking" or "business acumen," to understand the *why* behind the UI decisions. Although it's not our primary concern, we'll also pay attention to copy and messaging.

18.1 *First Impressions*

You can tell a lot about the app based on its presentation. The visual aspect of design hits us quickly. Based on this first impression, we decide if we want to stick around or go elsewhere. At this stage, we get an idea of the feeling the app is trying to communicate to us—is it serious or playful, trustworthy, or suspicious? These are just some of the questions that go through our heads in a split second.

As designers, our job is to build an experience consistent and in tune with the impression that the business is trying to communicate. As a result, during the critique, we should be on the lookout when a design reinforces or contradicts this consistency.

FIGURE: LAUNCHING YELP

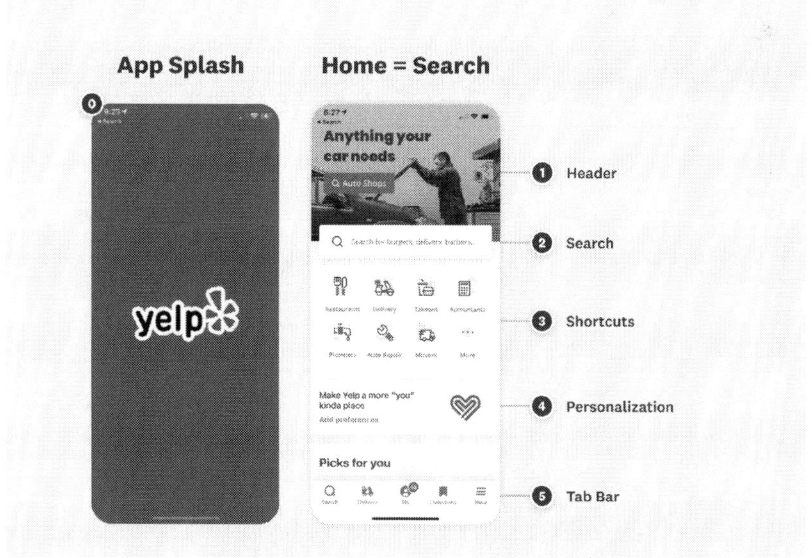

Upon opening Yelp, although it's quick, the splash screen has a subtle animation—the logo briefly recedes back before lurching forward. The combination of rounded logotype corners and the giant white outlines evoke a friendly feeling. Here are a couple of things to note on the landing page:

1. **Header.** It calls out less known Yelp coverage—auto shops. This suggests that Yelp is reinforcing the fact that it's more than just a place for restaurant reviews.
2. **Search.** The search bar had a slight shadow to indicate affordance and the input text suggests what the user can find on Yelp. The copy of "burgers, delivery, barbers..." suggests that the user can input a variety of different types of searches from dishes, to fulfillment methods, to services.
3. **Shortcuts.** Yelp uses a shortcut style menu here highlighting seven offerings and a button for more. The first three offerings are all food related: Restaurants, Delivery, Takeout. I suspect these are the core flows for the app. However it's also interesting to see Accounts, Plumbers, Auto Repair, and Movers. I wonder if these categories are dynamic and change based on season and/or market.
4. **Personalization.** This app banner asks the user to add preferences. Personalization is always a good strategy and we'll look into this a little closer in the next few sections.
5. **Tab bar.** After the splash screen, the user lands on "Search" (as opposed to the traditional "Home"). Since I haven't used Yelp in a while, I have 44 notifications on my account. Is this good or bad? It's hard to tell from this page but we'll find out once we take a closer look at "Me."

We got some useful information from the landing page. Before we dive in, sometimes it's helpful to step back before going forward. In this case getting out of the app and searching for "yelp" on the App Store can give us additional cues about Yelp's positioning.

FIGURE: YELP ON THE APP STORE

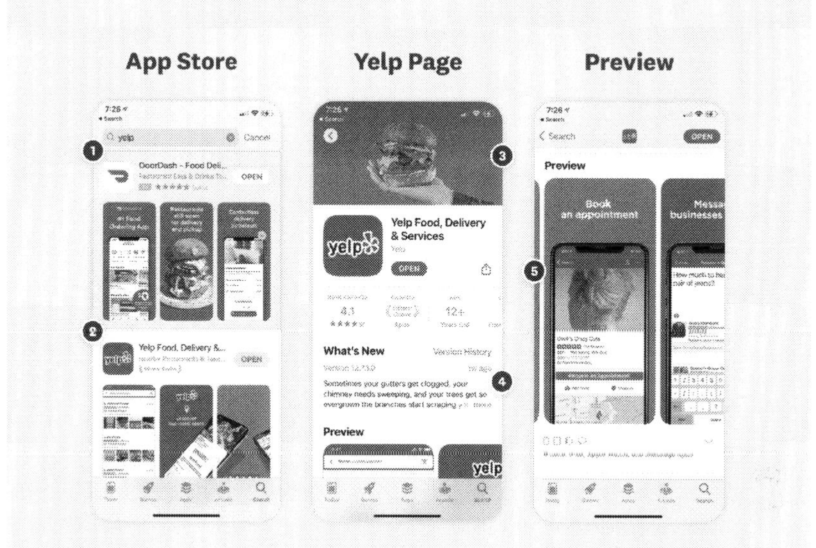

There are a few interesting things to notice here:

1. There's competition from DoorDash, since it's using "yelp" as an ad keyword.
2. Yelp includes its value proposition in the title: "Yelp Food, Delivery & Services."
3. The header of the App Store page is a giant burger (similar to the one from DoorDash, perhaps juicy burgers entice more app downloads).
4. The "What's New" copy colorfully addresses how the team has cleaned up the app to make it better while also highlighting services the app can help you find.
5. The preview screenshots give us a variety of services that Yelp is trying to promote, like finding home pros and getting quotes.

When you're doing the app critique, you don't always have to go back to the App Store or the Play Store. It's likely that the interview will be focused more on the app itself than anything outside of it. But gaining additional context can be a good move, especially if this is a popular app that everyone is familiar with.

Now let's get back into the app. To do this, I intentionally closed Yelp and launched it again—looks like the header has changed for me. I close the app again and reopen to see just how many different header variations there are.

FIGURE: HEADERS

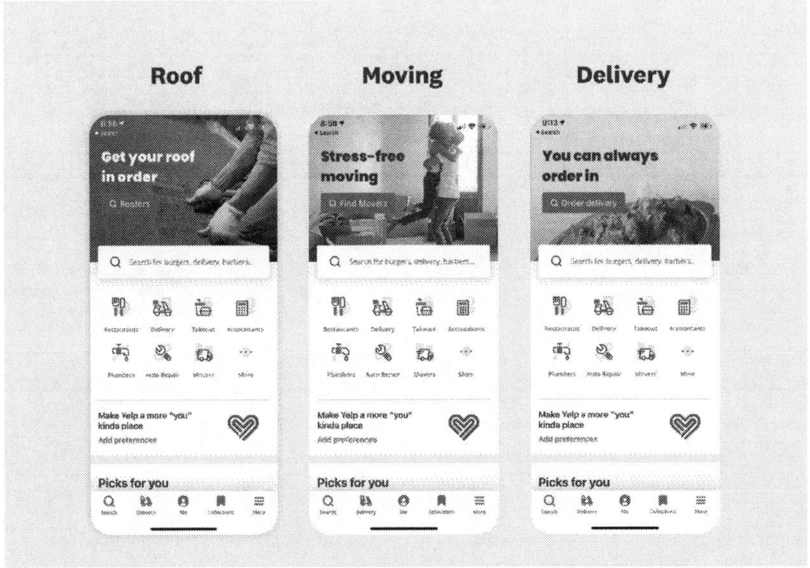

Judging by the different header styles, Yelp is trying to reinforce the image that it's more than just a food app. Having used Yelp in the past, I remember the header also used to change based on day of the week or even time in the day, like suggesting brunch options on Saturday morning. It's an interesting approach. Using context to predict what the user is trying to do removes friction and can get them to take action faster.

FIGURE: UNDERSTANDING HIERARCHY

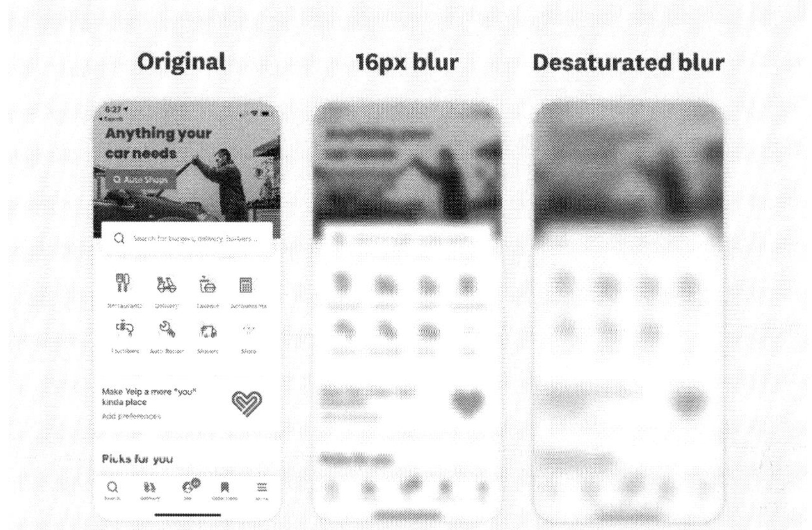

Visually, the header is positioned in a primary spot in the app real estate. Not only does it take up a significant portion of Home upon landing, but it also uses bold colors like red, blue, or white and an image to stand out from the rest of the page.

When assessing hierarchy, one trick you can use is to squint or look at the app from an arm's length. What do you see then? What shapes are prominent, and what jumps out to you the most? If you're practicing the app critique on your own, I recommend taking a screenshot, blurring, and desaturating an image as useful ways to assess hierarchy.

In our example, the header takes on a shape of its own, and the Auto Shops CTA does tend to blur in with the rest of the image. Next, although it's further down the page, the personalization heart stands out due to its shape, size, and the whitespace around it. Elements such as the navigation shortcuts, search, and the tab bar are lower in hierarchy.

18.2 *Navigating the App*

We took some time to familiarize ourselves with Yelp overall and got some interesting data points from the landing page. Now let's look around. What else can we do? Going through an app's navigation will help us get a better sense of the content and how it's structured.

FIGURE: DELIVERY, ME, NOTIFICATIONS

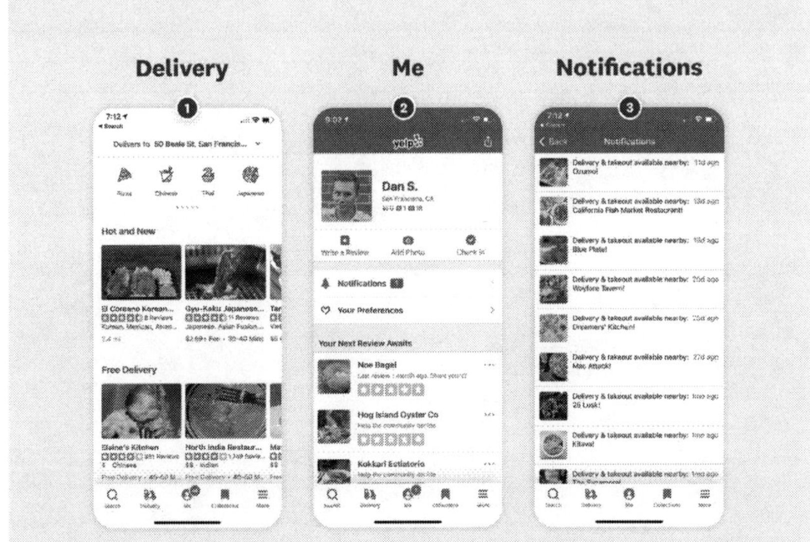

1. **Delivery.** Since most restaurants are either closed or operating at minimum capacity, it's no surprise that delivery is made prominent as an item in the Tab Bar. One interesting visual element you'll notice going through the app is that the icons here use a different style than Home and Search. I suspect these styles are probably an evolution of Yelp's visual language. The carousel on the top implies there are about 20 restaurant categories available, though arguably, it can be visually simplified by removing the carousel dots at the bottom.
2. **Me.** When I was going through the app the first time, I cleared my notifications, and this screenshot reflects that; however, after a few hours I'm getting new notifications.
3. **Notifications.** It's useful to see notifications all in one place. However, the usefulness of the content itself is debatable. Is the content relevant to me because I've visited these places in the past, or is it closer to an ad promoting a service? Looking at the notifications as a whole in this format makes them all look the same. Since they all blend in, it's hard to spot the difference or if there's something important I should pay attention to, thus reducing the efficacy of these. There's an opportunity here to further personalize notifications and lean in on the visual design to reinforce how much choice the user has when they're ordering takeout or delivery. Alternatively, some of these notifications could

also get cleared over time so as not to provoke user anxiety with the amount of things they need to clear out or check up on. Just like taking up room on Home to promote engagement, notifications too are a quick growth tactic to incentive use. However, there's a certain point where their efficacy plummets, as is seen here when there are way too many notifications to go through.

FIGURE: NAVIGATING YELP: COLLECTIONS, MORE

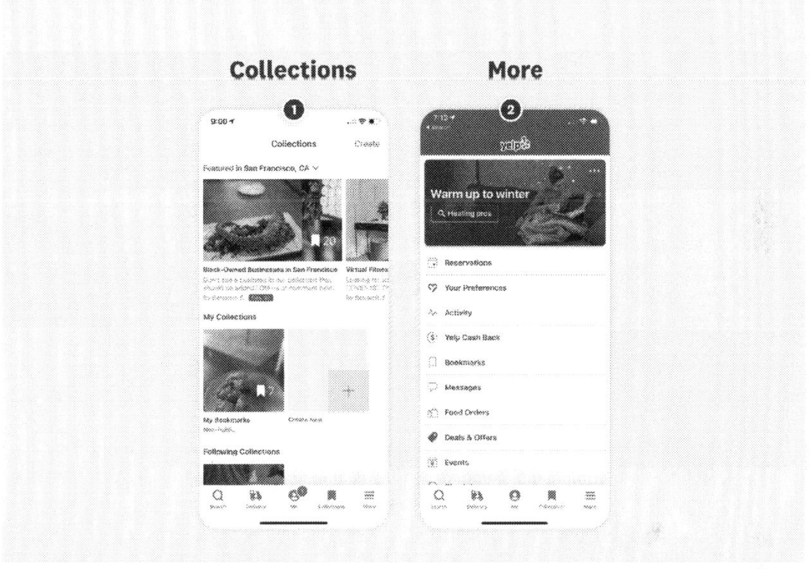

It looks like a collection is a method of organizing similar things, or at least similar to the person who's creating a collection and then either keeping it private (as My Bookmarks suggests with the "Non-Public" label) or making it public.

I typically liken the More page as a kitchen sink drawer for miscellaneous items. Yet it is a little strange to see a banner, "Warm up to winter." Most likely this is another growth tactic to promote other services. Visually, the row icons are inconsistent: some use hairlines, others have thicker borders, and some are filled.

18.3 *Exploring Personalization*

We've now done a surface dive on Yelp. Primarily focusing on Search, briefly popping to the App Store and then returning back and exploring the app via the tab bar navigation.

Next up, I'm curious about how Yelp is trying to improve its recommendations via personalization. As previously mentioned, getting personalization right can be useful for a business as relevant content leads to higher engagement and user retention. However it's how apps implement personalization that makes all the difference.

FIGURE: PERSONALIZATION ENTRY POINTS

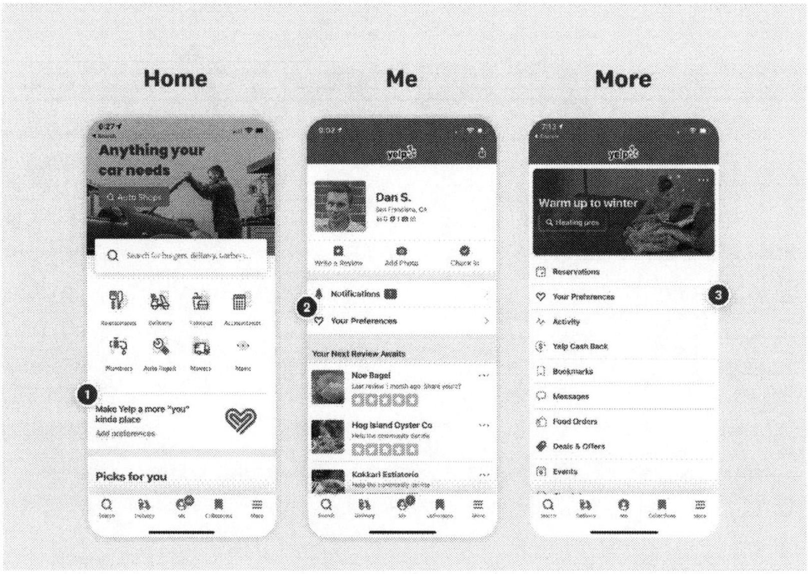

We briefly covered this in earlier critique but it bears repeating: there are multiple entry points into personalization on pages. In this case, we have Home, Me, and More.

Given the high prominence of the personalization banner on Home, it's likely this is a main entry point for the feature. I suspect Yelp is trying to temporarily promote the feature in order to drive engagement. Logically having preferences under a Me tab makes the most sense. I suspect "Your Preferences" is included in More in order to promote this feature.

FIGURE: BROWSING PERSONALIZATION PAGE

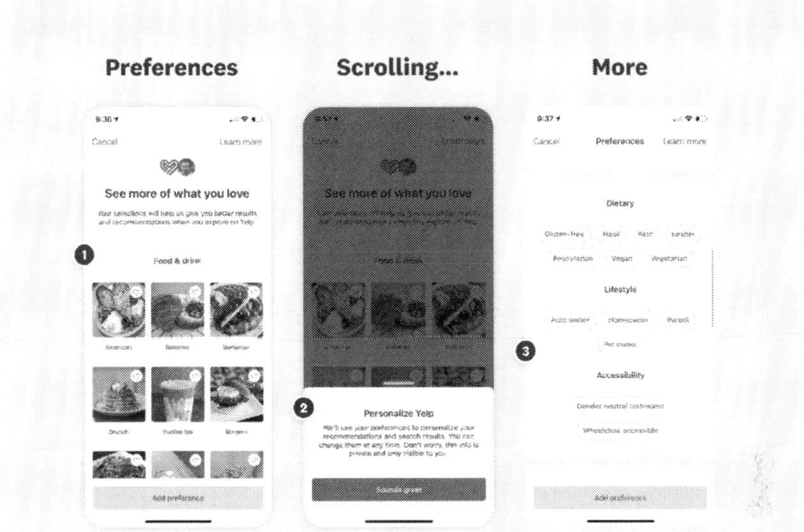

In this case, Yelp is essentially asking the user to complete a survey of what they prefer to do. Tapping "Learn more" gives us an explanation of the feature (2). This all makes sense if a user is choosing options in the "Food & drink" category (1). However things get less clear once we scroll down the page. Are dietary needs, lifestyle, and accessibility *preferences* (3)?

FIGURE: GETTING STRANGE RESULTS

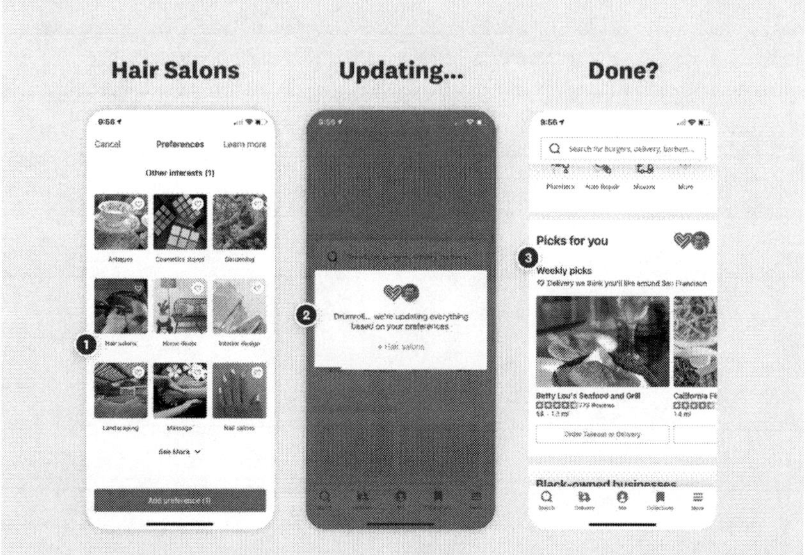

What about Hair Salons? My assumption is that if I pick hair salons as a "preference" (1), Yelp will be smart enough to point me to places that are open nearby. The tap interaction feels responsive as the heart on the top right turns red and pops in. I tap on Add preferences and get excited by the drumroll message (2).

Unfortunately it looks like something went wrong somewhere. Not only did I not get any hair salons, but somehow I got suggestions for food delivery (3). If I was a user, I'd lose trust in this feature fast. I suspect this is a bug. Maybe there were no salons available, and Yelp tried to pick the next best option—but it didn't take my input into consideration.

In general, Yelp does a good job of asking users to provide feedback in bite-sized portions. I wonder if a similar approach can be used here for personalization. It's useful to have this page as a way to confirm what things I've already shared with Yelp. However, filling it all out in one go feels cumbersome.

One way to simplify this interaction is to break up the questions into small chunks that can be sprinkled throughout the app. Alternatively, preferences can be assumed based on user interaction. For example, if I'm searching for restaurants and I have tapped on Indian the last five times I've used the app, it should know I prefer this type of cuisine, and show me relevant options.

18.4 *Ordering From a Restaurant*

Now, let's take a look at one of the Yelp app's core flows. Imagine I, the user, am looking for a takeout option in a new part of town.

FIGURE: GETTING TAKEOUT

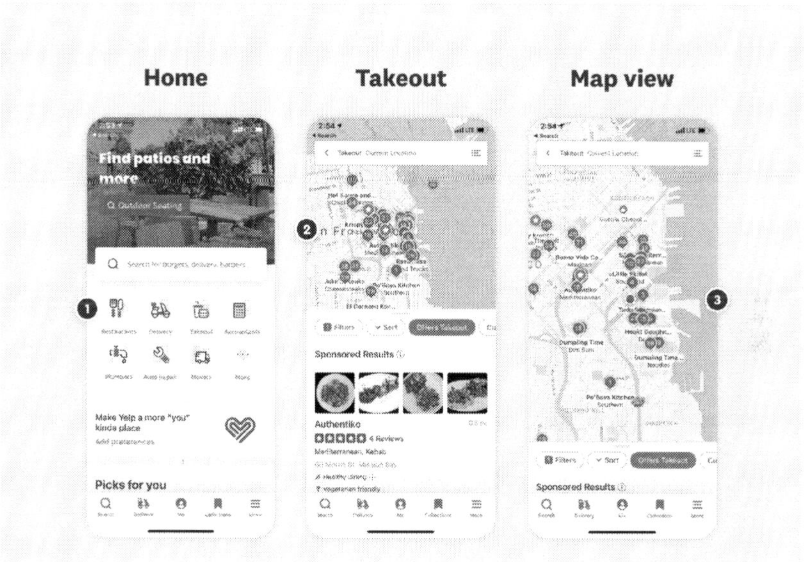

One way to quickly find a restaurant is to make sure I'm only looking at places that have a takeout option (1). Tapping on Takeout on the Home page brings up the split map/list view (2). This view gives me primarily two paths to take: the map or the list. I don't want to go far, so while the default radius of the map is useful to see all the options, I need something closer.

By tapping on the map, the sheet moves down and the map zooms in. This is a solid interaction as Yelp is trying to remove the extra friction from pinching and zooming. But I want something really close to where I am, so I pinch to zoom in even further.

FIGURE: DECIDING ON A PLACE

After zooming in, the pins update and I get a better sense of what's nearby. I zoom in again and entertain the idea of sushi, but after tapping on the restaurant and seeing only three stars, I have second thoughts. The map and the card view is a nice touch, as it allows users to navigate restaurants in different ways. However, it's not apparent why Death by Taco is number one and the nearby Nama Sushi SF is numbered 25.

The filtering mechanism on the bottom sheet (3) is also not very intuitive, because although Offers Takeout is on, tapping on the Filters pill shows that Offers Takeout is selected there as well. Duplicating the same content feels confusing.

After deciding on Death by Taco, I tap on Order Now (4) expecting to select a dish. The Order Now copy is clear, feels strong, and is a good way to guide the user towards the next step.

FIGURE: CHOOSING WHAT TO ORDER

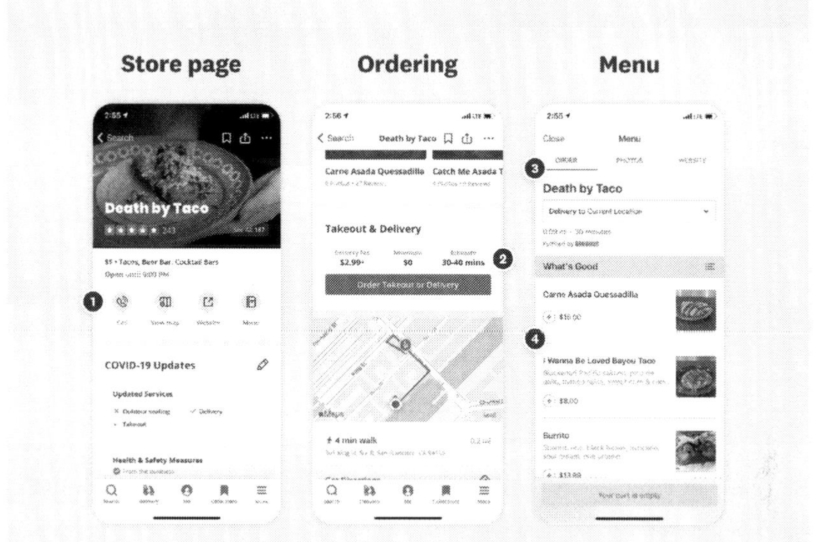

After tapping Order Now I land on the restaurant's page. There's a lack of clarity here as to what the next primary action should be (1)—didn't I just press order now?

Scrolling through the page we see that there is another button, Order Takeout or Delivery (2). Strange. Didn't I already have Takeout selected? Why do I need to select it again—and now there's an option for delivery too? Some of this friction could have been easily avoided by letting the user skip directly to the last screen (3) when pressing Order Now.

On the menu (4) I decide to add an item, but it looks like tapping on the + brings me to yet another view (as opposed to adding the item to my cart directly).

FIGURE: ADDING MY DISH AND CHECKING OUT

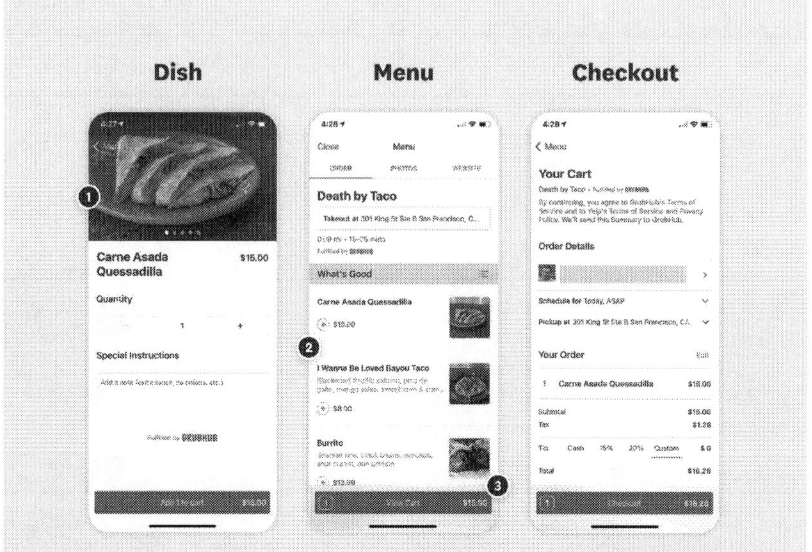

Inside the detailed view of the dish I wanted to add, it's nice to see photos (1), however the reviews are missing, and I'd have to go back to the Store view and then find the dish again if I want to read them. That's on top of the friction of having to order from the detail page, and not the menu page. After tapping "Add to cart," I'm landed back on the Menu.

Everything is good to go, however the quantity next to the Carne Asada Quesadilla (2) didn't update when I added it to my cart. Maybe it's only reflected in the cart? Tapping on View Cart (3) confirms that's the case. The Quesadilla is there, my details and payment method are up to date, and I'm ready for Checkout.

In this flow we took a quick pass at how someone may use the app to find takeout nearby. There are many ways of going about this use case and I would encourage you to explore additional scenarios here, such as considering dietary preferences or user mobility. Using Yelp in different geographies can be helpful in understanding usability in different kinds of places. So don't restrict yourself, and consider multiple core use cases and variations on these when you're practicing.

18.5 *Parting Words of Advice*

In this critique, we walked through a common framework to evaluate an application based on its visual design, interaction design, and product strategy. We also tangentially covered motion design and considered copy.

◇ IMPORTANT Remember, depending on the company and the role you're applying for, you may want to emphasize certain aspects of a critique over others.

This is just one way of running a crit. Based on how you approach this exercise, you may come up with an entirely different flow and evaluation. What's important is to have a rigorous framework in the first place to evaluate the app against.

19 Whiteboard Challenge

STORY

It's 1 p.m. I'm nervously standing by the whiteboard fidgeting with a marker. I'm only five minutes into the whiteboard interview but it feels like an hour has passed. What was the prompt again? I'm sweating. Is there air conditioning or do they blast heat on purpose? Anyway, I draw a persona and start making flows. Whoops, 40 minutes later I find out it's the wrong persona, wrong flow, and I'm a hot mess.

Since that one awkward time, I've done many whiteboard interviews and had the opportunity to interview new and seasoned designers using the whiteboard challenge. I've seen some common mistakes but also best practices emerge from those interviews. While this interview is different from your everyday whiteboard sketch, it doesn't have to be an enigma. Here's a systematic approach to take on the challenge, avoid common mistakes, and prepare effectively.

19.1 *Whiteboard Challenge Format and Criteria*

Whiteboard interviews typically range from 30 minutes to one hour. Usually you'll be interviewed by one or two designers. Similar to the take-home exercise,[§15] the whiteboard design challenge is meant to evaluate your skills in a short amount of time with a focus on interaction design and collaboration.

Your interviewers will assess you on:

- **Problem definition.** How well can you explore the problem space and identify big problems to go after?
- **Solution finding and idea generation.** How quickly can you explore multiple creative options without being married to any one idea and identify the best one to develop further?
- **Interaction design knowledge.** How well can you make trade-offs between platforms, or global and local interaction patterns? Is your story and interaction flow coherent?
- **Collaboration.** How well do you work with your interviewers by responding to their prompts and getting them interested in the approach that you're taking?
- You'll also need to be aware of your main constraint: **time**. Whiteboard interviews usually last almost an hour—but with initial setup and questions at the end, time will fly. You'll need to budget appropriately to show strong reasoning and meaningful concepts.

Just as with the app critique, how you come across, your level of self-awareness, matters. Usually you'll complete one whiteboard interview per company however at some places designers may have to complete two different whiteboard challenges. Typically the first challenge will assess your generative skills while the second interview will focus more on MVP scoping and/or getting the feature to the finish line with engineering.

19.2 *Going on the Journey Together*

Since whiteboards are an artificial challenge, it will be up to the interviewer to properly set you up. As the candidate, you'll be driving the interview. However, since prompts vary and companies have different expectations, clarify expectations with interviewers up-front:

- What outcomes do they expect to see?
- How do they want to be engaged?

- What role will they play in the process: are they designers, product managers, engineering peers, users of the product, stakeholders, researchers, or someone else?

Write down their response and what you won't cover so that objectives are visible and clear from the start. At its core, the whiteboard is a highly visible space to build shared understanding quickly. Use this to your advantage.

19.3 *Approaching the Challenge*

Once you have an understanding of the interaction model, the process itself can unfold as predictably as the traditional double diamond[125] design model that's so often taught in school. Since you'll be pressed for time, you'll need to make the call on what steps to accelerate, where to skip, and where to dive into the details.

125. https://uxdesign.cc/how-to-solve-problems-applying-a-uxdesign-designthinking-hcd-or-any-design-process-from-scratch-v2-aa16e2dd550b

FIGURE: THE DOUBLE DIAMOND DESIGN MODEL

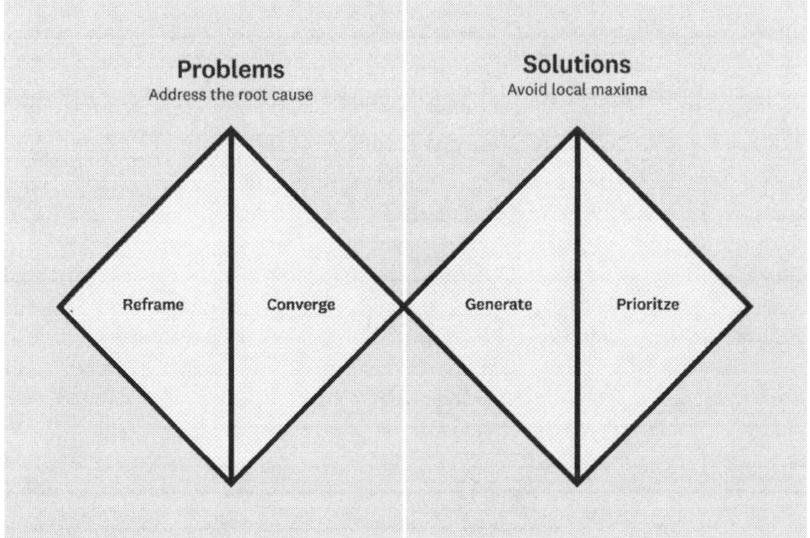

The double diamond design model. *Source: Dan Nessler*[126]

For those not familiar with the double diamond model, it's a simplified model of the design process that's essentially boiled down to four steps:

1. **Understanding the problem.** Challenging existing assumptions, asking questions, clarifying.
2. **Defining the problem.** Reframing the existing brief based on answers from the previous steps.
3. **Exploring solutions.** Brainstorming multiple divergent solutions to avoid local maximum, not judging ideas, and keeping things as open as possible.
4. **Converging on a solution.** Picking a particular solution to go after and spending time fleshing it out.

Like all models, it's not perfect. It doesn't account for all the nuances of the design process, but that's OK because the whiteboard interview isn't about going through nuanced details like visual design and such. Instead, this exercise is more about getting a glimpse into your design approach, specifically how you think through complex interaction design[§3.4] challenges.

126. https://medium.com/u/409333d18adc

During one of my interviews, the candidate kept drawing and redrawing a border of a window, emphasizing that they're particular about how things look, thinking about 1px borders and shadows. While detail is important to design, the reality is that there's no way to adequately convey this detail, nor is it required for a whiteboard challenge. Show your visual skills in your portfolio or in the design exercise.

19.4 *Managing the Whiteboard Space*

Just like when you're presenting your portfolio, you also want to position yourself in a good spot for a whiteboard. This means having enough space for you to write while having your interviewers clearly see what you're doing. You should also keep track of time, ideally with a timer on your watch.

The surface area of your whiteboard should be proportional to the amount of time you'll spend on it.

FIGURE: MANAGING SPACE AND TIME

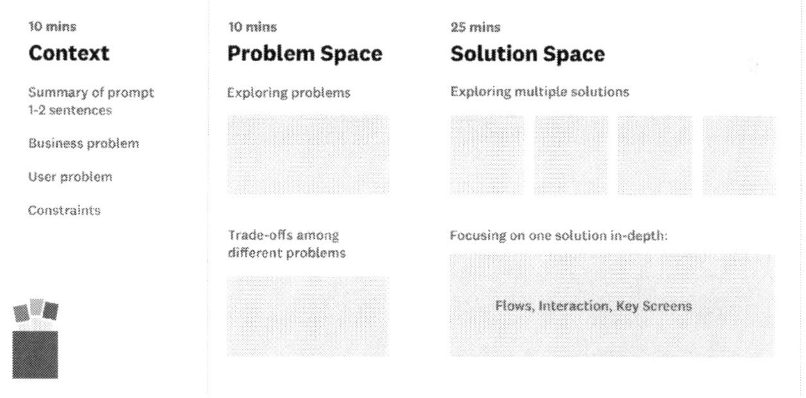

The surface area of your whiteboard should be proportional to the amount of time you'll spend on it.

SETTING THE CONTEXT

The first step to any design solution is to understand the problem. Just like in your portfolio project summary slide, you want to summarize the context:

- What is the prompt? What are you trying to solve for?
- What are the business objectives?
- What are the user objectives?
- What are the constraints?
- How do we measure success?

At this stage, you may treat your interviews as stakeholders. They can be your business or research counterparts. Ask questions to understand the problem fully from multiple perspectives and document this on the whiteboard.

When you wrap up: summarize key context points, tell your interviewers what you're going to do next, and ask if there's anything unaddressed that they'd like to see. This ensures everyone is in sync and no lingering questions (which can derail you later) remain.

NARROWING PROBLEM SCOPE

At this point you might have more problems than you have time to solve for. That's a good sign. Usually, in defining the context you'll discover many opportunities to go after.

This step is an opportunity (no pun intended) to demonstrate your **product thinking** by narrowing options to the critical few leading to outsize impact. Show how you think about impact and the criteria you use to evaluate a problem space.

Here are some basic frameworks:

- **Impact versus cost.** The impact to the business and the user will be high, while the time spent developing this feature will be low.
- **Forward momentum.** Building this feature will pay down tech debt and position the team to learn and iterate faster.
- **Ideal experience.** If there are no explicit constraints, what would the ideal solution look like?

Alternatively, you might also be asked to not think about constraints at all (for example, unlimited engineering resources) and to create the best solution. In that case your constraints are driven by user needs, which you want to note down.

IMPORTANT Finally, beware of the **curse of knowledge**. Take the time to remind yourself of the main goal and pick one big problem that you can solve well in the allotted time. It's tempting to fight on multiple fronts, but you won't have the time for that here. Choose meaningful focus over diffused diligence.

GENERATING IDEAS

Now for the fun part—exploring many varying solutions by lifting constraints. Suspend disbelief and generate lots of solutions. The beauty of whiteboards is that you can draw lots of ideas and then either erase or narrow down the list to a promising few. If you get stumped, don't be afraid to start sketching. The very act of sketching on the whiteboard and describing as you're drawing can yield additional ideas. Go for quantity over quality at this phase.

CONVERGING ON A SOLUTION

Once you've considered the world of possible solutions, you can start narrowing your scope down to a few promising options. Now's the time to go deep. Again, it's important to refer back to your original objectives. Did you miss anything? Look back to ensure the solution you're about to expand on hits on the key pain points you've learned during the problem phase.

As you're sketching out your solution, think in journeys and flows. How would someone interact with the service or the product? How would the interaction flow from one screen to the next? At this point you're usually not expected to think through the edge cases as you're sketching out a happy path.

19.5 *Finishing on a High Note*

Even with great time management, there are usually more problems and more solutions to explore, so it's very likely that you'll run out of time. If you've been tracking time yourself, pause ten minutes before the end of the interview to take a pulse check—what do the interviewers want to see next? Do they want you to proceed further, or is this a good place to stop?

If you are at a stopping point or if you've actually "completed" the whiteboard challenge with time to spare (congrats, a rare feat!) take a moment to summarize and mention how you might have approached the process differently. Balance this self-reflection with time for additional questions that you might want to ask your interviewers.

As an interviewer, I'm also reflecting on our time. Could we work well together? How well did you respond to my feedback? Was your approach different from mine? Can you help me overcome my gaps? Have I learned something new here?

19.6 *Common Whiteboard Mistakes to Avoid*

When interviewing designers, I see many common mistakes made repeatedly. It doesn't matter if the designer is fresh out of school, mid-level, or senior. Here are a couple of issues that stand out and can be easily fixed.

OVERKILLING IT WITH CONTEXT

As part of the product design interview, it is important that you establish a strong foundation that's predicated on context and the problem. But you can also go overboard with this and run out of time, so you don't get to any solutions or you take a very superficial pass at the solution phase.

This is a problem of time management. Context setting and problem definition should take less than half of the interview time. For example, in a one-hour session with 15 minutes for questions, roughly 10 minutes should be used for understanding context, about 10 minutes for problem exploration and definition, and most of your time (about 25+ minutes) on sketching and iterating through solutions.

JUMPING INTO SOLUTIONS TOO SOON

The flip side of too much context is doing too little. Jumping into solutions without considering the broader context leads you to dance between possible solutions and possible problems. It leads to a dangerous path where you spend a lot of time on a solution and invent the problem for it. Make sure your foundation (context, problem) is solid first.

OVERFITTING AN EXISTING PATTERN

Some designers have tried to use patterns from one app (for example, Facebook) as an answer to the whiteboard prompt. While this approach is generally sound and you will use analogous apps for inspiration, beware of trying to fit a pattern that doesn't make sense in the context you're solving for. Think through the problem from first principles—what must hold true for this pattern to work? If the context isn't right, consider a different pattern.

THINKING COMPONENTS, NOT JOURNEYS

Instead of thinking about the experience as it's presented to users, some designers think about components and patterns instead of journeys. While thinking about hand-off is important, if you don't have the overall journey right, it doesn't matter if your UI can be componentized, as you'll still be solving the wrong problem. Get the journey right first.

NOT VOCALIZING YOUR THOUGHTS

The more clearly you can verbally communicate what you're doing, the easier it is for the interviewer to understand your process and provide feedback.

◇ IMPORTANT Strike the optimal balance of talking, sketching, and facilitation. This can be hard to do at first, which is why I recommend practicing (more on that follows).

NOT TAKING ADVANTAGE OF INTERVIEWER FEEDBACK

On the flip side, you don't want to speak so much that it leaves little breathing room for your interviewers, with no opportunity for them to interject. Interviewers are your best source for answers, and they're right there! Don't miss out. Lead them through your process, but also be sure to pause, clarify, and engage them with questions. Your job is to strike the optimal balance of talking, sketching, and facilitation.

NOT ADDRESSING INTERVIEWER FEEDBACK

Generally, whiteboard prompts start open-ended with a wide field of opportunities. As you work through the prompt, I'd like to see how you react to my feedback. Are you receptive? Do you "yes, and" or do you try to brush it off or, worse, skip it? Responding to feedback effectively is just as crucial as having a solid process with good solutions.

BLAMING THE WHITEBOARD INTERVIEW

No interview is a perfect assessment of your skills. As interviewers, we know this and take it into account by assessing candidates holistically across multiple interview types. However, getting defensive and blaming the whiteboard challenge when you're still interviewing isn't an effective use of your time. Ask questions and build rapport instead.

> After a decent whiteboard interview, I left ten minutes at the end for the candidate to ask me questions. Instead of asking questions or talking about how he might have done it differently, he proceeded to bad-mouth the interview and blame the whiteboard for his poor performance.

19.7 *Solid versus Amazing Whiteboard Execution*

Once you've mastered the basics, it's time to think about what can take your whiteboard execution from good to great.

SOLID EXECUTION

A good whiteboard execution hits on many of the things we have already talked about—proper framing, generating solutions, and collaboration.

You've taken the time to understand the problem by looking at it through multiple lenses from the business, user, and engineering side. You've defined a specific audience or persona to design this solution for. You've pushed back on the initial statement by reframing it, perhaps making it broader or more specific or by discovering a new problem altogether. The interviewers agreed this was the way to go.

Based on your problem you've generated many different high-quality ideas quickly. You didn't dodge any questions—you answered all of them and clarified with the interviewers to make sure their questions were addressed. In the end you made good on time, enough to give you a moment to step back and reflect on what you could have done better.

AMAZING EXECUTION

Amazing execution builds on top of solid execution. Usually, I've seen this come from design leads who have a rich interaction design vocabulary developed over years of solving complex design problems in different industries.

In this case, you not only solved the initial problem quickly but you also exhausted your interviewer prompts, leaving them with nearly no questions. You've impressed them with your level of thinking and creativity by coming up with unconventional solutions that not only solved the problem but also anticipated other issues that you've mitigated for.

Although you stated the approach that you would follow to your interviewers up-front, you weren't rigid. You struck the right balance of moving faster through certain sections, skipping some, but also deliberately taking longer in other parts to make sure no one got lost. In the end, you finished the whiteboard exercise with plenty of time to spare for questions, leaving your interviewers impressed by your execution.

19.8 *Practicing Better with Whiteboard Prompts*

The best way to get better at whiteboards is through practice. Baseline yourself initially to gauge your progress. If you haven't done any whiteboarding, grab a marker and start sketching. Don't worry about perfection, just get familiar initially.

The prompts vary depending on the company and the space they're in. Some exercises range from pragmatic to design fiction. Interviewer guides usually include the prompt, variations, and questions interviewers might ask, plus grading criteria. As an interviewee, you'll be presented with the prompt up-front and then be asked to walk the interviewer through the process. Here are a couple of starter prompts to experiment with:

GROWING GARDENS, GROWING BUSINESS

- **Prompt.** Growing Gardens targets suburban families who are interested in gardening but have little to no formal knowledge. The business primarily sells plants but is also extending into additional products (pots, fertilizer) and services (landscaping). Create an application to help people learn more about gardening and getting them to to begin to garden.
- **Assessment.** As an interviewer I'd like to see how you think about the opportunity space, which platform you decide to use for this prompt, and how you balance user and business needs.

DESIGNING AN INTERIOR FOR AN AUTONOMOUS VEHICLE

- **Prompt.** An automaker, Edison, has been experimenting with a completely new car design for their model Z vehicle. This car is fully autonomous, so doesn't require any human interaction. As a designer, you've been asked to reimagine the car interior. What should the interior look like?
- **Assessment.** I'd like to see how you think about blue-sky projects, and how you define a problem space and generate novel ideas accordingly.

TIME-TRAVELING TOURISM

- **Prompt.** Scientists recently discovered a way to time travel. People can now go back and forward in time without any consequence to the timelines—no need to worry about the butterfly effect. As one of the first designers of the time machine, you've been tasked with creating an experience for time-traveling tourists. What experience would you create?
- **Assessment.** The open nature of this prompt gives you many possibilities to go after. You'll need to think through constraints, analogous experiences, and how to scope the problem meaningfully.

19.9 *Baselining Your Whiteboarding Skills*

Now that you have some prompts and core criteria, you can start practicing by yourself. Imagine you're running a think-aloud usability study, but instead of moderating, the participant is you. Record your first-time through and be sure to time yourself. Play back the recording and look for patterns where you pause, don't speak, or speak too much.

Take a photo of the whiteboard and do a self-evaluation based on the criteria we mentioned in the beginning:

- What did you wish you could spend more time on?
- What did you miss?
- What's not clear?
- Did you go over or under your time limit?

Use the combination of your recording (audio and video) and the photo of the whiteboard to grade yourself. Note areas of strength and opportunities for improvement. It's important to isolate areas of weakness and focus on closing those gaps. That said, don't forget to highlight your strengths during the actual whiteboard interview.

After your baseline, and a few more practice runs (which you can easily do in a week), it's time to practice with a fellow design friend (or two). Take turns, let them be your interviewer and have them probe you on the design details. Then evaluate them. The nature of switching roles will help you see the problem from a different perspective.

20 Whiteboarding Remotely

If you've been asked to do a whiteboard challenge in 2020 or 2021—and perhaps even beyond—chances are it's taking place remotely. Like the on-site version of this challenge, typically you'll have about 30 minutes to an hour to complete this interview. Instead of a traditional whiteboard in a conference room you'll be given a few options as to which tool you want to use.

In general, these options fall into two categories—analog or digital. Analog tools such as a notepad or an actual whiteboard may feel familiar and fast. Digital tools that allow you to share the document live in the cloud may make it easier to collaborate.

TABLE: WHITEBOARDING OPTIONS

TOOL	PROS	CONS
Whiteboard	Just like the real thing at a regular interview setting.	If you don't have one already, buying a large whiteboard can get pricey. May not be readable through a laptop camera.
Paper notepad	Can be a great way to sketch out ideas, cheaper than buying your own whiteboard.	As with the whiteboard, camera quality will play a role in how your sketch looks.
Tablet (e.g. iPad)	Using a tool such as Procreate allows you to quickly sketch ideas.	Requires you to maneuver the device so that it's visible to the interviewer.Taking notes may take longer compared to sketching.
Design tool (e.g. Figma or Sketch)	No new tools to learn, easy to move around, sharing the file on the cloud makes it easier to collaborate.	Be careful not to waste time polishing pixels.

TOOL	PROS	CONS
Whiteboarding tool (e.g. Miro, Mural)	Easy to get started with sketches quickly, and cloud share aids collaboration.	Getting things precisely mocked up may take a long time and may not feel as fluid as a dedicated design tool.

If you're not sure which tool is best, pick the one you're most comfortable with. Interviews can be stressful enough and you won't be doing yourself any favors if you try to learn a new tool at the last minute.

20.1 *Set Your Environment up for Success*

If you're choosing to go the analog route, be sure to test your camera set-up and quality ahead of time. It may be worth it to invest in a standalone camera, as opposed to the one that comes with your laptop, because you can easily reposition the camera to point to your notepad or whiteboard while still seeing the interviewer on the screen. Alternatively, you can dial into the meeting with your computer and your phone—using your phone as a standalone camera to point to the sketch.

Modern design tools allow you to share your file on the cloud, which may make collaboration easier while conserving video bandwidth. As an example, if you're whiteboarding on Figma, you don't have to share your screen, thus conserving bandwidth. If connectivity becomes an issue you can turn video off and go with audio only.

Regardless of which tool you pick, you may still run into interruptions or connectivity issues. Make sure you account for those and think how you'll respond when they happen. Having a plan for these now will make it easier for you to navigate these speed bumps as they occur.

FIGURE: MANAGING A REMOTE WHITEBOARD

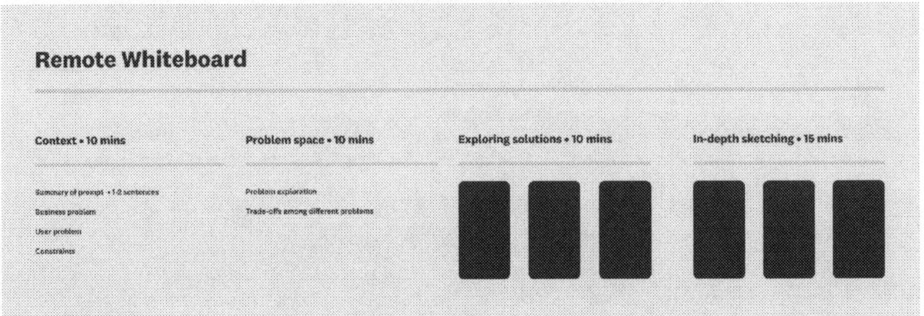

If you're using a design or whiteboard tool, you don't have to worry about managing space, but you should keep in mind how much time you spend on each section. Just as with the physical whiteboard, you don't want to spend so much time on context and problem framing that you run out of time to come up with solutions.

Although the double diamond model gives an illusion of a deliberate, contained design process, we know that this is rarely true in actual design practice. The whiteboard challenge is a miniature version of reality. You may have to sometimes briefly revisit a problem or clarify context. Be sure to push on your explorations and definitely make time to get into the details. The further you get, the more productive a conversation you'll have with your interviewer, who will be asking you increasingly harder questions to challenge your thinking. Take this challenge as an opportunity to show how you think and be sure to demonstrate those ideas in your sketches.

20.2 *Keep Collaboration in Mind*

One of the challenges of the whiteboard is that you may not be able to see the interviewer's body language. This becomes especially challenging if you're sharing your screen and the interviewer becomes a small rectangle off to the side. In these cases, it helps to pause and check in with your interviewer from time to time. Since you'll be primarily driving the interview, you can stop periodically to ask, "Are you with me?" or "Do you have any questions so far?"

◇ IMPORTANT As you know, the key criteria for a whiteboard challenge is collaboration. The remote flavor of this challenge offers a glimpse into how you may work with this designer in the future. Are they collaborative and encouraging? Make sure you write down your thoughts after the exercise.

20.3 *Practicing Remotely*

When you're solving design problems, one easy way to get a hang of things is to start with the simplest method possible. This could just be a notepad where you could sketch and document your ideas and process. As you get further along in your practice, I recommend switching to the final tool of your choice. This could still be a notepad, or if you do want to go the digital route (which I highly recommend), practice whiteboarding there. Consider your practice complete when the tools have become second nature, you've developed a robust system for solving design challenges, and can quickly frame up the problem and the solution.

PART V: AFTER THE INTERVIEWS

Interviewing is a process of continuous learning and self-reflection. Sometimes we find ourselves in the middle of an interview with one company just after having recently wrapped up a final interview with another company. Periodically stepping back and noting down your performance will help you continue to improve your interview skills and thus increase your chances of getting that dream role.

When you're interviewing, inevitably your application will get rejected. Rejection[§22] stings, but by conducting your own retrospective and by asking for feedback, you can use it to your advantage. Instead of repeating the same mistake again, you'll know what not to do next time. Don't skip the step of asking for feedback—it may make a difference between getting a job or not in your next interview.

Once you do get the role, don't stop. Accepting an offer too quickly can be a risk if the company has certain red flags (for example, poor culture or lack of runway). Be sure to schedule interviews of your own and do the due diligence[§23] to make a more informed decision while negotiating the offer.

21 Post-Interview Retro

You've wrapped up your final design interview! At this stage, you might have an interview lined up right after or you may be early in the interview process with other places. Regardless, it helps to step back and reflect on the day. Also, don't forget to close strong by thanking your interviewers for their time. Some say that thank-yous are passé. I disagree. Sending a specific and thoughtful email is an extra touch that reinforces your interest in the role.

21.1 *Figure: Post-Interview Retro*

5 mins **Celebrate**	5 mins **Improve**	5 mins **Learn**
What went particularly well in the interview? List highlights	What could be better? List lowlights	What did you find out? Are you still excited about the role?

To begin, grab a piece of paper and fold it twice to make three columns: celebrate, improve, learn.

21.2 *Celebrate: What Went Well?*

When we're in the middle of interviews, things happen fast. Sometimes there's little room for thinking, and if you're an introvert you may feel overwhelmed by the constant barrage of questions. So it helps to step back after the interview and celebrate the things that went particularly well:

- How did I set myself up for success during the interview?
- What question(s) did I pass with flying colors? What made it good?
- How did I closely connect with one of the interviewers?

> **STORY**
> During one exhausting day of interviews, I bonded with the founder over our mutual love of cooking, enough to exchange tips and recipes (and perhaps also to show that I was serious about it). In the spirit of bringing your whole self to work, it was a small thing that helped us connect.

For interviews that went poorly, look for highlights in specific moments. Capitalizing on things that you already do well helps build confidence in a process that sometimes feels opaque.

21.3 *Improve: What Could Be Better?*

As you step back, try to view through the eyes of an outside observer, as if you're watching yourself and the interviewer from the sidelines.

- How did you come across?
- What did you miss?
- What could you have done better?

How you frame your response matters. For example, if you're talking about conflict—make sure you communicate that you've learned from it and not blame the other party (even if they were to blame, it doesn't matter in an interview setting).

Other times, an opportunity for improvement isn't necessarily a mistake but a missed opportunity to put yourself in the best light possible. Perhaps there was a particularly thorny problem that you were able to solve because you made a connection that others didn't see, based on your previous experience or learning outside of work.

The point of this prompt isn't to beat yourself up over small mistakes. Instead, it's a chance to think about areas of opportunity and what's in your control. Prioritize and work on those first—your future interviewing self will thank you.

21.4 *Learn: What Did You Find Out?*

> *"I've learned that people will forget what you said, people will forget what you did, but people will never forget how you made them feel."*
>
> — Maya Angelou

Another thing to note is **what you learned** and how you **felt** during the interview.

STORY

"What's your favorite brand?" asked the hiring manager during an on-site interview. I paused to think, as brand wasn't my forte, but gave an explanation for why I thought Airbnb was doing meaningful work in experiences. "I hate Airbnb. What's your next one?" she shot back. Later she proceeded to tear apart my portfolio. This

> interview was enough for me to learn everything I needed to learn about this company's culture.

The interview is a two-way street. You and the interviewer get to know each other and build a shared understanding.

What looks good on paper may not be the reality. Alternatively, a seemingly subpar job description can be amazing because of the team. One of my colleagues shared a lesson in how her friends, a husband and wife, optimized their job search. The husband sought out new industries and companies that are on the cusp of making it big. The wife paid more attention to the immediate team members. Both ended up successful, but the wife was happier.

At the end of the day, it's about the people you work with, so it's important to ask yourself if after the interview you still want to work there:

- Does this culture resonate with my values?
- Can I be successful here?
- Does the environment set me up for success?
- Were there any red flags?

Look back on your original job criteria. Now that you've applied to jobs and interviewed at companies, was there anything new that you learned about your dream job or yourself?

22 Learning From Rejection

You've wrapped up your product design interviews and are now waiting to hear back. But a few days later you get that dreaded reply thanking you for your application, but it's "not a good fit at this time." What happened?

FIGURE: A GENERIC, CRYPTIC EMAIL

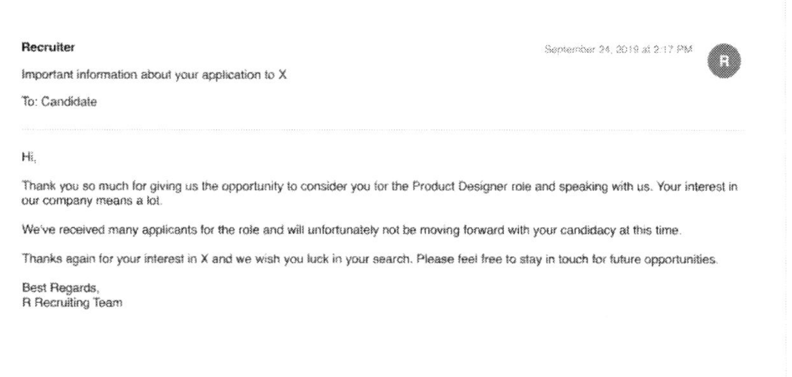
Recruiter
September 24, 2019 at 2:17 PM
Important information about your application to X
To: Candidate

Hi,

Thank you so much for giving us the opportunity to consider you for the Product Designer role and speaking with us. Your interest in our company means a lot.

We've received many applicants for the role and will unfortunately not be moving forward with your candidacy at this time.

Thanks again for your interest in X and we wish you luck in your search. Please feel free to stay in touch for future opportunities.

Best Regards,
R Recruiting Team

You might get this generic, cryptic email. 😨

It's easy to blame yourself and feel terrible as your thoughts race to think of what you did wrong. Before you get caught up, I would encourage you to take a deep breath and step back.

◇ IMPORTANT You can choose your reaction. If your friend went through a similar situation, how would you talk to them about it? Approach yourself the same way—self-compassion helps you take the learning in and bounce back stronger.

In this section I'll cover why candidates get rejected. Think of failure as a stepping stone—use it to improve your chances of success next time.

◇ IMPORTANT Rejection along your interviewing journey is inevitable. It means you're pushing yourself and not settling. How you handle it determines where you ultimately end up.

22.1 *First Step—Ask for Feedback*

So let's say you got an email similar to the one above. Now's a good time to follow up with the hiring manager or recruiter or both and ask for feedback (thus demonstrating self-awareness and a growth mindset in the process).

Here's a general template to follow:

1. Thank them for giving their time.

2. Mention how you're interested in the role and would like to be kept on the radar even if now's not the right time.
3. Ask for feedback. You'd like to improve and it would be helpful to know about your growth areas so that you can be an even stronger candidate the next time around.
4. Close by thanking them again for the opportunity.

Companies are hesitant to share feedback. In short, it might expose them to litigation if the candidate feels they've been rejected unjustly due to discrimination. Unfortunately this incentivizes most companies to avoid feedback altogether.

Most of the time, you might get a carefully worded response mentioning an area of concern in no specific terms. You'll need to read between the lines here. For example, if the recruiter said your soft skills need work—think of how you presented yourself or how you came across. It may be beneficial to cross-reference this feedback by asking a current or former colleague for their (radically honest) assessment.

The granularity of feedback will vary from nonexistent to vague, but even then I would still encourage you to ask for it as it may uncover your blind spots—mistakes that you're completely unaware of.

22.2 *Framework for Working Through Feedback*

Over time you'll accumulate different and potentially conflicting feedback. This is why it always helps to have a career roadmap for your next step in the journey. Some feedback will be relevant—some won't be. A roadmap helps you prioritize.

Figure: Breaking Feedback Down

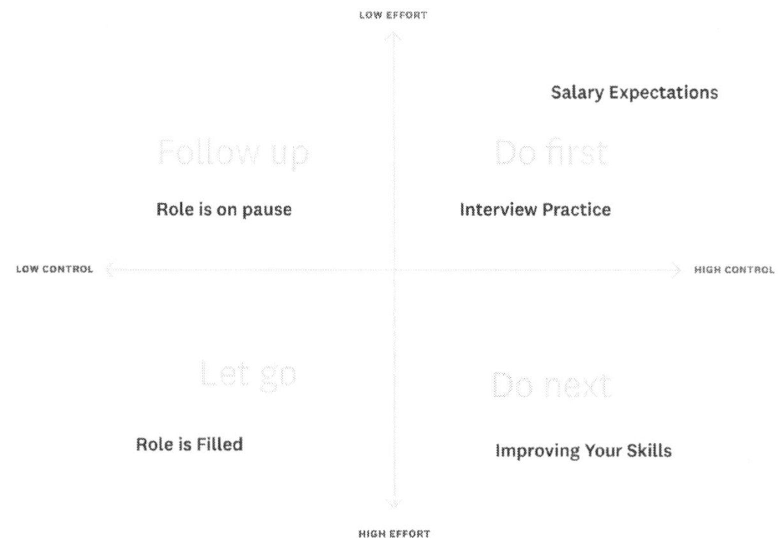

Break the feedback down into quadrants.

Another way to prioritize is looking at feedback through a dual lens of effort and control. Obviously, high-leverage actions need to be done first, but on the flip side, let go of things that you can't control—no need to stress out about things that can't be changed.

22.3 *Reasons for Rejection*

Although a company really wants to fill that vacant design role, the cost of a bad hire is high. Companies hire **conservatively**. So even though they need help (and they stretch existing employees to fill the gap), many choose to wait longer to **find a perfect match**. That's why it's important to leave a strong impression and convince your interviewers that you're the right designer for the job.

To be clear, "a perfect match" doesn't actually exist. Don't eliminate yourself by not applying to roles where you meet 70% of the requirements. If you have the skills, you can pick up the other 30%. What's important is to communicate to your interviewers that in addition to your know-how, you have the ability to adapt and learn fast.

You can ensure you and your interviewers are on the same page by asking them point blank:

> *"Is there anything that I said or didn't say that would make me not an ideal fit for this role?"*

This question usually breaks the wall and allows the interviewer to communicate what they've seen so far. Then you act on this feedback immediately and set the right impression.

Let's look at a couple more factors that are in your control that you can use to your advantage.

INTERVIEW PERFORMANCE

Even after having prepared and practiced ahead of time, you will still make some mistakes during interviews. That's OK. Things don't always go according to plan, so it's important to take the new learning in. If you haven't already done the post-interview retro,[§21] I recommend you start there.

You might discover areas that you want to practice or improve upon, such as the whiteboard exercise[§19] or the app critique.[§17]

While this book gives you a structure that you can take and adapt, I also recommend practicing with a design friend. This will help you see past your own blind spots and open up new perspectives.

> *"You find and win a great job against a pool of very competitive candidates who may want that job as much, if not more, than you do."*
>
> — Debbie Millman

Interviewing can feel like hard, thankless work. If you're good at your work, shouldn't they just hire you already? The truth is, even in our current age of design abundance, competition is high. So don't forget to practice and put your best self[§14] forward.

FEW "REAL-WORLD" PROJECTS

Design is a hands-on discipline—the closer you can get to tangible results in practice, the more convincing your argument to employers that you can do the work. In other words, the more "real" your work is (getting a product fully built, shipped, iterated upon), the more prepared you'll be, compared to "simulated" work environments (for example, only working with other designers on static mocks).

FIGURE: SPECTRUM OF DESIGN PROJECT TYPES

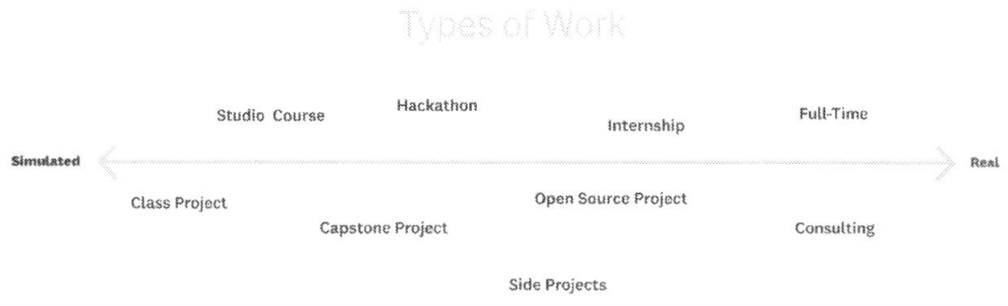

Based on your current experience, where in this spectrum do your projects fall?

If you're new to the field, getting the first job will be hard, as employers might feel like they're taking a bet on you. But you can alleviate their worries by showing proof that you've done this work before. My recommendation is to look at internships, side projects, open source projects, or hackathons—to name a few. If real-world experience is a barrier, continue filling your portfolio, showing that you're serious about your craft.

YEARS OF DESIGN EXPERIENCE

Even if you have the "real world" experience... you might not have enough. Everyone wants a senior designer with at least three-plus years of experience. But how do you get experience without experience? The reality is that most design jobs don't need a senior designer—mid-level or even entry-level designers can hit the ground running and deliver impact.

FIGURE: UNREALISTIC DESIGN JOB REQUIREMENTS

Product Designer

Requirements

Strong UX/UI skills

Experience with front-end development, including HTML, CSS and Javascript is a plus.

Proficient in Sketch, Photoshop, Illustrator, and MS Paint (required), or other design tools.

20 years of mobile experience ideally

These design requirements are getting out of control…

Dig deeper behind the title. What are the responsibilities, what kind of experience are they looking for? Can you deliver on these expectations or rise to the occasion? You can address the experience gap with examples that show how you were able to transfer your skills to solve increasingly complex challenges.

Companies aren't looking for someone with five-plus years of experience anyway. "X number of years" is shorthand for someone who's done the work, has experienced different environments, and is able to do the work without supervision. You can get that experience in two years, depending on where you work. Or you might stagnate and not reach a level of proficiency even in ten years—be careful where you work and which environment you choose.[§4.1]

LACK OF A SPECIFIC SKILL

Sometimes you might get rejected due to a lack of a certain skill or the company's need at this time; for example, they're strong in UX but need more visual designers. If so, this is an opportunity to get better at a specific aspect of your craft. However, maybe you also don't care about this skill (visual design, for instance), and if that's the case, you might look at opportunities where you can play more to your strengths while finding resources to help you level up your growth areas.

DOMAIN EXPERIENCE

Sometimes companies may hesitate to bring on designers who don't have deep domain expertise. For instance, your experience is in enterprise design, but they want consumer designers. Or a company may want someone with an intimate knowledge of the entertainment space, but you don't have that experience. As a result, these companies may discount your non-domain experience heavily.

The thinking goes, if this designer hasn't done the same thing elsewhere, they won't be a good fit here. **Nothing could be further from the truth**. Design is a fluid discipline. Some designers prefer to specialize in one domain, but many also expand and grow their skills in different industries.

> **STORY**
>
> During one interview, I was preparing for my next stage, when I got a call a day before saying it would be a waste of time for both parties if I showed up because they didn't think I had the skills necessary. The reason? They wanted designers with more consumer experience. This didn't stop me from getting consumer design offers elsewhere. So don't let one rejection deter you from applying to roles that may seem like a stretch.

So what does this mean for you? Have the conversation with your interviewers, show examples of where you transferred your learning successfully. These could be different domains (for example, consumer to enterprise), different platforms (web to mobile), or even different design disciplines (from graphic to service design).

SALARY

Occasionally you might price yourself out of the market. When it comes to salary, recruiters ask about this question up-front, usually during the phone screen.

There are a few ways you can answer this, but it helps to do your research up-front from multiple sources, such as LinkedIn, Hired, or AngelList, to get a realistic estimate of what you're worth and how much you should be thinking about as far as base compensation is concerned (especially when you're applying to startups who compensate heavily with equity).

Ultimately, it's a personal question. Sometimes it's worth it to sacrifice higher pay for learning. Ideally you can be in a role that gives you maximum learning and compensation, but that's not always possible.

FACTORS OUTSIDE OF YOUR CONTROL

Not everything is under our control. Sometimes the role might get closed due to budgets or other issues.

> STORY
>
> In one of my roles, after I gave a two-month notice, I started looking for a replacement by posting on job boards and going to design events. I found someone who not only had more experience but also had deep domain expertise. She interviewed for the job and things went well. Unfortunately, the role was later cut. It happens. You may be the ideal candidate the company isn't ready for.

Alternatively, a company might be in a low design maturity state. Your skills might not be valued enough or the role is scoped down tightly. In that case, the rejection may be in your favor, as it allows you to pursue better opportunities where design is valued more.

IMPORTANT Designers have more power than they realize. Yes, the field is competitive. Yes, there are many designers out there and, according to the latest #designtwitter, everyone is a designer. But many jobs also go unfilled. Certain markets and metro areas have more roles than designers. To paraphrase William Gibson, we live in the age of design abundance, but the roles are not yet evenly distributed.

22.4 *Some Rejection Is Healthy*

Sometimes a lack of rejections can be a red flag too. You might actually be setting your goals or aspirations too low if you're not getting a good dose of rejections during your interviews. Think of rejection as inoculation against further rejections, helping you get better over time.

23 What to Do When You Get the Offer

You've landed that dream design job after all those interviews. This may even be your second or third offer. In either case, good on you for coming this far. The hard work paid off and the tables have turned. Before you accept the offer, do some homework to set yourself up for a strong head start in your next job. Now you'll get to play the role of an interviewer to see if hiring this particular job will be best for your career.

When companies hire executives, they usually go through an intensive interview process of getting the dirt behind the candidates. You should follow a similar process. With an offer in hand, take the time to get your questions answered about the company, opportunity, and team so that you can make a well-informed decision.

◇ IMPORTANT Skip the email Q&A—set up a coffee chat (or a conference call) instead. Body language and voice can sometimes be more telling than the answers themselves.

23.1 *Interviewing Your Direct Team*

To start, you should talk with people you'll be working with daily—a fellow designer, engineer, or a product manager. If there's only one person that you can get to interview from your direct team, I would recommend talking with the product manager. So much of your day-to-day will be spent directly working with them. Understanding how they think about customers, design, and user research will help you get a much better clue of design maturity at the company.

23.2 *Interviewing Your Design Manager*

If you haven't had a chance to talk with your design manager§4.3 during the interview process, definitely make the time to do so now.

You should feel confident that this manager is someone who's going to help you grow. If something feels off, now's a good time to clarify. A good manager is like a coach—they're there to set you and the team up to play your best. They'll navigate tough decisions with poise. No manager is perfect, but finding someone you can get along with well will make a big difference over time.

◇ IMPORTANT If you're joining a small company such as a startup, consider requesting a skip level meeting by asking to talk with your manager's manager or the CEO of the company. In smaller settings the leadership team has an outsize impact and can make or break your experience. How they respond to your questions will help you better gauge the company's design maturity.

23.3 *Interviewing People Who Left*

Now of course, current company employees will be biased in favor of the company. It's rare that someone will tell you that the org isn't in good shape or that the work environment is stressful. So it helps to get a second opinion. Talk to a former designer if there was one. Sometimes interviewing the people who just left will give you an unbiased view of the workplace you're about to join.

> STORY
>
> When I was getting background info on one of my managers, I looked at his connections on LinkedIn. One of those connections—let's call him David—worked with my manager a few jobs ago. Coincidentally, David also worked closely with a CEO of another company that I interviewed with. Small world!

Take the time to search out those former employees—a few searches on LinkedIn, Twitter, or Google is all it takes.

23.4 *Questions You Should Consider Asking*

As you're reaching out to folks and setting up coffee chats, it helps to have a strong question list ready that gets to the heart of the matter. Just like interviewing users, you don't want to ask leading questions but instead get at the truth by asking about existing behaviors.

I recommend you get a clear signal on the work, work-life balance, the design team, the company's design maturity, and—if it's a startup—how much runway they have left.

THE WORK

Here are some good questions to ask your design manager.

- What are your expectations for me in the first month on the job?
- How quickly do we ship new features?
- How involved is user research in the design process?
- Have you had a designer before who made a mistake or was underperforming? How did you handle their performance issues?

THE PRODUCT

By now you should also have a good understanding of the company's offering. However if it's an enterprise company or a specialized niche, you may not get a complete sense of the product (unlike a publicly available consumer app for instance). In that case, it helps to request a product demo. Think of this as an app critique, now you're assessing the product to better understand the types of problems and opportunities available to you.

- How is the product sold?
- How much tech debt (and/or design debt) does the product have?
- What are the biggest opportunities for improving the product?

WORK-LIFE BALANCE

Working in a company that's a good fit can make a difference between coming to work miserable versus happy. Some organizations pride themselves in going above and beyond, pushing employees to work nights and weekends to achieve a greater mission. Other companies do the bare minimum and everyone leaves the office by six p.m. In the end, it's a personal preference.

- What is it like to work here?
- How many projects does a designer usually work on in parallel?
- What does a usual day look like for a designer working here?
- What was the last intense project that you worked on? What made it intense?

DESIGN TEAM

To understand your growth opportunity, it helps to understand the types of folks you'll be working with and how the design team is situated in the company.

- How is the design team organized within the company?
- Is there a head of design and who do they report to? If they're under product or engineering then design will always be in the backseat.
- How big is the design team? Are there plans to grow it? What roles are next to hire?
- What do you think is a current strength of the design team?
- What is a growth opportunity for the design team as a whole?
- How is the design team staffed? You'll want to learn if there are dedicated researchers, brand designers, content designers and so on. In smaller companies people will wear multiple hats, in larger companies you're likely to find more specialists.
- When does the design team come together (for critiques, team outings, and so on)?

Some of the questions that you'll ask will inevitably overlap with design maturity. Usually, in a company's early days everyone is a generalist and designers scramble to meet the changing needs of the company. As the org matures, processes become more established and the quality bar rises.

DESIGN MATURITY

Design is still a nascent discipline in many orgs. There are many different design maturity models out there, but suffice it to say companies with low maturity offer a different challenge compared to high design maturity companies. In the former you shape the process, in the latter you optimize and get better at your craft.

Both options may be a good fit for your career. It helps to learn more about the level of design maturity[§4.2] at this company.

- How are roadmaps or quarterly goals set at the company?
- When it comes to building features, who determines what to build?
- How much budget does the UX/design team get?
- What was the last project driven by UX research?
- What's the design to engineering ratio?
- Is there a design system in place?
- Is there a design ops team?

One thing to note—in smaller companies with little to no design resources, you may be the only designer. However, you can mature the design practice there quickly if their appetite for it is high. For larger companies, design maturity will be slower—given the layers and various stakeholders, it will take longer even if the impact might be more significant.

STARTUP-SPECIFIC QUESTIONS

If you have an offer from a startup, you should also ask about the company's burn rate and growth ambitions. Every startup carries risk, but that risk can be mitigated with a strong team, strong execution, and decent funding.

- How does the company make money or how do we plan on making money?
- Is the company currently profitable?
- What is our current burn rate—given the current size and funding, how long do we have before we have to raise another round?

Most startups fail. Yes, it may be glamorous to work at one to make a dent in the universe, but remember, not every company will succeed. And that's OK. It's nice to see one's equity amount to something, but see it as a bonus. The most important factor that will contribute to your well-being is the people you'll interact and work with daily.

23.5 *Making the Decision*

When you get an offer, take the time to zoom out before you zoom in. If you were to take this role, how will it help you achieve your current and future goals? Ultimately, we're all captains of our own ships. A good job is one that pays well, grows your skills, and advances your career. Of course, choosing a job isn't all about career aspirations either. Work-life balance is also key. In the end, you should weigh factors based on how important they are to you.

Remember the mapping your futures exercise[§5] exercise that we did earlier on? Now's a good time to reflect, since you've been through the process and a few weeks have passed by since then. Are your fundamental goals still the same? Have they changed with new information?

◇ IMPORTANT There will never be a sure thing or an ideal workplace. Companies reorg, teams change, projects shift. The best you can do is to look at core factors (such as culture) and the key people who influence the process so that even in the times of reorg, you'll still end up in a good place because the culture of the company§4.4 is one that resonates with your values.

CHOOSING AMONG MULTIPLE OFFERS

If you're in a lucky position of deciding among multiple offers, it helps to step back and think about the factors that are most important to you. It can be easy to get caught up and compare the roles based on superficial factors—office space, location, salary. With the exception of salary, some of these might not be important. And even with salary—minor differences may seem trivial compared to other factors, such as a great team and a short commute.

List the things that are important to you and see how companies stack up—logically, is there a clear winner? Emotionally, do you feel more at home or a better fit at a certain place?

Lastly, an exercise you can do is imagine yourself fully accepting a specific offer. Live out your next day as if you've already committed to it. Sleep on it. When you wake up—do you still feel strong about your choice?

If you've done your prior research, this step will be hard. If you're deciding between two great options, flip a coin and make a decision based on that. If you feel immediate regret based on the toss, then you know which option is truly important to you.

REJECTING OFFERS

Inevitably, for one reason or another, you'll have to reject a company or two—this one will be tough. If you absolutely know for sure that you don't want to continue or have a better offer that you've already accepted, reach out to the company that you're rejecting and let them know quickly. As bittersweet as this is, it's not the end of the world; the design industry is surprisingly small, so you never know when you'll run into these folks next.

24 Breaking Down Your Design Job Offer

When we think of negotiation, we think of it as the final step between you and the job. The reality is that we're always negotiating. Sometimes you're not even in the room. Your work, your portfolio, is negotiating on your behalf, especially in the beginning—so be sure to make it strong. Show that you've achieved outstanding results in the companies you were with and this will lead to proper leveling and help the employer set the right expectations for a salary range.

24.1 *Compensation FAQ*

WHAT DO I SAY WHEN I GET A CALL CONGRATULATING ME?

Stay positive and convey your excitement for the role. The next step is to get the offer in writing so you can pore over it in detail. The employer wouldn't expect you to commit on the spot, and it's reasonable to ask for time to think things over.

I'M NOT SURE IF I WANT TO WORK HERE...

If you're still on the fence about taking the job, get answers to your questions first by interviewing your future teammates. As part of your interviewing, you can also ask about job expectations and career ladders. What does success look like? Who is a good example of a strong designer there? Return here when you're mostly certain.

I'M LUCKY TO EVEN GET THIS JOB—SHOULD I NEGOTIATE?

Yes! It pays to ask.

◇ IMPORTANT According to Comparably,[127] only 52% of all designers negotiated their salary. Not negotiating is a guarantee that you won't get more. Studies also show that women also take the first offer at face value whereas men see it as negotiable. At least starting the conversation opens up the chance that you'll get a bump, and you won't regret leaving money on the table. Your subsequent promotions and raises will be in part based on that number. There's no shame in asking and no shame in later accepting the original offer.

HOW DO I GET MORE?

Aside from polishing your skills, the next step is to collect data to understand the market rate for designers. The goal isn't to squeeze every penny out of the company. Rather, you want to make sure there's a good match between your level of skill and the money that you're getting. You don't

127. https://www.comparably.com/public-culture/38/3/did-you-negotiate-your-salary

want to end up in a place where you drive a hard bargain, get the money, end up not performing, and get let go as a result.

HOW DO I FIND OUT HOW OTHER DESIGNERS ARE COMPENSATED?

The best resource is real compensation from other designers. Ask your friends or even friends of friends to get a rough estimate. Hired's Salary Calculator[128] and W2 filings[129] are also good resources for actual salary data. If you're going the startup route, take a look at AngelList,[130] as jobs come with transparent equity and salary ranges.

Levels.fyi[131] is a good resource, as it has a granular side-by-side comparison of salaries across (mainly large) tech companies. Similar to Hired, Levels is starting to verify salaries through official documents. It also graphs ranges for tech salaries based on level, helping you better understand how different companies do compensation. Less reliable info comes from self-reported salaries on sites such as Glassdoor, LinkedIn Salary, and Comparably.[132] Your best bet is to look at aggregate salary per level.

SNAPSHOT OF YOUR WRITTEN OFFER

Your compensation package will consist of multiple levers you can pull:

- **Compensation.** Combination of cash, equity, and sometimes a starting bonus with a promise of a performance bonus.
- **Title.** A series of levels that determine your salary range.
- **Benefits.** Medical and voluntary insurance. This is a major perk that can help you save major money compared to buying it yourself.
- **Vacation.** Some companies offer unlimited time off, others allow you to sell your time off, and some tie vacation to employee band.
- **Perks.** These can be some nice-to-have extras, such as free lunch at the office, flex work, learning budgets, and so on.

If you have multiple offers, it helps to do a summary of all the financial benefits that you get in order to do a side-by-side comparison.

Remember though, the most important things (for example, industry experience or access to expertise from mentors) won't be stated in your

128. https://hired.com/salary-calculator
129. https://h1bdata.info/index.php
130. https://angel.co/
131. https://www.levels.fyi/
132. http://comparably.com/

offer and are hard to quantify. These are personal, so be sure to take stock of intangible benefits that are valuable to you. Small things like a culture of remote work or a flexible working-hour policy add up quickly.

That's why when you're looking for work, it helps to start with the end in mind. Have a north star for the next step in your career—it aids you in narrowing down options and making tough calls based on factors critical for you while not getting distracted by shiny but meaningless add-ons.

24.2 *The Compensation Package Breakdown*

When you receive your compensation package, you'll be leveled at a band, which comes with a range; for example, associate product designer makes $100K–$110K base salary compared to a product designer who might make $110K–$125K. In general, the company that you're considering should have an objective standard for determining salary ranges, and you can always ask how they've arrived at their decision.

Years of design work serves as a rule of thumb when it comes to compensation, but years of experience doesn't always equate to expertise. Ability to ship products that led to phenomenal outcomes does. Prove that you can perform at a certain band and have deep expertise that the company doesn't have—you'll get compensated appropriately.

BASE SALARY

Base salary is usually shown as a pre-tax annual number. If you're moving to a new area, be sure to factor in your cost of living plus various taxes. According to Hired's State of Salaries 2019 report,[133] the average tech salary is highest in the SF bay area at $145K. However, Austin, TX, wins out since it has a better cost of living and so the same salary brings more purchasing power. In addition to your base salary, it's helpful to understand how often the company does performance reviews, as these are additional opportunities to recalibrate your salary. Typically they happen either once or twice a year.

BONUS

You may also get a one-time signing bonus, usually conditionally if you stay on for the full year. Sometimes you may also get a promise of a per-

133. https://pages.hired.email/rs/289-SIY-439/images/hired-state_of_salaries.pdf

formance bonus at the end of the year, so you can ballpark how much potential extra money you might get. Take that with a grain of salt though—these bonuses are not guaranteed.

BENEFITS

When we think of compensation, benefits don't immediately come to mind. However, getting benefits like medical insurance coverage can quickly add up, helping you save $15,000 or more for individual coverage.

Some other perks that you might encounter:

- 401K budgets to help you manage retirement.
- Learning budgets that you can spend on workshops or conferences.
- Snacks and lunches at the office saving you both time and money.
- Discounts with other partner companies.

Quantifying benefits and their financial impact can be tricky, but you can always do some back-of-the-envelope calculations to rough-size the money and time you can save.

EQUITY

In addition to offering salaries, companies, especially startups, offer equity as another form of compensation. Typically, early-stage companies weigh heavily on equity but pay lower in base. Of course, this isn't legal or investment advice, so always check with your lawyer and/or if you have questions.

Generally, you'll encounter these equity types:

- **Public stock.** Although the stock price of a company will vary over time, the benefit of public stock is obvious: it's real money that's worth something today.
- **Restricted stock units (RSUs).** You wait to get the shares, and once they vest, you don't need to buy them.
- **Incentive stock options (ISOs).** You get the right to buy shares in the future with a preferential tax treatment. Your offer will state how much you will have to pay per share (strike price), but you will have to fork over some cash to get your equity.

To understand how much your equity is worth, you'll need to understand how much you're getting out of a total pool of options outstanding and how much the company is currently valued at. You'll also need to have conviction that this value will rise over time (hopefully in part due to your efforts). You may also want to talk with your recruiter or your future manager about how much your shares are valued at a specific valuation to determine how much you could stand to make as the company grows.

You don't get equity all at once but instead accumulate it over time—aka vesting. A typical vesting schedule is four years, which means you'll get all of your shares in four years. Usually there's a one-year cliff where you get 25% of your equity package at the end of year one. After that you get 1/48 of your equity vested every month until you reach year four.

While it's exciting to work for startups, the chances of making it big are rare. The reality is that nearly all startups fail, some break even and get acquired, and a select few hit it big. Even with the select few, 2019 was a year of lackluster IPOs as companies' stock significantly decreased after going public. That said, Facebook's IPO wasn't an early blockbuster success either. So treat equity as a nice bonus, not as a 100% sure thing.

If you want to learn more about how equity works, take a look at Holloway's Guide to Equity Compensation.[134] Candor also has an article on equity education,[135] and they provide a nifty equity calculator[136] to help you figure how much your equity is worth.

25 Negotiating Compensation

Start with the end in mind. Before entering a negotiation, think through the factors that are important to you now. You don't have to have a five-year vision—not many do. But having a solid plan for your next year, what you want to learn, and the type of work you want to be doing will help you meaningfully make trade-offs.

25.1 *Not a Zero-Sum Pie*

When we think of negotiation, it's not unusual to think of it as a zero-sum game. One player takes most and another is left with less. But that's a losing proposition. You should reframe a negotiation as a conversation to

134. https://www.holloway.com/g/equity-compensation

135. https://carta.com/blog/category/equity-education/

136. https://carta.com/blog/value-equity-offer-startup-equity-calculator/

come up with a win-win situation for both parties. This will lead not only to a good short-term outcome for you but also to long-term goodwill down the road when your next assessment comes.

◇ IMPORTANT A good negotiation should feel like a productive collaboration between two teammates.

Stay enthusiastic about the role throughout the negotiation process as you're building rapport with the recruiter. Thank them for the concessions as you're approaching the offer together. Mention that you appreciate their willingness to listen and be flexible. Graciousness goes a long way—don't miss an opportunity to make the other party feel fabulous. You've already built trust throughout the interview process; use the negotiation as a way to further reinforce your goodwill.

In turn, **be willing to listen**. Empathy is a designer's master skill. If you can truly understand their issues, and the true issues behind those, you can come up with a creative way to solve the compensation problem while putting them at ease and moving closer toward your end goal.

◇ IMPORTANT Practice negotiating. This is a difficult and crucial conversation. Sometimes you might trip up and not get the right words out during a crucial moment in negotiation. Do a mock interview with a friend. Dedicate a little time here, where the stakes are low. With practice, the negotiation will feel closer to a natural conversation, allowing you to think and respond quickly with empathy and enthusiasm.

25.2 *Understanding Your Level*

Your total comp is determined by a company's leveling framework. The more senior you are, the more experience you have, the more money you'll get. At higher senior levels your compensation will be predominantly based on your performance and will be closer tied to your equity.

In certain organizations, being brought on at a certain level sometimes acts as an anchor. That is if you're starting out at mid-level you may need to prove yourself for a long amount of time before getting promoted to a senior role. That said there is also a risk of coming in at a level that's too high or setting yourself for a bar that you cannot meet.

After you join the company, the leveling document will be used as objective criteria to evaluate your performance and determine whether you're not meeting, meeting, or exceeding the criteria set forth. While the common hustle advice is to "fake it 'til you make it", sometimes there is no making it. Instead you'd be better off in a place that strikes the right balance of playing to your strengths while giving you an opportunity to grow without so much stress that you're not able to do your job.

Every company will have their own leveling guide which in great detail shows what one needs to do in order to perform at a certain level.

TABLE: INDIVIDUAL CONTRIBUTOR DESIGN LEVELS

LEVEL	EXPERIENCE	EXPECTATIONS
Associate (L1-L2)	Experience primarily comes from academics or bootcamp. This is usually an intern or a co-op position.	Just starting out working in design in a professional capacity. Able to take direction.
Mid-level (L3-L4)	Usually a university graduate or someone with a few months of experience from previous internships.	Strong grasp on fundamentals developing collaboration skills, taking on projects of increasing complexity. Operates at a team level.
Senior (L5-L6)	Usually about 7-8 years of work experience.	Defines and reframe problems, gets to the heart of the matter, reliably comes up with strong solutions without supervision. Operates at a department level.
Staff or Lead (L7)	8+ years of industry experience but at this point the years of experience matter less than impact.	Usually leads a team of designers under them, creates new frameworks, comes up with ideas that solve multiple problems. Operates across departments.
Principal (L8)	Same as above.	Created new brands, potentially defined industry trends, leads the company with other C-level counterparts.

Leveling will differ by company and one company's L5 is another company's L4. Resources such as levels.fyi[137] are helpful in understanding how one's level transfers over from one company to the next. Companies also usually break down role titles into granular levels. These levels are usually not exposed externally (e.g. Product Designer II) but they are important internally as they assign you to a specific band that's tied to salary.

137. http://levels.fyi

FIGURE: LEVELS FYI DESIGN LEVELS

Companies level designers differently but in general they all follow a similar trajectory. *Source: Levels.FYI*[138]

Make sure you do your research, learn what other companies pay for the band you've applied for. Beyond the numbers, peel back the layers. Is there additional know-how you can get on the compensation conversation? Is the company uncompromising on baseline salary but flexible with stock options? Blind[139] is a good resource to look into this info.

You won't have all perfect info at the end of the day but closing some gaps of this knowledge will put you in a stronger position during the negotiation.

25.3 *Demonstrate Your Strengths*

Negotiation starts when you first start applying, so look for opportunities to reinforce the unique skills and knowledge that you bring to solve a specific pain (or multiple pains) for the company.

When I was applying through job boards (which is one of the worst ways to apply, by the way), I was able to score an interview at

138. https://www.levels.fyi/?compare=LinkedIn,Amazon,Google,Facebook&track=Product%20Designer

139. https://www.teamblind.com/

> a well-known tech company due to advanced prototyping that I'd done previously. It was demonstrating the work in-person and letting the interviewers use my prototypes on their own that helped land an amazing offer.

Think of negotiation broadly. It's not something that happens just at the end—a strong start can make a huge difference toward your final comp and leveling. But let's say you already are at the end—it doesn't hurt to reiterate the unique value that you bring.

◇ IMPORTANT If you want to get compensated highly, you need to understand a company's key pain points. Show that your unique strengths can resolve these issues.

Inevitably you will get pushback around cost, but reframing the discussion from cost to an investment for the company will help you steer the conversation in the right direction.

25.4 *Use Multiple Offers to Your Advantage*

If you're in a lucky position to have multiple offers, be sure to compare and contrast. Talk with the recruiter about matching your highest offer's salary. At this point you have some advantage here, as a company would hate to lose a qualified candidate to a competitor. Beyond salary, you can negotiate equity or maybe sweeten the deal with a one-time signing bonus.

Understand that interviewing candidates is a long process. They've just gone through rounds of writing the job description, reviewing candidates, going through phone screens, and getting designers to spend their time interviewing you and other candidates. Finally, they narrowed it to one offer—yours. This whole process usually takes money and time, and time is the most painful factor. They'd rather not go through a month and a half of work again.

◇ IMPORTANT If you don't have multiple offers outstanding—don't let this deter you from negotiating. Even starting the compensation negotiation process already increases your chances of getting a favorable outcome.

ACCELERATE THE INTERVIEWING PROCESS

Sometimes you'll end up in a position where you're still interviewing at one company but you've already got an offer at another. Be sure to let the company who's still interviewing you know that you're already at the offer stage elsewhere. This adds a bit of (valid) pressure on them to accelerate the interviewing process. Ideally, as early in the process as possible, let the other company know that you're late in the interviewing cycle with someone else. This will help you line up all your offer letters at the end.

WHAT IF THERE ARE NO OTHER OFFERS?

Lastly, you might not have any offers outstanding or anything to match against. You may even be out of a job, so anything will look good right now. Alternatively, you might get an offer from a place where you'd love to work and the starting salary is already high. What do you do? Two things—conditionally agree or restructure your offer based on things critical to you.

25.5 *Conditionally Agree*

The first step in negotiation is understanding the needs of your client. Since you'll be working closely with a recruiter and they have a quota to fill, you can assure them that you're serious about the offer by saying you'll accept it right away if they can get you X. X can be anything that's important to you and is not just restricted to salary.

Saying no can feel like placing an ultimatum. As we've talked about earlier, a negotiation is like a conversation (but with high stakes). If you're getting close to what you hope you're getting, you can say no in a non-confrontational way—"Thank you for showing flexibility on salary, this seems appropriate. Could we talk about other things that factor into compensation?"

Again, this will reinforce the image of your flexibility and allows you and the other party to examine compensation in a safe way.

25.6 *When Your Dream Job Won't Budge on Comp*

You've played your cards right, done your homework, and negotiated with multiple offers, but still the company won't budge. Hey, at least you've tried and you're still ahead of most folks who don't even ask. You still have a couple of options.

SHIFT AMOUNT OF SALARY VERSUS EQUITY

If you're negotiating with a startup, the company simply may not have the money to give you a higher salary, as everyone is already taking a pay cut. Potentially, this is an opportunity either to ask for an increase in equity if you think your compensation package isn't in line or to better understand how subsequent rounds of raising money will affect your compensation.

Finally, as a method of last resort you can also scale down salary in favor of equity or go the reverse route and ask for more cash with a lower equity stake. In doing so, you need to understand how this will impact your future performance reviews. Are you only going to be compensated with raises in extra cash, or can extra equity come into play as well?

FOCUS ON GROWTH

Regardless of where you are in your career, optimize for growth. Given the choice between a job that pays slightly more and one that helps you grow more—go for the latter. It's easier to negotiate for a raise or a higher salary when you have the skills and the results to back it up.

So how can you negotiate for growth? Bring up the fact that you're excited to learn and contribute on key projects. This could be access to key individuals (mentors, for example), specific projects, or teams that can be high impact. These things may cost little to nothing for the company, while giving you long-term potential for your career.

25.7 *Final Words on Negotiation*

When you're joining a company, you're not just getting paid—you're also buying into their culture.§4.4 Ideally, you'll end up in a place that has good salary, good work, and good people. The day-to-day will be far more important to your long-term sense of achievement and success. If you're always stressed about the commute, or if it feels like the co-workers don't have your back, it will eventually translate to not just worse performance—it will ultimately lead to burnout, forcing you to look for another job.

IMPORTANT Negotiation is a critical skill for designers. It's not just something you magically get better at during a few critical moments where it counts. We don't get to practice it as often as we need. Aside from practicing, it helps to learn what to practice. If I had to recommend one book on negotiation, it would be *Never Split the Difference*.[140] Written by an FBI hostage negotiator, the tactics are made applicable to many areas of life, "in the boardroom or at home."

25.8 *Additional Resources*

To learn more about design levels and how various companies structure them:

- Intercom's individual contributor design levels[141] and design manager levels,[142] in addition to being open available and detailed, have specific objectives and growth tasks tied to each level.
- Basecamp's Titles for Designers.[143] Although Basecamp is a small company by startup standards, their design framework is rigorous. Aside from describing what are the different expectations of designers, it also publicly lists the names of designers at those levels.
- DoorDash's Head of Design, Helena Seo, shares her thinking and approach toward creating a leveling system[144] at the company.
- progression.fyi,[145] a collection of open source company ladders, includes some for design, such as BuzzFeed and Zendesk, among many others.

140. https://www.goodreads.com/book/show/26156469-never-split-the-difference
141. https://docs.google.com/document/d/1qlH-eNkP4rNFoM1eCsHQNwRTWrP9Yg1-XUqWHPTKAkg/edit
142. https://docs.google.com/document/d/1zqeuCgTL7zTcQRSgv-xoyndgiTyFchspncWDb3I0tbI/edit
143. https://web.archive.org/web/20201028105028/https://basecamp.com/handbook/appendix-03-titles-for-designers
144. https://doordash.engineering/2019/09/03/designing-a-career-ladder-for-product-design/
145. https://www.progression.fyi/

26 Leaving Your Job on a High Note

You've accepted an offer, negotiated it, and now all that's left is to tell your current company that you're moving on. First off—congrats! Success in design is often nonlinear. It's not about going to an expensive university to end up working for a prestigious company. Great designers know that. They've oftentimes experienced different cultures, worked with different people, and have seen industries shift. They understand that you can't learn everything in one place.

Here is how you can quit well, set your current team up for success, and prepare for your next opportunity.

26.1 *Finishing Strong*

The first person to tell about your leave is your manager. It's likely that they'll try to persuade you to stay and offer some sort of incentive, such as a higher salary. If your current job isn't meeting your needs that you hired it for, stick to your principles. People usually don't quit over salary. If you got to this point, it's likely that there's a list of things that aren't going well at your current job. It's bittersweet to say goodbye and venture into uncharted territory, but if you've done your homework, the move will be worth it.

◇ IMPORTANT Ask yourself: If somebody were to pick up your job today, how can you set them up for success?

Depending on where you're working, the law is usually flexible. In the United States, many states have "at will" employment, which means you can quit or get laid off at any time. You don't even have to have the conversation with your boss; just write your letter of resignation and be done with it.

It would be, however, a disservice to your team to leave so abruptly. This is especially true if you're the only designer at the company. If somebody were to pick up your job today, how can you set them up for success? Can you pay your expertise forward? One of the things that I appreciate in my current role is the strong design system that a prior team has put together. Even though I didn't have the opportunity to overlap with them, their work stood the test of time on its own.

26.2 *Recommend a Good Match for Your Current Role*

We leave jobs because they don't serve our needs well, but this doesn't mean that this job can't be a perfect fit for someone else. So if you know someone who's interested, let your team know—doing so will help them get back their footing quickly.

> **STORY**
>
> When I decided to leave one of my jobs for grad school, I started actively looking for a replacement. I reached out on local UX job boards and pitched the job at a number of design events as well. Eventually I met a designer who was not only excited about the role but also had relevant industry experience. I introduced her to the company, helping her get a head start on the interview process.

26.3 *Saying Goodbye*

If you already have regular one-on-ones with co-workers, now's a good time to sync up for the last time. Take advantage of these to express your gratitude and thank your co-workers. This is your last opportunity to give feedback, highlight their successes, and share the good times you've had together.

One of the things that I appreciate about our design industry is its tight-knit sense of community. Investing in and developing professional relationships, regardless of the company, is key. These people may follow you later. Or you may follow them to another role in a new company. You never know. Companies come and go, but relationships last.

On that last point, make sure to send out an email thanking folks, and leave contact info (usually a personal email) to stay in touch.

26.4 *When You've Had Enough*

On the other hand, you may totally hate your job. This gig has been driving you nuts. You feel underappreciated and overworked. No one really seems to care. If that's the case, resist the urge to (metaphorically) flip a table.

Yes, this situation isn't good. A two-week notice isn't required but is typical. Do the best you can and wrap things up. As Tina Seelig recounts in her book, *What I Wish I Knew When I Was 20,*[146] an employee who was quitting refused to help during a critical time and as a result, "the damage she did to her reputation during the last weeks of her employment dwarfed all the positive things she had done in prior years." Take the time to wrap things up as best you can and move on.

26.5 *Take the Time to Reflect*

While the recruiter or even the hiring manager at the next role might pressure you to start as soon as possible, don't give in. The time that you spend between your (now) past job and your future job is just as important. Use it wisely to rest and reflect on your experience.

If your previous job has caused you to burn out (or if you've burnt out multiple times already), then rest should be top priority. Don't try to do much work during this period. Disconnect fully. Catch up on what you've been neglecting.

Once you're refreshed, take the time to reflect. This is a good time to revisit your original job framework:§5

- Where are you in your career now?
- What has worked well or not so well in your prior jobs?
- What skills§3 do you want to grow in your next job?

◇ **IMPORTANT** Getting clear and writing the questions and answers out will help you frame the narrative of your previous job and tie up any loose ends. You'll also get a better signal of which opportunities to pursue in your next role. And when you're ready, start planning your onboarding.

27 Starting Your Job Strong

In tech jobs, two-year stints are becoming the norm. If you started working at 21 and retired at 65, that's potentially 22 jobs and 22 different onboardings. This number may be higher if you've worked for startups, since some companies don't even make it past the first year. Regardless of the company, ramping up to a new role poses unique challenges. Although com-

146. https://www.amazon.com/dp/B07Q83G41J

panies usually have an onboarding process in place, many of them are short and aren't role-specific. Don't leave this crucial part of the process to chance. By structuring your own onboarding, you'll be able to build strong relationships, avoid pitfalls, and create momentum toward great work and your next promotion.

◇ IMPORTANT Every onboarding will be different. Depending on the size of the company some phases may take about a month each. Some phases may be a quick affair while others may drag a little as you get into the details. In a small startup your onboarding may be compressed to a week or even a few hours. So take these as a starting point and be sure to adjust them to your context.

27.1 *Before You Start*

It may come as a surprise, but your onboarding starts with your first interview.[§10] Treat it as an opportunity to ask questions as if it's your first day working at the company. Of course, you won't learn everything here, so be sure to follow up with interviews of your own after you get the offer. When you accept the role, ask your manager if there's anything you should study ahead of time. Even if there isn't, this shows initiative on your part to get going fast. You want to be sure to do two things before you dive in:

- **Close the previous chapter.** When you're transitioning to a new role, take the time to rest and reflect. Even a small break will give you enough distance to close out the previous work chapter and savor the future possibilities of your new role. Don't make the mistake of jumping right in without proper recovery—you won't be able to start off as strong, and you may even burn out in the long run.
- **Create your learning plan.** After a period of rest, plan what you need to learn and accomplish by the end of day one, week one, month one and so on. Adjust your plan as you gain new knowledge, of course, but planning now will help you keep your career priorities in mind, especially when you hit the inevitable snags. Even if there are none, this shows initiative on your part to hit the ground running.

27.2 *Phase 1: Be a Sponge*

During this phase, you'll be in full-on learning mode. It might be tempting to start fixing things right away, but knowing the context, the system, and its people will help you push for change effectively later.

Key objectives for this phase include:

1. Gather context.
2. Set expectations with your design manager.
3. Get to know your squad (product, engineering, data science, research, and so on).
4. Meet the design team.
5. Learn the product and design rituals.
6. Learn your part of the system.
7. Start designing.

USE YOUR NEWCOMER ADVANTAGE

Newcomers are usually given a lot of leeway. Don't miss out on this opportunity to ask "stupid" questions. Your co-workers will feel valued sharing their knowledge, and you'll gain their respect along the way. It's too early to tell if things look good or bad. Outright criticism might even make you look foolish since you don't yet know the full context of decision-making. But don't lose your beginner's mind. Ask questions to get to the root cause—how did we get here? As you collect info from various sources, start building your own model of the situation at hand.

GET TO KNOW YOUR MANAGER

The first thing you want to do with your manager[§4.3] is agree on role expectations. You'll need to drive this conversation with your manager to learn about their standards: what counts as underperforming, meeting the bar, and going above and beyond? Depending on your level,[§25.2] the standards will be different. This will be one of your crucial conversations this phase. It's also good to cover these topics:

- Advice on how to succeed in the role.
- Organizational challenges to be aware of.
- Tracking and documenting work performance.
- Opportunities for support and training.

Beyond setting up regular one-on-ones with your manager (usually on a weekly basis), find out about their working style. What forms of communication do they prefer? When should they be called in for help? Understanding your manager's style will help you broach serious topics and avoid missteps during difficult conversations later.

Bonus: If you're up for it, share the 90-day plan (or a version of it that you're comfortable with) with your manager to let them critique and identify gaps you might have missed.

MAKE THE MOST OF ONE-ON-ONES

One of the best ways to start building relationships with your co-workers is to schedule informal one-on-ones on their calendars. Use this as an opportunity to leave the building and get some fresh air while getting to know them. What makes them tick? Why are they excited about their role?

- **Learn what your team expects from you.** Different engineers will have different expectations. Learn how your product manager's experience has been shaped by other designers (not just at this company). How was research engaged? Understanding and setting realistic expectations with your team will help you commit to reasonable goals while giving you an opportunity to also go above and beyond.
- **How can design help?** Not everyone understands design. Informing your team of your expertise will help them reach out to you in times of need. This isn't just a one-time conversation. You'll need to remind people about your skills, but the best reminder isn't verbal—it's doing the work itself.
- **Trust is built over time.** There's no easy way to take a relationship from 0 to 100, but you can start by understanding what's personally important to a team member. What do they hope to achieve? Asking something as innocuous as "How can I help?" can also uncover deeper issues at hand.

LEARN THE PRODUCT AND DESIGN RITUALS

As a designer, you'll want to get up to speed on the process of doing the work. Here are some starter questions to bring up with the design team:

- Where is the source of truth for design?
- How is a project kicked off and by whom?
- How are bugs or issues filed?

- Is there a formal design review process?
- How often do design critiques happen?
- How is the design system used?

Don't worry if you don't have it all covered before you begin your first project. Doing the work will help you resolve many of these questions and potentially raise better-informed questions along the way.

LEARN YOUR PART OF THE SYSTEM

In addition to connecting with your team, you'll want to learn about your part of the system. For example, if you're joining an e-commerce company to do work on checkout, learn everything about that experience. Dig up the design and the documentation, and start formulating your own opinions and questions. What makes sense? What seems puzzling? Don't rely solely on internal knowledge; be sure to also look at industry trends, patterns, and techniques that exist outside of your organization.

◇ IMPORTANT To make sure you truly understand, I recommend creating a system flow or a concept diagram to capture the bigger picture as well as the details.

REFLECT ON YOUR EXPERIENCE

You will now have a better sense of the company's culture during this period by observing how people act. As you're wrapping up your first phase, step back to reflect on your experience:

- Beyond the work itself, how does it feel to be here?
- What did you learn during this time?
- What new info do you need to be learning?
- Who are your go-to resources for help?
- What support exists to help you get up to speed quickly?

As you're reflecting on your experience, you might also want to update your plan to reflect your newfound information.

27.3 *Phase 2: From Learning to Execution*

This phase, you'll start to shift toward execution.

Key objectives for this phase:

- Learn about adjacent teams.
- Continue building relationships with your immediate team.
- Learn how your part of the system interacts with the larger whole.
- Wrap up and retro your first project.

LEARN ADJACENT PARTS OF THE SYSTEM AND THEIR PEOPLE

As a product designer, your top priority is to create a seamless experience for the customer, not ship the org chart.[147] This means you'll have to signal to other teams where their work breaks in your part of the flow or where you see potential collisions occurring.

- **Full customer journey.** In the first phase, you got to know your part of the system. Now it's time to dive into the customer journey from beginning to end. Consider mapping out this experience by looking at the system from different perspectives: How does the experience look for new users? What about for intermediates or power users? If your product is on multiple platforms, consider capturing those as well.
- **Collision resolution.** As you learn the system, you'll encounter various problems and collisions in the experience itself. What process is in place today to get them resolved? Does the current organizational structure hinder or support cross-functional work? How can this be improved?

DEVELOP YOUR EXISTING RELATIONSHIPS AND HANDLE CONFLICT

In phase one, you kicked off relationships using the one-on-one format. Now's the time to continue building relationships as you do the work.

- **Design partnership.** As you dive into doing the work, you'll play different roles, from leading and facilitation to coaching and support. Be on the lookout for how you can help support partners in research, data science, and engineering. Getting into the details of the work will help you pave the way for smoother projects and make everyone feel like they're treated fairly.

---

147. https://medium.com/@donorem/shipping-the-org-chart-3319181be9bd

- **Handling conflict well.** It's natural to encounter signs of conflict at some point, such as a teammate who disagrees with you and fights for their opinion or a PM who's unwilling to let go of their pet idea. These are all par for the course. The earlier you get to your first conflict, the faster you'll advance the relationship.

By focusing on first principles and understanding the problem, you can help drive productive discussions and turn conflict into a positive force. This way, you'll consider different perspectives and make a well-informed decision.

SHIP YOUR FIRST WIN AND DO A RETRO

When you wrap up your first feature, do a mini retro. What problems did you encounter? What did you wish you'd known when you started? By this point, you may be already working on another project. Apply the lessons learned from your first project here.

27.4 *Phase 3: Accelerate Impact*

By the end of this phase, you'll be a trustworthy, well-versed insider who's up to speed on process, team, and the inner workings of the organization. Your challenge will be to keep this momentum going.

Key objectives for this phase:

- Become efficient.
- Amplify impact.
- Reflect on your onboarding.

BECOME EFFICIENT AND AMPLIFY IMPACT

As you're working on projects and collaborating with your team and other teams, you'll start to understand the best way to communicate (maybe it's Slack or informal desk chats) and when to share the work. Continue finding, noting, and removing barriers that slow you (and the team) down.

- **Beyond efficiency, look to be effective.** To make an impact, you'll need to uncover the spirit of the intent (the true business need and the customer value), consistently deliver on the work, and amplify impact across the entire organization. Proper problem framing and understanding the full context of the situation will be key.

- **Learn company priorities.** How far does the company plan? How does the organization react to bugs? By documenting and bringing up issues, you can get a better sense of how the company makes decisions, which in turn will help you properly frame your ideas.
- **Build allies.** Lastly, don't forget to continue building your relationships. Whether it's informal coffee chats with your peers or skip-level meetings with your manager's manager, understanding the struggles they're facing and helping them will make you more successful.

REFLECTING ON YOUR ONBOARDING

As your third phase nears the end, do a final reflection:

- How do you feel?
- What went well?
- What didn't work as well as you expected?

Don't forget to give onboarding feedback and help set the next designer up for success. This will make everyone's experience so much better. Good luck on your first days on the job and beyond!

ADDITIONAL RESOURCES

If you're interested in learning more, take a look at *The First 90 Days: Proven Strategies for Getting Up to Speed Faster and Smarter*[148] by Michael Watkins. It was the original inspiration for this section and covers onboarding in depth. While it generally gives advice to set up managers for success when transitioning, many of the strategies are useful for individual contributors as well.

28 Land Well and Own Your Career

By now, you should know the nuts and bolts of how to land your dream role. From taking stock of your various skills, building your identity, structuring your portfolio, and navigating the various interview types, to reflecting on the feedback and wrapping things up with negotiation and a strong start.

148. https://www.amazon.com/dp/B00B6U63ZE/

As we know, design is never a linear process from A to B, and often there's a big, messy middle. Knowing how to get to your dream role comes with an understanding of what skills you bring to the table and how to properly communicate them in various stages of the process. Reflecting on your experience throughout these stages is key, as usually new information comes in to help us steer our job search in a favorable direction. While each journey is unique, having a destination in mind makes navigation easier.

28.1 *Is Remote Work Here to Stay?*

Over the course of writing this book, in the midst of the COVID-19 pandemic, the way we get work done (and how we interview) has shifted dramatically. The journey has been redefined. Gone are the days of in-person interviews—now you can talk to many companies all from the comfort of your home.

Of course this brings new challenges. It's hard to get a feel for a place when all you see is a bunch of faces in rectangles on Zoom. Networking is no longer an in-person affair but has been pushed online as well. Maybe location isn't as critical as we once thought. If we can get our job done remotely, especially in the midst of a pandemic, then this can usher in a whole new world of flexible work arrangements, opening up opportunities outside of the traditional tech hubs of the world.

28.2 *When Should You Start Looking?*

A common question that I sometimes get from folks who are already working is, "What's a good number of years to stay at a job before you start looking?" Ideally, you're in a place long enough to make an impact, and you outgrow the position or the company. There's nothing left to learn, there's not a clear or appealing path to growth, and you may see a more fruitful opportunity elsewhere. Sometimes this means being at a job for a few months, other times it means working at the same place for a decade.

Of course there are exceptions to this. The company may be doing poorly, is downsizing, or it has a toxic environment that wasn't apparent during the interviews. This could all happen, and there's no imperative to stay at a company that doesn't invest in you. Today's world offers designers *a lot* of challenges to address. The trick is to find the right alignment given your strengths and needs.

In her excellent book, Ask Me This Instead,[149] Kendra Haberkorn recommends candidates ask themselves why they would want to run away from a particular job. Sometimes these reasons can be obvious. Other times you might need to do a little soul searching to think about what you value in work and see if these values have changed since you last searched for or accepted a job.

I encourage you to write your reasons out. Similar to the interview retrospective exercise[§21] and your reflection[§27.4.2] at the end of your onboarding—think about the things that are working, what could be improved, and what you've learned. In doing so, you may not actually need to look for work, potentially many of these can be fixed on the job through some conversations with your manager. Kendra also suggests asking yourself what job you would run towards. After all, you don't want to leave a place out of anger just to find yourself in a new role that's just as bad or worse. Preparation is key—and figuring out what you really want and really value is part of that.

Lastly, you don't have to be actively looking for opportunities to stay in touch with your network. Develop the relationships before you need them. Talk to recruiters and your peers. Reach out to hiring managers you admire, especially when you're already in a great role you love. Since you're already working, there's no undue pressure to find a job immediately and settle in a less than perfect arrangement just to pay the bills. These conversations will be a lot more enjoyable and will help you get a pulse on the industry and where it's headed. In the words of Harvey Mackay, "Dig your well before you're thirsty."[150]

28.3 *Own Your Future*

If your job search is over and you've signed an offer, you might wonder, "What's next?" First of all, congrats, landing a role can be a challenging process and you've proven yourself to be a top candidate. And don't let that imposter syndrome get in the way—the decision to hire you has been

149. https://www.holloway.com/b/ask-me-this-instead

150. https://www.amazon.com/Your-Well-Before-Youre-Thirsty/dp/0385485468

made. Now it's important to concentrate on the work at hand, to accelerate and grow.

When some time has passed, I always encourage folks to revisit their ideal role template. Take a pulse check about every six months or so. Are the things that brought you to this job still there, or have things changed? Depending on the company and market, the rate of change may be drastic. Or maybe there were no changes to the company at all but perhaps your own needs have changed. Revisiting your original dream role North Star will help you continue steering your career in the right place with new information.

Landing a dream job with a great salary is just the beginning. It's what you do afterwards that will set you up for success, whether it's in your current job or the next one. Take another look at your skills and traits. If you're interested in getting promoted, make sure you bring that up with your manager so that you can work on a development plan together.

Design is a changing discipline. While fundamental principles of human behavior remain the same, technology is changing rapidly. Stay up to date, continue learning. These core skills will help you perform well on the job and will also make you a strong candidate so that you can write your own ticket and define your future.

Bon voyage! You got this!

29 Appendix: Resources

All the resources that were mentioned in the book in one place.

- Product Design Skills, Traits, and Responsibilities[§3]
    - T-shaped designers[151] as popularized by IDEO.
- Craft Skills for Designers[§3.4]
    - *About Face: The Essentials of Interaction Design,*[152] 4th ed., by Alan Cooper, et al. It's a great handbook to refer back to, as well as a primer for anyone new to design.

---

151. https://chiefexecutive.net/ideo-ceo-tim-brown-t-shaped-stars-the-backbone-of-ideoaes-collaborative-culture__trashed/
152. https://www.amazon.com/About-Face-Essentials-Interaction-Design/dp/1118766571

- Apple's Human Interface Guidelines.[153]
- Android apps Material Design.[154]
- Jakon Nielsen's 10 Usability Heuristics for User Interface Design.[155]
- *Observing the User Experience: A Practitioner's Guide to User Research*[156] by Elizabeth Goodman, et al. A useful read on research techniques that lays out the core fundamentals while arming you with practical tips.

- Collaboration Skills[§3.5]

  - *Meeting Design: For Managers, Makers, and Everyone*,[157] by Kevin Hoffman. A book specifically about meetings. I know what you're thinking: what could be more boring than attending a meeting—reading a book about it. But it's a solid read that helps you reframe how you facilitate and conduct meetings, helping you ultimately save more time.
  - *Designing Together*,[158] by Dan Brown. All about how to collaborate as a designer, working with different styles, and how to take work together to achieve a better outcome.
  - *User Experience Management*[159] by Arnie Lund. More applicable for managers, it's also a good read when it comes to understanding how individual designers fit into a larger company's ecosystem.
  - *Emotional Intelligence*[160] by Daniel Goleman. A definitive book on the topic of emotional intelligence, awareness of self, and how to use emotional intelligence to connect with others (it's not just about being "nice").

153. https://developer.apple.com/design/human-interface-guidelines/ios/overview/themes/
154. https://material.io/design/
155. https://www.nngroup.com/articles/ten-usability-heuristics/
156. https://www.amazon.com/dp/B008QWEH62/
157. https://www.amazon.com/Meeting-Design-Managers-Makers-Everyone-ebook/dp/B0754NL9R3
158. https://www.amazon.com/Designing-Together-collaboration-management-professionals/dp/0321918630
159. https://www.amazon.com/User-Experience-Management-Essential-Effective/dp/0123854962/
160. https://www.amazon.com/Emotional-Intelligence-Matter-More-Than/dp/055338371X

- Strategic Skills§3.6
  - How to have impact as a designer.[161] An Intercom blog post by Paul Murph that outlines the formula for impact.
  - *UX Strategy: How to Devise Innovative Digital Products That People Want*,[162] by Jamie Levy. A step-by-step guidebook for how to create great products.
  - *Outcomes Over Output*[163] by Joshua Seiden. A short read on distinguishing deliverables and outcomes, with a few case study examples.
- Professional Traits§3.7
  - Carol Dweck's book *Mindset: The New Psychology of Success*[164] is an excellent read about what it means to have a growth mindset, compared to a fixed mindset. This concept has been popularized in the media and may seem like old news; however, I sincerely recommend the book, as the rich stories bring it to life.
  - The power of believing that you can improve.[165] The Ted talk By Carol Dweck.
- How Design Maturity Impacts the Type of Work You'll Do§4.2
  - Level Up,[166] by Heather Phillips[167] (design director at Abstract). This questionnaire enables a company to self-assess its design maturity across multiple phases from process. Each question has four answers corresponding to how mature a company is based on its stage (process, communication, employee development, and so on).
  - Design Maturity Model: The New Design Frontier.[168] A report by InVision in which they interviewed and conducted a large-scale study across many companies, from small startups to large corporations.

---

161. https://www.intercom.com/blog/product-designer-impact/
162. https://www.amazon.com/UX-Strategy-Innovative-Digital-Products/dp/1449372864/
163. https://www.amazon.com/Joshua-Seiden/dp/1091173265
164. https://www.amazon.com/Mindset-Psychology-Carol-S-Dweck/dp/0345472322/
165. https://www.ted.com/talks/carol_dweck_the_power_of_believing_that_you_can_improve
166. https://designerfund.com/levelup/questionnaire/
167. https://www.linkedin.com/in/heather-phillips/
168. https://www.invisionapp.com/design-better/design-maturity-model/

    - UX Maturity Stages[169] by NN/g is a detailed, two-part article on how a company evolves from design immaturity to design enlightenment. Of note is that while growth can sometimes come fast and easy in the first stages, in the last phases, it takes more than a few years to reach the peak, and few, if any, companies ever reach it.

- Your Future Design Manager§4.3

    - *The Making of a Manager: What to Do When Everyone Looks to You,*[170] by Julie Zhuo. While the book is geared toward first-time managers, it's still a good read for individual contributors, especially those reporting to a newly minted manager.

- Assessing Company and Design Culture§4.4

    - Although it's more engineering focused, Key Values[171] is a useful resource for getting a sense of product culture at startups. Sites like Comparably and Glassdoor are also good resources, but take the feedback with a grain of salt as most reviews tend to skew negatively.
    - Kim Goodwin, a design consultant, defines four types of cultures:[172] adhocracy, clan, hierarchy, and market. Kim defines each and provides recommendations for how to gain credibility and influence for each culture. Another way of looking at these types is through your own lens—which culture resonates with you more.
    - More on Angel Streger's philosophy of design and Growth Design[173] from First Round.
    - Katie Dill, VP of design at Lyft shares 8 Principles on Scaling a Design Team[174]—a good read on what makes a design team successful in an organization.

---

169. https://www.nngroup.com/articles/ux-maturity-stages-1-4/
170. https://www.amazon.com/dp/B079WNPRL2/
171. https://www.keyvalues.com/
172. https://www.creativebloq.com/netmag/kim-goodwin-designing-culture-8135475
173. https://firstround.com/review/defining-growth-design-the-guide-to-the-role-most-startups-are-missing/
174. https://www.behance.net/blog/lyfts-vp-of-design-8-principles-on-scaling-a-design-team/

- Designing at a Large Company, Agency, or Startup§4.5
  - According to John Maeda's Design in Tech Report 2019,[175] there were 19 agencies bought in the last 12 months reported. So if you do end up at a large company, you may find yourself working for an agency inside the company or working closely with them. Or if you start your work at an agency don't be surprised if you become part of acquihire.
  - Looking to learn more about different types of agencies? Take a look at SoDA, a membership organization that has a list of agencies[176] known for their high-quality work.
- Designing Consumer or Enterprise Products§4.6
  - Interested in learning more about enterprise design? Check out the Enterprise Experience conference[177] by Rosenfeld Media, which brings in many well-known speakers in the field.
- Company Location and Surrounding Ecosystem§4.8
  - Hired's 2018 report[178] in the U.S.: Seattle, Austin, and Denver are some of the top cities for relocation for tech workers.
  - Holloway's guide on Remote Work[179] is a good resource for anyone figuring out how to navigate the remote work experience.
- Design Impact, Ethics, and Diversity§4.11
  - Clayton Christensen is well known for his jobs-to-be-done theory, and one of his seminal books on the topic is *The Innovator's Dilemma*.[180] But did you know that he also wrote the book, *How Will You Measure Your Life*?[181] In this book, Clayton admonishes readers to think about their guiding principles when making decisions so that they stay true to themselves and not end up in jail.

175. https://design.co/design-in-tech-report-2019-no-track/#17
176. https://www.sodaspeaks.com/members
177. https://rosenfeldmedia.com/enterprise2020/
178. https://hired.com/state-of-salaries-2018
179. https://www.holloway.com/g/remote-work/about
180. https://www.amazon.com/Innovators-Dilemma-Revolutionary-Change-Business/dp/0062060244/
181. https://www.amazon.com/How-Will-Measure-Your-Life-ebook/dp/B006IDOCH4/

- More on Jeff Bezos' framework[182] in the 2010 Princeton graduating class address.

- Mapping Your Design Futures§5
  - Now that you're familiar with the job criteria, take a step back to brainstorm what aspects of that criteria are important to you. You can use this job evaluation template[183] to get started. One way to think about your next role is to think about it in the context of your previous positions. What lessons did you learn there? What was useful and what wasn't as useful? What do you want to do more or less of?
  - If you want to learn more about applying design thinking to your life, take a look at *Designing Your Life: How to Build a Well-Lived, Joyful Life*[184] by Bill Burnett and Dave Evans.
  - If you're interested in futures thinking, take a look at *What the Foresight*[185] by Alida Draudt and Julia Rose West. We commonly think about the future on a linear scale, where things improve gradually over time. But this book challenges this notion by introducing multiple futures.

- Uncover Your Superpowers§6.1
  - How to Find Your Design Superpower[186] by Heather Phillips.

- Portfolio Formats to Consider§7.4
  - Folio[187] by yours truly. A quick-start portfolio design deck for Sketch, Figma, and Keynote.

- Prototype Your Portfolio§7.6
  - Inverted Pyramid: Writing for Comprehension[188] by Nielsen Norman Group.

182. https://www.princeton.edu/news/2010/05/30/2010-baccalaureate-remarks
183. https://docs.google.com/spreadsheets/d/1jipbAyAOKd-Gb5slQWJH7KwUyxNVC7j2vKLzHy9BaMU/edit?usp=sharing
184. https://www.amazon.com/gp/product/1784740241/
185. https://www.amazon.com/What-Foresight-personal-explored-preferred/dp/1537424866/
186. https://www.fastcompany.com/3062056/how-to-find-your-design-superpower
187. http://getafolio.com
188. https://www.nngroup.com/articles/inverted-pyramid/

- Promote Your Portfolio§7.7
  - The dribbblisation of design[189] by Paul Adams, on Intercom. On the dangers of following trends too closely.
- Using Referrals§8.2
  - Why Your Inner Circle Should Stay Small, and How to Shrink It,[190] by Scott Gerber. Counterintuitive advice from HBR on networking and the power of making fewer connections.
- Networking Authentically§9
  - *How to Win Friends and Influence People*[191] by Dale Carnegie. The classic in the field, still just as relevant today.
  - *Never Eat Alone*[192] by Keith Ferazzi. Although it has mixed reviews, Keith does a great job of providing tips and frameworks you can use to meet people. At the heart of it is the genuine message that we're better off connecting and sharing resources rather than hoarding away our contacts.
  - *Networking for People Who Hate Networking*[193] by Devora Zack. For those shy persons jumping into their first event, this is a great step-by-step guide. The book leads you through a series of exercises to make networking fun and enjoyable, especially for those of us who would actually prefer to spend our time (and eat) alone.
- Auto-Piloting Your Job Search§8.6
- Profile submission
  - Hired[194]
  - Underdog.io[195]
  - Woo[196]

189. https://www.intercom.com/blog/the-dribbblisation-of-design/
190. https://hbr.org/2018/03/why-your-inner-circle-should-stay-small-and-how-to-shrink-it?_lrsc=8a867d81-ec2f-4916-bb7e-b15f30106782
191. https://www.amazon.com/How-Win-Friends-Influence-People/dp/0671027034/
192. https://www.amazon.com/Never-Eat-Alone-Expanded-Updated/dp/0385346654
193. https://www.amazon.com/Networking-People-Who-Hate-Underconnected/dp/1605095222
194. https://hired.com/
195. https://underdog.io/
196. https://woo.io/

- Job boards
    - Designer News[197]
    - Authentic jobs[198]
    - Coroflot[199]
    - AIGA[200]
    - CreativeGuild[201] by Creative Mornings
- Final Interview Preparation§11
    - *The Upside of Stress: Why Stress Is Good for You, and How to Get Good at It*[202] by Kelly McGonigal.
- Cross-Functional Interviews§14.4
    - BuzzFeed's list of design interview questions.[203]
- Acing the App Critique§17
    - Jobs to be done and personas[204] by NN/g. A short read on how to use both methods effectively.
    - *Discussing Design*[205] by Adam Connor and Aaron Irizarry. This book goes into the mechanics and the nitty-gritty of critique facilitation.
    - *How to Make Sense of Any Mess*[206] by Abby Covert. A short read that arms you with basic information architecture tools and techniques.
    - *Elements of User Experience*[207] by Jesse James Garrett. A quick read that breaks down a design problem into multiple layers: visual, skeleton, structure, scope, and strategy.

---

197. https://www.designernews.co/jobs
198. https://authenticjobs.com/
199. http://coroflot.com/
200. https://designjobs.aiga.org/
201. https://creativemornings.com/jobs
202. https://www.amazon.com/Upside-Stress-Why-Good-You/dp/1101982934
203. https://github.com/buzzfeed/design/blob/master/recruiting/interview-questions.md
204. https://www.nngroup.com/articles/personas-jobs-be-done/
205. https://www.amazon.com/Discussing-Design-Improving-Communication-Collaboration/dp/149190240X
206. http://www.howtomakesenseofanymess.com/
207. https://www.amazon.com/Elements-User-Experience-User-Centered-Design-ebook/dp/B004JLMDOC

   - *About Face: The Essentials of Interaction Design,*[208] 4th ed., by Alan Cooper. A hefty volume of nearly 700 pages, it's a solid reference for all things interaction design.

- The Take-Home Design Exercise§15
- Photography
   - Pexels.[209] Bills itself as a free and *inclusive* photo and video library.
   - Unsplash.[210] One of my favorites, and the go-to resource for high-quality photography.
   - Pixabay.[211] Over a million images and videos shared, free for personal or commercial use.
- Illustrations
   - Humaaans.[212] A customizable illustration library by Pablo Stanley. Use is free for personal and commercial use.
   - Blush.[213] Founded by Pablo Stanley, it's a customizable illustration resource that allows you to remix, change colors, and find illustrations for different occasions.
   - Undraw.[214] Similar to illustration libraries already listed but with less focus on the character and more emphasis on staging.
- Maps: Your project may not require maps, but if it does, spending a little time customizing a map could be another way you can differentiate your design:
   - Mapbox.[215] Probably one of the most robust APIs out there. With Mapbox studio you can customize tons of things. The learning curve may be a little steep at the beginning, so I recommend you take a couple of pre-existing Mapbox maps and customize those first to get a feel for it.

---

208. https://www.amazon.com/About-Face-Essentials-Interaction-Design/dp/1118766571
209. https://www.pexels.com/
210. https://unsplash.com/
211. https://pixabay.com/
212. https://www.humaaans.com/
213. https://blush.design/
214. https://undraw.co/illustrations
215. https://studio.mapbox.com/

    - Google map styles.[216] You can select a theme or you can come up with a brand-new style, customizing things like buildings, landscapes, points of interest, roads, transit lines, and water.

- Breaking Down Your Design Job Offer§24
    - Hired's Salary Calculator.[217]
    - W2 filings[218] for a source of truth on actual numbers.
    - AngelList[219] for startup equity and salary range.
    - Holloway's Guide to Equity Compensation.[220]
    - Cartas' Equity education[221] and Equity calculator[222] to figure how much your equity is worth.

- Negotiating Compensation§25
    - *Never Split the Difference.*[223] Written by an FBI hostage negotiator, the tactics are made applicable to many areas of life, "in the boardroom or at home."
    - Intercom's individual contributor design levels[224] and design manager levels,[225] in addition to being open available and detailed, have specific objectives and growth tasks tied to each level.
    - Basecamp's Titles for Designers.[226] Although Basecamp is a small company by startup standards, their design framework is rigorous, and aside from describing what are the different expectations of designers, it also publicly lists the names of designers at those levels.

---

216. https://mapstyle.withgoogle.com/
217. https://hired.com/salary-calculator
218. https://h1bdata.info/index.php
219. https://angel.co/
220. https://www.holloway.com/g/equity-compensation
221. https://carta.com/blog/category/equity-education/
222. https://carta.com/blog/value-equity-offer-startup-equity-calculator/
223. https://www.goodreads.com/book/show/26156469-never-split-the-difference
224. https://docs.google.com/document/d/1qlH-eNkP4rNFoM1eCsHQNwRTWrP9Yg1-XUqWHPTKAkg/edit
225. https://docs.google.com/document/d/1zqeuCgTL7zTcQRSgv-xoyndgiTyFchspncWDb3lotbl/edit
226. https://basecamp.com/handbook/appendix-03-titles-for-designers

- DoorDash's head of design, Helena Seo, shares her thinking and approach toward creating a leveling system[227] at the company.
- progression.fyi.[228] A collection of open source company ladders, including some for design, such as BuzzFeed, Zendesk, and many others.

- Starting Your Job Strong
  - *The First 90 Days: Proven Strategies for Getting Up to Speed Faster and Smarter*[229] by Michael Watkins, has advice that's applicable to managers and individual contributors alike.
  - Shipping the org chart[230] by Dag Olav Norem.

30 Acknowledgements

A frequent question I get from folks is, how long did it take to write this book? Although the content took only two years to put together, the reality is that I've been thinking about the topic of design, careers, and development for over a decade. And although my name is on the cover, rest assured many people supported me on this journey; there wouldn't be a book without them.

First and foremost, I'm grateful for the support of my family. I spent a fair amount of time writing parts of the book while on vacation, which sometimes meant locking myself away in my room for hours on end. Thank you for being patient with me during this time.

A big shout out goes to the fantastic team at Holloway. Courtney Nash helped start the conversation encouraging me to write. Her support and guidance helped me create a strong narrative from beginning to end. Taking the book to the finish line was no small feat either, and I have to thank Joshua Levy and Rachel Jepsen for helping me get there.

Big thank you to Fabricio Teixeira and Caio Braga at UX Collective for supporting my writing over the past few years. Shout out to Fabricio for feedback and encouraging words which buoyed me to continue writing

227. https://doordash.engineering/2019/09/03/designing-a-career-ladder-for-product-design/
228. https://www.progression.fyi/
229. https://www.amazon.com/dp/B00B6U63ZE/
230. https://medium.com/@donorem/shipping-the-org-chart-3319181be9bd

during a challenging time in my career. And of course, I'm indebted to everyone who has read my articles, shared the work, downloaded the templates, and provided feedback.

I also want to thank all the reviewers who have taken the time out of their busy schedules to read this book and provide insightful feedback: Nancy Duan, Sylvia Yu, Adam Connor, Melissa Hui, Julie Stanescu, Chris Shu, Zain Ali, Marissa Louie, Aniruddha Kadam, Sanchit Gupta, Susan Rice, Timmy Chiu, Tanner Christensen, and Tanaya Joshi. Special thanks to Hang Le and Angela Liu, who went the extra mile and were generous with their time and knowledge to make this book stronger.

I wouldn't be here without my mentors and managers who helped my early career development: Michael Rawlins, Bob Thomas, Chris Cox, Pamela Hostetler, Gregg Tyson, David Vonesh, Marc Fusco, Melissa Teitler, and Glenn Britting. I'm grateful to my alma mater, Carnegie Mellon University, which set me on a whole new path that I wouldn't be on were it not for the rigorous MHCI program. To the team at Instacart, which helped me grow exponentially over the past few years with the help and support from: Ryan Scott Tandy, Brett Rampata, and Himani Amoli.

Thank you to everyone who has helped me on this journey so far. If we haven't had a chance to connect just yet and you have some words of advice or feedback, I encourage you to reach out!

—November 2020

About the Author

Dan Shilov is a product designer with over a decade of experience creating products for consumer and enterprise companies across web, mobile and wearable platforms. When he's not hard at work pushing pixels, he mentors designers and speaks at local design organizations. Over the course of his career he's interviewed countless designers and design managers and seen them all struggle through various parts of the interview process. As a result, he's been sharing his insights and documenting interview best practices to help designers put their best foot forward in order to land their dream job. Dan holds a master's degree in Human Computer Interaction from Carnegie Mellon University.

About Holloway

Holloway publishes books online, offering titles from experts on topics ranging from tools and technology to teamwork and entrepreneurship. All titles are built for a satisfying reading experience on the web as well as in print. The Holloway Reader helps readers find what they need in search results, and permits authors and editors to make ongoing improvements.

Holloway seeks to publish more exceptional authors. We believe that a new company with modern tools can make publishing a better experience for authors and help them reach their audience. If you're a writer with a manuscript or idea, please get in touch at hello@holloway.com.

Made in the USA
Columbia, SC
13 June 2024

10d96ea4-1854-4858-999d-ed573e8e0c6fR01